THE DEER HUNTER'S FIELD GUIDE:

Pursuing Michigan's Whitetail

THE DEER HUNTER'S FIELD GUIDE:

Pursuing Michigan's Whitetail

John H. Williams

Momentum Books Ltd.

Cover design by Don Ross

Photographs by John H. Williams

Illustrations by Roger Miller and Edward McGlinn

Momentum Books Ltd.
6964 Crooks Rd.
Troy, MI 48098

ISBN 1-879094-24-X Paperback Edition

Dedicated to my wife, Annette
Not only does she tolerate my pastimes—
She actually encourages them

Contents

Illustrations

Author's Note

Hunting, for my father, was a sport. It was something he did for a week, or so, each year. He seldom read about it; he seldom talked about it. He never really became proficient with the weapons he used, and he knew practically nothing about the animals he hunted. The vast majority of the hunters I've known are like my father. I strongly hold the opinion that hunting demands much more of me. Things often happen very quickly in the field. Have I developed my full capability with the weapons I shoot? How's that animal going to react when hit? If wounded, where is it most likely to head? If need be, am I capable of tracking it in this habitat? My conscience demands that I be able to affirmatively answer these, and many other similar questions, long before I ever head into the field.

Hunting, and hunting the whitetail in particular, is much more than a sport to me—it's a love. It is the reason I became a biologist. It's the reason I shoot my shotguns and rifles once or twice a week year-round. It's the reason I shoot my bow as often as I can, usually four or five days a week. It's the reason I read as often as I find time. For me to go out and hunt an animal, any animal, without being prepared to the best of my abilities is something I will not do.

I have an insatiable desire to know the animals I hunt and to know how to hunt them. Fair chase and the need to hunt properly are very important to me. The kill, if one occurs, is always a moment of sadness. For me there are deep-seated ethics that this sport demands. For the group of sportsmen (and women) with whom I associate, these ethics are transformed into an ethos: we will not compromise our values and our love for this sport.

I was hunting caribou on the Ungava Peninsula in northern Quebec a few years ago. My guide's name was Louis (Louie) Ribe. The first thing Louie asked me when we met was why I'd come there—what did I want? "I want the first animal I take (you're allowed two caribou on a license) to be such that when I remember it ten or twenty years from now I'll still be proud of it, still glad that I took it. I want the second animal to make the book, or I won't shoot," I said. Louie smiled, as he did so readily, and said simply, "OK." We had a wonderful hunt.

I took a beautiful bull the second morning, and we looked at literally hundreds of others, none of which would make "the book." On the seventh day of the hunt we were on a high ridge shortly after daylight. After glassing the surrounding tundra for most of the day, we saw many fine bulls but none like we wanted. Finally the cold and the wind got to me and I retreated over the ridge behind us. Almost immediately I spotted animals on the next hillside. Instantly I knew that the largest of the ten bulls was something special!

Louie's native tongue is French, but from the moment we met and he learned I was English-speaking he never slipped; he always spoke beautiful, articulate English. Now, training the spotting scope on the big bull, he began an excited monologue in French. As soon as he looked at me he realized I couldn't understand a word he said. He gave me a big grin and said, "There's your book. There's your new world record!"

The big bull and his bachelor group were nearly a mile away and lying down near the crest of the hill. We left everything except my rifle and our binoculars and started off at a run. We managed to keep some large boulders between us and the bulls for a ways. A copse of cedars then prevented the bulls from seeing us, and finally more boulders. We'd gotten within four or five hundred yards and I began to feel confident that we were close enough for a shot. Then suddenly we heard water. Between us and the bulls was a raging torrent! Sheer vertical walls of fifty feet or more and whitewater stopped us. We were now within three hundred yards. With the 7mm Magnum that distance normally wouldn't have been a problem. But the wind racing across the tundra was brutal and when I told Louie I couldn't be sure and therefore would not risk the shot, he put his hand on my shoulder and said, "I'm sorry."

Louie and I looked through our binoculars and watched the biggest caribou bull either of us had ever seen walk slowly over the hill. As he disappeared, Louie bade him farewell and said softly, "Go in peace my friend, and have a good winter."

I know one thing for sure, Louis Ribe can hunt with me anytime he likes. Without flag-waving or preaching, I sincerely hope I've imparted Louie's philosophy—and mine—throughout this book and the special kind of respect for the sport of hunting, illustrated by my experience on the Arctic tundra.

John H. Williams

Foreword

As an editor of outdoor publications, I long wondered why no one had ever written a comprehensive guide to deer hunting in Michigan. This is, after all, a state that last year counted 725,000 firearm deer hunters, 270,000 archery deer hunters, and 103,000 muzzle-loading deer hunters. It is a state with a fall deer herd numbering around 1.5 million animals. It has a deer hunting tradition that spans many generations. Yet, so far as I have been able to determine, no one had ever assembled a complete manual on Michigan deer hunting— until John H. Williams wrote the book you are holding.

The work he has created has been worth waiting for. It is a distillation of knowledge accumulated through twenty-five years of deer hunting in Michigan by an astute observer. Williams augmented his personal knowledge of deer hunting with extensive research on the white-tailed deer and interviews with wildlife biologists throughout the state.

The end product is a thorough account of all aspects of deer in Michigan from the biology of whitetails to effective strategies for hunting them. Williams discusses firearms, ammunition, sights, and archery equipment for deer hunting; the importance of scouting; how to choose a deer hunting stand; where and how to hunt deer whether in farmlands or wilderness or any kind of country in between—in short, just about everything a hunter needs to know about deer hunting in Michigan. It adds up to a lot of sound advice for beginners and veterans alike, advice that is abundantly illustrated with recountings of hunting incidents from the author's own wide experience.

Williams' book is a long-awaited and valuable addition to Michigan's sporting literature.

Kenneth S. Lowe, Editor
Michigan Out-of-Doors

Preface to the Second Edition

In the four years since *The Deer Hunter's Field Guide: Pursuing Michigan's Whitetail* was first published much has changed. Deer, deer herds, habitat, management decisions, hunters, and society are all living, evolving entities. None of them, nor their interrelationships, ever remains the same for long. It's therefore time for the second edition of this work, with updated information.

Since 1990, Michigan's deer herd is down. In 1990, the DNR estimated a statewide whitetail population approaching two million animals; in 1994, it's believed to be roughly 1.2 or 1.3 million. We had too many deer in 1990 and the DNR knew it. A lot of this reduction was, therefore, "by design" of the DNR; some of it was by design of Mother Nature. In late April 1992, a spring snowstorm that dumped eight to twelve inches of snow across most of the northern Lower and the west-central U.P. was then followed by two weeks of abnormally—almost winterlike—cold weather. This was simply too much for many yearlings and they perished. It also severely impacted spring "greenup," delaying it badly at a most critical time for all pregnant does. Many lost their fawns right then. Over Memorial Day weekend, and for the next week, Mother Nature decided to finish what she'd earlier begun. Newborn fawns were subjected to freezing rains and cold temperatures for a solid week. The entire fawn crop in the west-central U.P., and much of the northern Lower, was lost. Such a drastic reduction was not anticipated by the DNR.

Now, and for at least the next several years, hunters are going to see far fewer doe permits, block permits, and probably some changes in the licensing format as well, although just what these changes might be hasn't yet been determined. The hardest hit areas were the west-central U.P. and the northeastern section of the Lower. Deer numbers in a wide band across the entire length of the U.P. are actually up and, in some sections, up considerably. Most of the north-western Lower, and southern Michigan (with only a couple exceptions) have only slightly lower numbers. In Part IV, I'll address these changes in greater detail.

I'll guarantee, the herds will bounce back; our state biologists are working hard to see that they do. Despite what often amounts to a lack of support from DNR administrators and Lansing politicians, our biologists, in my opinion, continue, as usual, to do a wonderful job.

Preface to the First Edition

The Deer Hunter's Field Guild: Pursuing Michigan's Whitetail is intended to provide the Michigan sportsman with the latest, most comprehensive information on the white-tailed deer. Further, I have attempted to do this in a manner both entertaining and readable. Many facets of deer hunting, readily found in great detail in other books on the subject, are treated only briefly. Instead, this book is designed to focus on those aspects of the sport that are traditionally glossed over. I comprehensively discuss the whitetail's biology to meet the hunter's needs, and make it very specific to our state. The facts about the rut, for example, would not be the same about deer in the Deep South, where the breeding season is much longer.

I have drawn from the latest available research—many of the facts discussed here were not fully understood or even known as recently as five years ago. Chapter 2 deals with the issue of management as it has evolved in Michigan, and should give you some insight to where we are today.

In Part III, I have covered in detail such subjects as how to select a stand—what factors you should consider and why, when you should sit in certain locations, and when not to. I also give considerable attention to how one should hunt under a variety of weather conditions. In Chapter 10, I explain not only the importance of preseason scouting but, more importantly, just how it is done. Then I take the reader one step further and explain the most powerful tool you can use in scouting, "The Hunting Habitat Map." Addressing the specialized needs of the Michigan hunter, I go into great detail delineating those hunting techniques and strategies that will be most productive for each region of our state, be it the farmlands, the more rural areas, or the true wilderness regions of the Upper Peninsula. Much more is included in separate chapters on trophy hunting, hunting in your own neighborhood, and hunting in the late season.

The county-by-county descriptions in Part IV are unique. The research for this section took me over eighteen months to complete. During that time I spent more than 180 days on the road, racked up more than one hundred thousand miles on my research vehicle, amassed several hundred pages of notes, made hundreds of telephone calls throughout the state, taped more than one hundred hours of observations and thoughts, and conducted more than two hundred interviews.

I have experienced Michigan deer herds by traveling throughout the state in a way few ever do. My hope is that you, the reader, are satisfied with what you find in the following chapters and that this book will help your pursuit of this magnificent animal. I would also be very pleased if what you find between these covers gives you an even greater admiration for the Michigan whitetail.

Acknowledgments

In September 1987, when I began writing *The Deer Hunter's Field Guide: Pursuing Michigan's Whitetail*, I naively believed I would simply just write a book—that is, it would be no big deal. In the many months since that beginning, I discovered how difficult such an undertaking is, and how much I owe to so many who helped me in this endeavor.

First, I want to thank Kenneth Lowe for writing the Foreword. If it weren't for Ken and his encouragement over the past fifteen years, I'm not certain I'd still be writing today. I want to thank the people at Momentum Books: Bill Haney for the faith that he showed in the potential of this project; Scott Johnson for his professionalism and his ability to tie up the many loose ends that I had left; Judy and Ed McGlinn, the editors, for their meticulous attention to detail. The efforts of these folks have certainly strengthened the end result.

My sincere thanks to Joe Frankum, who very unexpectedly passed away in September 1990, for his many hours of laboring over copies of rough manuscript and his many insightful suggestions. The Upper Peninsula is so vast and varied that if it weren't for Jim Hammill, Dick Aartila and Jim Cook, I'd have been unable to maintain my direction—thanks, you were truly a great help.

The final copy could never have approached its ultimate level of quality were it not for the efforts of many experts in the field. My thanks to the following for both their time and their expertise: John Ozoga, Louis Verme, Jim Hammill, Dick Aartila and Joe Frankum. A very special thanks to John P. Chancey for his many hours spent proofreading the rough draft. My gratitude to Roger Miller for his drawings. To all our state biologists and technicians not mentioned by name, my sincere thanks. If this material is judged to be useful and accepted by our state's sportsmen, it's a credit to you; it could not have been completed without your assistance. While the contributions of these and many others are gratefully acknowledged, I alone accept complete responsibility for any conclusions drawn or the manner in which information has been presented and for the accuracy of this material.

John H. Williams
June 1990

Part I

The World of the Whitetail

The Animal —Behavior and Habitat

What is this animal, the white-tailed deer, that evokes so much excitement, interest and devotion in the Michigan sportsman? Why on earth did more than one million men, women, and children, from all over the state, head into the woods and fields of Michigan last fall in its pursuit? *What is at the heart of this fascination?*

To answer these questions, we should first learn a little functional biology about the whitetail and something about its life and its ways. What we learn may also help us to become better hunters. First off, the whitetail is technically known as an Artiodactyla, or even-toed ungulate. This evolutionary species had its origin during the Eocene epoch, some thirty-six to fifty-eight million years ago. As other competing groups foundered, the ungulates successfully adapted to a great many different terrestrial habitats; the group's diversity increased as did its individual numbers. Within this highly adaptable group was a smaller group, the ruminants, to which the whitetail belongs.

The Ruminantia, those animals with multichambered or compound stomachs, first made their appearance some twenty-five million years ago in the early Miocene epoch. Within this suborder, the specific family to which our whitetail belongs is known as the Cervidae. This group first appeared some thirteen million years ago and has changed greatly since. Early fossil records indicate that the first identifiable Cervidae were quite small, standing roughly eighteen inches high and weighing fifteen to twenty pounds. Today this diverse and highly successful group is found throughout most of the world (it is largely absent from Africa, Australia, and some of the world's remote island groups), and contains approximately thirty-seven different species of deer. The North American members of the group include the white-tailed deer and mule deer, as well as the moose, elk, caribou, and a host of exotic or alien species.

Cervidae are characterized by being relatively slim of body and long-legged. In all species except the caribou, normally only the males grow antlers. Antlers, as opposed to true horns, are grown and shed annually, and are composed of the fastest growing bone known. During the months of June and July a large white-tailed buck's antlers can grow by as much as a half inch, or more, a day.

It is widely believed that some predecessor of the modern-day whitetail made its way across the Bering Strait land bridge connecting northern Asia with North America during the Pleistocene epoch, roughly one million years ago. During the ensuing period the animals spread and evolved into several different South, Central and North American species, including our whitetail. From bone fragments found by archaeologists throughout Michigan, we know that the modern-day whitetail has resided here since just after the last glacial melt-back some 15,000 years ago.

The deer in Michigan—the northern woodland whitetail—is technically known as *Odocoileus virginianus borealis*. This is the largest of the whitetails. While average *borealis* bucks weigh anywhere from 150 to 225 pounds, exceptional specimens of more than 300 pounds are taken. The largest whitetail ever shot was taken in Minnesota in 1926. In November of that year, Carl J. Lenander Jr. shot a buck that field dressed at 402 pounds. Minnesota's Department of Conservation calculated the deer's live weight at 511 pounds! No larger deer has ever been reported anywhere.

In addition to being the largest, *borealis* has the widest distribution of any of the some thirty North and Central American subspecies as well. (There are additionally seven or eight South American subspecies.) Besides being found throughout Michigan, *borealis* is also found in all or parts of Maryland, Delaware, New York, New Jersey, Connecticut, Rhode Island, Massachusetts, Pennsylvania, Ohio, Indiana, Illinois, Wisconsin, Minnesota, and the Canadian provinces of New Brunswick, Nova Scotia, Quebec and Ontario. Its numbers and current range are expanding as well.

Both from a biological perspective and from that of the hunter, the best way to gain an understanding of the whitetail is to learn about the social organization in which it lives, for you cannot adequately grasp one without the other. Whitetails are gregarious; that is, they seek each other out and seldom, if ever, do they live alone. But the relationships are complex and dependent upon sex, lineage, age, and time of the year. There is not just one big collection of deer, but rather two, and possibly even three separate subgroups. These groups are: the female or matriarchal group numbering anywhere from eight to twenty individuals, the male or bachelor group numbering anywhere from three to eight individuals, and perhaps what could be considered the immature male group as well. Some would say that this third collection does not constitute a group at all—and, technically, perhaps it does not. Immature bucks, from twelve to eighteen or twenty months of age, are best described as "social floaters"; unsure of their exact role and place, they rather loosely "associate" with but do not really "belong to" any given group. (I'll discuss this later in some detail.) Probably the best way to understand the development of, and interactions within, the whitetails' world is to follow the deer throughout the various seasons of the year, beginning with the spring.

Spring: A Time to Recoup Losses

For the purposes of studying our deer, we'll consider spring to be that period of time that begins with the breakup of winter. In a typical year, this will be late March or early April. The snows have already melted or are melting fast. Deer in the southern portion of our state are already eagerly switching over from a harshly imposed lifestyle of browsing to the much preferred style of grazing. The fresh, protein- and energy-rich green shoots of spring are voraciously consumed as the deer's metabolism—the rate at which energy is burned—kicks into high gear from a winter's low. Winter coats are being shed; fat deposits, if any remain, are being dumped and, for the first time in months, a positive nutritional balance—more energy in than out—is being attained. In the northern two-thirds of Michigan the deer, especially the does and last year's young, have now broken out of their yarding areas—those pockets of dense thermal cover that are the very lifeblood of our northernmost herds. The bucks will follow in a week or so.

If it weren't for our northern coniferous stands—principally cedar and hemlock—we'd have no northern herds of deer. But now, having overbrowsed them badly, the deer are seemingly eager to flee their confines. They begin a movement back to their traditional summer ranges.

While the animals of the north can't yet find much to graze on, they do now at least have the luxury of sufficient browse, something they really haven't had for at least three or four months. Now they have aspen and birch, maple and oak, white pine and jack pine, as well as many other foods unavailable just days before. The browse that will be eaten is matchstick size in diameter, or smaller. Such food has a very high ratio of nutritious bark fibers to the far less valuable cellulose interior fibers of larger twigs.

Due to the ever-increasing amounts of daylight (photoperiod), the deer's bodies are undergoing pronounced chemical changes at this time as well. The pituitary gland, also known as the master gland, is stimulated by the increased sunlight (through the optic nerve). In the bucks, this gland then releases the somatotrophic hormone that starts the buck's annual cycle of antler growth. In the does, the pituitary also stimulates the adrenal and thyroid glands. The resultant increase in metabolic activity of the doe is responsible for a tremendous surge in the development of her unborn fetuses.

Her soon-to-be fawns are now 130-day-old fetuses. Since their seventh week in utero, their organ systems have all been in place, but even at this late date they weigh only two pounds apiece and measure roughly a foot long. At birth, following a two-hundred-day gestation and roughly seventy to eighty days from now, the young will weigh six to eight pounds, and have a forehead to rump measurement of twenty inches. They'll stand some fourteen inches high at the shoulder. In order for the fetuses to attain such dimensions, however, the dams must first ingest large quantities of energy-rich foods. As soon as it's possible (available), she'll nearly double her dietary intake and consume anywhere from ten to twelve pounds of energy-rich grasses, forbs, and leaf materials daily.

The normal routine of this doe will be to feed heavily twice a day, and somewhat more sparingly two or three more times in between. She, along with other members of her immediate familial group, will feed heavily from daylight or just before, until nine or ten in the morning, then heavily again beginning about four in the afternoon. She'll bed down during colder nighttime periods. If her little band has wintered in an area far removed from its normal summer range, it will continue to move in that direction.

Such movement is much more pronounced as we move north throughout our state. In southern Michigan, the average spatial adjustment from summer to winter range will be one mile or so. Throughout the northern Lower Peninsula, it will vary widely, but normally be two to five miles. In the Upper Peninsula, some deer will move as far as forty miles between summer and winter ranges. The average movement is probably about eight to twelve miles. Essentially all the deer in any given area are, at this time, doing the same thing. As mentioned, the does along with last year's fawns will be in their matriarchal bands. The mature bucks will be with other bucks, perhaps as few as two or three or as many

Diagram 1.1
Example of spatial and habitat adjustment between summer and winter ranges

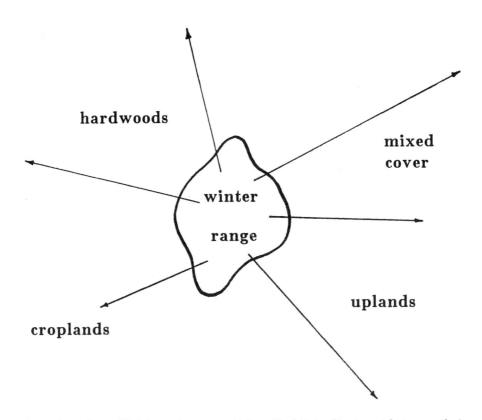

Deer throughout Michigan show a spatial and habitat adjustment between their summer and winter ranges. These adjustments are much more pronounced for our various northern herds than for our southern herds. Nonetheless, the patterns are representative of the movements found anywhere in the state. As illustrated, only a small percentage of the available range supports essentially all the deer during the wintering period. It is thus the winter range in Michigan that most accurately reflects the overall carrying capacity of the region. The better the winter range, the more deer the overall area can support, other factors being equal.

as six or eight and, while not with the does or other bucks, they'll all be in small groups moving away from their wintering areas. This distribution pattern is shown schematically in *Diagram 1.1*.

From all external appearances our doe is not yet pregnant. It is not until roughly two weeks before she'll deliver that her udder will swell and become pendulous. She's not even showing enough of an increase in abdominal girth at this point to tell by visual inspection, although she soon will. Upon their arrival at their summer range, the doe and her group will continue to maintain a somewhat loose and casual type of interaction. Some may drift off to explore the perimeters of their range, but they'll come and go as they like, and they'll be centered in the area that the matriarch, or dominant doe, considers to be home. Precisely where, within this range, they'll wander will probably be more dependent upon where the best food is located than any other factor at this time.

Each band of does has a matriarch. This position of authority is bestowed upon her based on age; in an ideal world each female in the group will thus get her day. In contrast to the bucks' bachelor groups, each matriarchal group is composed of directly related individuals. There will be two, three or more of the matriarch's female offspring, plus their female offspring and immature male offspring ten months old.

As mid-May approaches, the small band of does becomes increasingly irritable. They'll soon drift apart, each to a separate area within their range. If a pregnant doe has young from last year they will at first follow her to her chosen birthing area; this will be roughly the same area where they themselves were born just one year before. As birthing time becomes imminent, the dam will run her yearlings off as well. (See *Diagram 1.2*, which illustrates the matriarchal group's spatial arrangement at this time.)

Isolated now, the doe is ready to give birth. When the final moment arrives, she'll pick an area—probably but not always well concealed—and she'll either lie down on her side or simply stand. Times vary, but the average birth takes somewhere between ten and twenty minutes. As soon as the fawn is expelled, the doe nuzzles it, grooms it entirely, and eats the afterbirth. Within minutes the fawn crawls to the dam's udder and suckles. Feedings thereafter will occur two or three times daily, with the fawn taking about eight ounces of milk at each feeding.

Diagram 1.2
Example of spatial distribution of a summer range for bucks and does

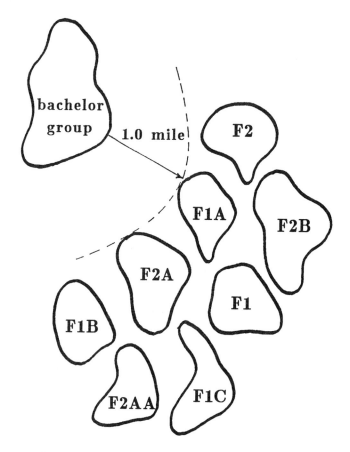

F1 is a mature female that is mother to F1A, F1B, and F1C.
F2 is a mature female that is mother to F2A and F2B.
F2A is a mature female that is mother to F2AA.

This schematic representation of a typical herd's distribution during the birthing and early postnatal period is based upon research observations from the Cusino Research Station at Shingleton. The adult doe, just prior to parturition, isolates herself from all others. The year-old fawns, during this period of the dam's complete isolation, then run the corridors that form between the boundaries of the adults' birthing areas. These subadult animals may rejoin their dams and newborn siblings within four to six weeks. The various nuclear families will then remain isolated for another month or so before gradually reforming the larger matriarchal group. The adult bucks remain isolated in their own selected habitat throughout this entire period; the two groups will not intermingle until much later in August. Throughout Michigan, well over 80 percent of all fawns will be dropped within one week either side of June 1.

If our doe is not a primipara (pregnant for the first time) juvenile (one year old), she will, in all probability, deliver twins. Four to six hours after having done so, she'll lead the fawns from the birthing area, moving them to separate locations anywhere from one hundred feet to two or three hundred yards, depending upon her experience level and the habitat. The act of birthing, despite the doe's cleansing of both the fawns and the immediate area, results in the soiling of the earth with fairly large quantities of amniotic fluid, urine, feces, and blood. If left here the fawns would be at increased risk. Moving them is a behavioral adaptation for the purpose of reducing predation.

Within twenty minutes of their birth, healthy-born fawns are capable of standing, and within an hour they are capable of walking, on very shaky legs, for up to a quarter of a mile. Once moved, however, and placed into new bedding sites, the fawns will sleep. The doe, tired herself, will move off another hundred to two hundred yards and rest. She'll return to care for each in turn, and she's always alert to any sign of danger. An angry doe

Fawn. Is there anything more beautiful in all of nature than a newborn fawn? Note this one's eyes. All fawns have blue eyes for their first week to ten days before they turn deep brown.

is a formidable foe to most predators; nonetheless, the first seventy-two hours of a fawn's life is a perilous time.

Fawns from first-time dams are at especially high risk, as are fawns from severely malnourished dams. In the case of fawns born to primipara dams, the risks are the result of the dam's inexperience. Research shows that up to 37 percent of these fawns perish, while that percentage declines with increasing experience in the doe until only 7 percent are lost to dams six years old or older. Malnourished does can be found in any age group (but are more commonly young animals themselves), if the range on which they live is of poor quality. Fawns born to these dams are in jeopardy due to their frailty from the start, and overall as many as 60 percent to 70 percent may perish.

For the first ten to fourteen days of their lives, the newborns' reaction to danger is simply to freeze. Their spotted coats and coloration render them very difficult to see and their body odors are quite minimal. As time passes the doe will gradually move the young closer and closer together until, after four weeks, they're bedding together, although the dam will still keep her distance for a little longer. As they develop, the fawns begin to mimic their dam's feeding activities and they slowly begin grazing on soft greenery and forbs while continuing to suckle.

Summer: The Easy Life

By their eighth week, the fawns obtain fully 50 percent or more of their caloric intake through grazing and browsing. Although they won't be fully weaned until at least their twelfth week, they are now placing much less of a physiological drain on their dam. The doe, with lessened demands on her, is now sleek and fit. With adequate habitat, she's quickly regaining the weight loss incurred during earlier heavy lactation. Additionally, with the heightened awareness that her fawns are showing and their increased physical abilities, keeping track of ever-present danger is less of a task for her; living is easy. Parasites, both external and internal, are problematic with an assorted array of fleas, ticks, lice, mites, liver flukes, tapeworms, roundworms, nasal bots, mosquitoes, black flies, and so forth. To otherwise healthy animals here in Michigan, these critters represent more of a nuisance than a real threat—a parasite never kills, or even seriously handicaps, its host.

The fawns are growing rapidly. From birth, they doubled their weight in two weeks, quadrupled it in a month, and now at twelve weeks they weigh roughly fifty pounds each. They are now independent ruminants. No longer dependent on mother's milk they freely sample, by trial and error and by mimicry, a wide variety of foodstuffs. The real mainstays of their diet at this point, however, are the highly energy-rich new foliage of oak, red maple, aspen, birch, and other trees as well as the quickly ripening summer fruits.

Within four to six weeks of their birth, our fawns' older siblings have been in attendance, and this family of four or five has been freely roaming over the mother's selected range. Now they increasingly encounter other deer, as their small family unit begins converging with their more distant kin that share adjacent areas. The dam is still ever protective, however, and is present whenever needed to assure that her fawns are not unduly harassed by others. As the smaller units continue to mingle and merge, it is again the matriarch who calls the shots. She decides when to move, when to rest, what to eat and when, and where to drink; all are subservient to her lead.

Since leaving their yarding (winter concentration) areas, the small band of does has had minimal contact with adult bucks. As shown in *Diagram 1.2,* the bachelor group of bucks drifted off and has been summering in a separate portion of the available range. This is believed to be the result of a slightly different morphology and hence nutritional requirements as well as of different preferences, but much more research needs to be done before this can be said with certainty. Regardless of the reasons, this separation obviously serves to spread the herd over a much larger percentage of the available range, and it leaves those areas of highest nutritional quality to the does and their fawns. This separation of range is probably much stricter in heavily forested regions, such as Ontonagon and Gogebic counties in the U.P., than it is in agricultural areas or areas of high-quality range. This occurs from a purely nutritional viewpoint since the surplus caloric levels found in agricultural areas would minimize the need for separation and dispersal so essential on poorer range. It's also apparent that in areas where bucks are very heavily harvested, i.e., the Lower Peninsula, there will be fewer bucks to separate and, in fact, buck groups may be entirely absent.

The male group shares a much larger range than the does—roughly one to five square miles for the bucks and seldom more than one square mile for the does—but this is highly dependent upon the quality of the range. Sometimes, especially in southern Michigan, it is much smaller. Within this range a bachelor group will consist of from three or four individuals to as many as eight or more. Since leaving the wintering areas our bucks have bulked up their bodies considerably; this is particularly true of two- to four-year-olds. Weight gains of as much as 25 percent or even 30 percent in animals of this age range are the general rule. Assuming adequate nutritional levels and moderate population densities, both of which serve to stimulate antler development, the bucks' antlers have been developing rapidly since April. By late August prime-age bucks, those three to eight years old, are toting impressive sets of velvet-covered headgear. All of this leads naturally to a discussion of dominance, for this is the sole purpose of antler development.

Nothing in nature with such a profound physiological drain as antler development will enhance the animal's chances of survival if it doesn't lead to an advantage; antler development does exactly that. Antler development and pure physical strength lead directly to dominance, which is directly related to breeding ability—the right to pass along genetic fitness. When the rut arrives, it is the dominant males who do the majority of the breeding. Despite some common literature (and the hype given to it) that's been written of late, antler development is principally a function of nutrition and age; genetics or heredity play a very minor role. Since the males within the bachelor group are generally not closely related, there is more difference in maximum body and antler size among these animals than there is among the direct lineage-related does. Within the relatively small geographical area from which any group's bucks are drawn, however, these differences are minimal indeed and of little consequence. Given a common range (same essential nutritional level), age is then the primary factor in determining individual body and antler size. Hence, while it's true that antler/body size is the primary factor in determining dominance among bucks, this is essentially saying that dominance is age-related within that group.

Establishing dominance is most stressful among similar-size animals; it will ultimately be determined in these cases by pure aggression. Some bucks (and does) are simply more aggressive than their peers and through an array of body signals, as well as actual physical acts, these animals assert themselves upon their associates.

Fall: Life's Fast Track

By late August, photoperiodism again rears its head and abruptly ends the tranquility that has marked the summer season. Rising testosterone (a male sex hormone) levels in the buck's bloodstream mark the cessation of antler development. The velvet, that living membrane in which the developing antlers have been encased, suddenly dies. Essentially, this covering is nothing more than an external circulatory system that has been steadily feeding nutrients to the growing antlers. Now the system shuts down and the circulatory flow at skull level ceases. Once this occurs the buck will rub the drying velvet from his hardening antlers.

Up to this point, the developing antlers have been soft and could have been easily damaged. The buck has been careful not to let this happen, but now he seeks to shed the velvet. He'll do so by gently rubbing his antlers against any small tree or bush. Such rubs may be within cover or out in the open; the buck simply rubs wherever he happens to be when the urge strikes him. These rubs do little damage to the vegetation involved. They are accomplished quickly, within ten or fifteen minutes, and carry no significance whatsoever to other deer in the herd, buck or doe. Bigger bucks rub a week to two weeks sooner, or even earlier, than do smaller subordinate bucks.

At this point the various herds of deer, having lived separately all spring and summer, also begin to intermingle. It is the prime-age bucks who get wanderlust, and since all other deer are submissive to them, they now wander freely into the range of any matriarch within the area. With buck-doe ratios running roughly 1:4 throughout the Upper, all the way to perhaps 1:17 or even 1:20 in areas like Gladwin and Osceola counties, it's obvious that there are always a lot more does than mature bucks. The bucks, who have been living in relative harmony with each other, now become short-fused. Confrontations are much more frequent. Generally speaking, simple body language (stereotypical posturing) quickly settles such encounters. The direct stare with ears dropped back is the most frequently employed, and is often sufficient to dissuade a subordinate. More aggressive postures include the "high-head" and "low-head" threats, and clearly tell the recipient of the threat that if he or she (both bucks and does employ these gestures) does not give ground, more aggressive behavior is certain to follow.

When gesturing goes unheeded or more aggressive action is required, the front leg kick is frequently employed. The aggressor, from any angle, delivers a swift upward thrust of a foreleg into the offender. Rearing is another common tactic, and is frequently employed by antlerless bucks or bucks in velvet. It also is employed year-round by does. Throughout most of the year, threat postures, and some actual physical acts, are common to both bucks and does. In the fall, however, the bucks are far more prone to use their now polished and hardened antlers. A "low-head," hard stare is usually all that is needed, but when two bucks of near equal rank confront one another, sparring or actual fighting will usually ensue, particularly if the bucks are unknown to each other. When such encounters occur, the other deer in the area watch intently. Bucks and does alike, who are at some distance from the commotion, will often come on the run to investigate, seemingly to see who the victor will be.

It is this type of physical confrontation that the hunter who "rattles" antlers tries to imitate, and it should be obvious why this hunting procedure will be much more effective for Michigan archers than gun hunters—such natural encounters are going to occur with the highest rate of frequency in mid-to-late October. It also stands to reason that the more bucks in the area—in other words, the more even the buck-doe ratio—the more intense the competition for breeding rights, and the more effective the rattling technique will be. It thus follows that areas such as our northern Lower Peninsula are unlikely places to try this particular hunting technique, due to their extremely skewed buck-doe ratios.

While it does not often happen, sometimes neither stereotypical posturing nor sparring can settle a dominance quarrel and an actual fight will ensue. Often these are bloody and vicious encounters. A farmer in Tuscola County, in early November 1982, found on his place a seventeen-point buck that had been badly gored at numerous points along his front shoulders and side. Several of his antler tines were broken as well. The buck had apparently died of those wounds, as do several of our very best bucks each year.

Such a confrontation will most assuredly occur whenever an older monarch shows any sign of weakness. Brute strength and power bestow dominance to bucks; timidity and respect for age have no place here.

The entire fall period—from the time the bucks first begin stripping their velvet—is hectic and helter-skelter for the bucks, mature and immature alike. At the same time the bachelor group is breaking up its amicable ways, the yearling bucks that still reside with their mother's group are undergoing the same physiological, and hence psychological, changes that the big boys are experiencing. Up to this point, these small (teenage, if you will) bucks have been dominated by their older female relatives. Now they must make a decision; either they can remain submissive, and hence emasculated, or they must move off, out of the family group. Lineage-related bucks cannot become dominant over their female relatives. The poor fella is in a bind; he's got the urge to breed and hence be dominant, but at every turn he's thwarted within his group. He probably is dominant over his age-class siblings and cousins, but he's submissive to all adult does within the group and they hound him relentlessly. If he chooses to accept that role he may stay within the group as a psychological castrate, but seldom will he do so. Most choose to leave.

The resulting fall dispersal of young bucks is a perilous time for them. Depending upon the quality of habitat and surrounding deer densities, the young buck's dispersal can be anywhere from five or ten miles to nearly one hundred. The youngster's ambivalence is clearly shown in some radio telemetry studies in which the animals have drifted way off only to wander back within a couple weeks, just to leave once more. This random movement among small bucks through unknown territory, coupled with their obvious inexperience, is undoubtedly a major reason why they're so readily tagged by hunters each fall.

In areas where there's a good age-class distribution among the bucks, the bachelor group breaks apart at this point. Each buck, especially the more dominant, goes his separate way. At this point they are loners, but it's important that they advertise their breeding availability to the local doe population. There are two ways in which this is done: one is through the formation of rubs, the other is by the making of scrapes. I said earlier that the rubs made by bucks shedding their velvet—cleaning or polishing rubs— were of no interest to other deer. But there's another type of rub made now, anytime from the second week of October until the end of November here in Michigan. It is important and it is known as a breeding rub.

When making a cleaning rub, the buck gently, almost tenderly, rubs his antlers over the brush or tree. Ever so carefully the velvet is stripped away and that is the end of it. In a breeding rub, the buck is in a fury; he attacks the object he rubs and tries to destroy it. In the case of bushes and small saplings, the buck will very often break them right down to the ground and trample them. In his rage he rubs not only his antlers through the vegetation, but also the glands found around the base of the antlers, the forehead and the top of the head. The secretions thus left identify the maker of the rub to all others. Although there are exceptions, a couple things about breeding rubs are true. Generally, the bigger the buck, the bigger the tree, sapling or bush he'll attack. Secondly (and there's a lot of variation here), it's usually true that the bigger the buck, the more rubs and scrapes he'll make. Lastly, it's generally the most dominant (or Alpha) buck in the area that makes the vast majority of the markings—again both rubs and scrapes. There is also special significance in where these rubs are placed. The location of cleaning rubs has no significance; they can and will be found anywhere. Breeding rubs, however, are placed where other deer can either watch them being made or readily see them at a distance. They're placed in openings, on the edges of openings, or along well-used runways. (See Chapter 10 regarding the significance of breeding rubs in scouting.)

The other marking sign of significance is known as the scrape. A scrape is a patch of ground that is thrashed and laid bare by the buck. Again, generally, the bigger the buck the bigger the scrape. A big buck will make scrapes that measure at least two feet by three feet and frequently they'll be even bigger. The buck paws up the ground with his hoofs, cleaning away all the debris in the process. He'll then rack it with his antler tips, and urinate on it. The urine runs down his hind legs and mixes there with the heavy secretions exuding from the tarsal glands, which lie on the inside of the hind legs. Once this mixture is deposited, he'll again paw the earth, thus creating (generally) a batch of very strong-smelling mud. Some early scrapes are such that this ground disturbance is all there is, but generally a scrape that the buck really intends to monitor is also placed under the limb of an overhanging tree (both hardwoods and conifers are used). In addition to what I've already described, the buck then thrashes the limb and, just as with a breeding rub, he deposits scent from his head glands on it. He'll then repeatedly check and freshen these scent posts at least twice a day, providing he's not in the company of an estrous doe. A dom-

Breeding Rub. Breeding rubs are placed where other deer can either watch them being made or readily see them at a distance. In a breeding rub, the buck is in a fury; he attacks the object he rubs and tries to destroy it. Generally, the bigger the buck, the bigger the sapling, tree or bush he'll attack.

Breeding Scrape.   A scrape is a patch of ground that is thrashed and laid bare by the buck. The scrape is then scented with a mixture of urine and secretions from the tarsal glands on the buck's hind legs. A big buck will make scrapes that measure at least two feet by three feet.

inant buck may have as many as seven to ten, or more, scrapes, generally set in a line covering a quarter of a mile or more. (Again, see Chapter 10.)

It is the purpose, of course, of the scrapes to attract the estrous doe's attention. The doe, acutely aware of her environment, locates the scrape. When estrous arrives, if she decides to breed with that buck, she'll wait nearby for his return. Hunters naturally give a lot of attention to scrapes, and a lot of bucks are taken off of them, but there's an awful lot of confusion surrounding them also. Let's attempt to clear it up.

Research at the Cusino Wildlife Research Station at Shingleton in the U.P. has indicated that, over the years, the mean date of the rut there is November 18. This means that 50 percent of the does are bred before that date and 50 percent after. (More than 80 percent of all does are bred within the month of November.)

Since it's believed that the mean date in southern Michigan is a few days later, this should mean that if scrapes are indeed used as I've described, our gun hunters should do well hunting over them. The fact is, however, they do not. Our archers do far better hunting scrapes than do riflemen. I'll explain why this is so, and tell you exactly when scrapes will be most effectively hunted.

As estrous activity begins throughout the doe population, it starts out very slowly, peaks rapidly, then diminishes greatly until finally dying completely some sixty days later (see *Diagram 1.3*). Roughly three weeks prior to this, however, testosterone levels peak in our bucks. As a result, you have the entire buck population living at a feverish pitch, ready and willing to breed but with no one to breed. The bucks go crazy; they make breeding rubs; they get into knockdown, drag-out battles, and they make scrapes. In their uncontrolled ardor, they religiously check those scrapes hoping to pick up that hard-to-find doe in estrus.

Finally the big day arrives and does start cycling in. Soon, within six or seven days, there are does in estrus everywhere. The big buck can now find a doe in estrus around practically every corner; the function of the scrape has been served and, despite the fact that the rut is anything

Diagram 1.3
Estrous frequency in does, and testosterone blood levels in bucks

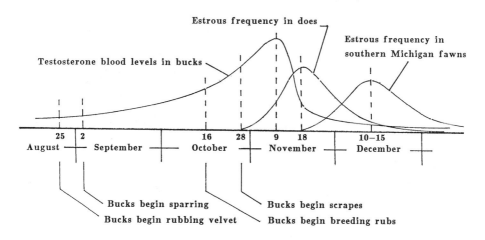

In order to assure that all of the does available to breed are in fact successfully bred, it is essential that the bucks settle their dominance disputes before the does actually become receptive. Nature accomplishes this task by bringing the entire buck population to a feverish pitch prior to the actual "rut," or breeding season. The bucks are then prepared to concentrate solely on the important breeding behavior when that critical time arrives. Hunters should really concentrate on scrape hunting during this early prebreeding period, which occurs two to three weeks before most breeding. A significantly different situation exists in the southern Lower Peninsula, where we have a breeding period with two peaks (see curve for southern Michigan doe fawns). These six- to eight-month-old does will cycle roughly thirty days later than the adult southern Michigan does. Since these yearlings comprise roughly 50 percent of the southern Michigan population, a major breeding period occurs in mid-December each year, in addition to the one roughly 30 days earlier in mid-November. Fifty percent to 60 percent of southern Michigan's doe fawns (six to eight months old) will then be bred. This bimodal, or two-peak, phenomenon diminishes in importance rapidly as we move north—only 5 percent to 10 percent of this same age group will be bred in the Upper Peninsula.

but over, the buck stops checking—he no longer needs to! The message is very clear; the time to hunt over scrapes is from their very first appearance (these dates will vary from year to year, but roughly October 14 to 19 in southern Michigan, October 11 to 16 in northern Lower, and October 5 to 10 in the U.P.) until roughly November 1 or 2 in the U.P.,

Buck and Doe. When a buck finds a receptive doe, he will stay with her for as long as she is in estruous. They'll breed repeatedly, perhaps a dozen or fifteen times altogether in a twenty-four hour period.

and probably about opening day of the gun season in southern Michigan. Beyond these dates, scrape hunting is going to be far less effective. For the bowhunter, scrapes can be truly effective.

The activity level of our psychologically mature bucks—meaning a buck that is dominant within his range regardless of his chronological age—has been very high since early October. He eats little, sleeps little and quarrels often. Life's pace quickens even more as that magical day draws ever nearer when the first doe cycles. When he finally finds a receptive doe, providing that he's mature and she agrees to stand for him, he'll mount her almost immediately. Copulation takes only a matter of moments—thirty seconds or so and it's all over—but the relationship itself is far from over.

The buck will stay with the doe for as long as she is estrous and they'll breed repeatedly, perhaps a dozen or fifteen times altogether in a twenty-four-hour period. As soon as she cycles out, however, she will go her way and he goes back to searching for other receptive does. Such intense, non-stop activity for the buck goes on throughout the entire rut. In the six weeks from early October until the end of the rut, a dominant buck may well lose up to 25 percent of his body weight. He will have entered this period of time in prime condition. With a sleek and polished coat, he was fat and healthy; now the rut is past and he is spent. Most authorities agree that this unbelievable level of activity is responsible for the shortened life expectancy of bucks—irrespective of hunting—as compared with does.

The does on the other hand have been largely on the periphery of all this activity. Each was the center of a buck's undivided attentions in her own turn, but largely ignored both before and after. She's now ready for winter, and in excellent shape. If in early August the average doe weighed 100 pounds, she'll now weigh 120, and she's changed from her red coat of summer to her gray coat of winter. The extra insulation is already beneficial on these early cold, frosty nights.

While it's true that she's now pregnant with two small embryos (while first-time dams frequently have a single fawn and triplets are not uncommon among mature does, 85 percent of all does will have twins), nature has devised a grand scheme to help her through the meager winter months ahead. The embryos grow very slowly, thus presenting a minimal drain on the doe's system throughout the winter months ahead.

Throughout Michigan, over 90 percent of does age one and one-half and older will be pregnant. This will be true no matter how old the doe; there is no truth to the myth of the "old dry doe." Does continue to breed and bear viable young throughout their lifetime, except in those years when they're extremely malnourished. In fact, research has shown that the older the doe (read more experienced), the more prolific she'll be in terms of successfully rearing her young. In southern Michigan, 50 percent to 60 percent of doe fawns six to eight months old will be pregnant too. As we move north the numbers of these young animals that are pregnant decrease rapidly; throughout the U.P. only 5 percent to 10 percent of these animals are impregnated.

Coincident with this chaotic breeding activity—the dispersal of young bucks, the physiological strain on mature bucks, as well as the temporary disruption of the bachelor group—the deer have also been the subject of our intense hunting efforts. This effect varies greatly throughout the state. For does and fawns in the U.P., it's been pretty much life as usual since only a small percentage are harvested (15,000-plus in 1992). In the northern Lower there's somewhat higher pressure applied to them with 40,000-plus being taken in 1992; in the southern Lower the pressure varies greatly depending upon area (nearly 30,000 were taken in this region in 1992). With the bucks, of course, it's a different story. It is estimated that fully 80 percent to 90 percent of our legally antlered bucks are claimed each year in southern Michigan. Anywhere from 65 percent to 75 percent are taken in the northern Lower (the kill is generally higher in the southern counties in this region and lower in the northern counties), and roughly 40 percent are tagged in the Upper. Statewide, this legal kill has been running between 125,000 and 187,000 bucks annually over the past decade. There is no reason to believe that we're exceeding the deer's ability to at least maintain their current population levels, provided we can maintain the carrying capacity of the habitat. As I'll explain in Chapter 2, this remains a serious question.

Winter: Don't Fool with Mother Nature

If Mother Nature follows the normal course of events, winter starts gradually. In the U.P., snows begin to accumulate slowly about mid-November and continue into late January. The deer have begun to settle down from the chaotic fall. The rut is past, and now is the time for the big bucks to try and recoup their losses; they feed voraciously. Bachelor groups have reformed and taken on new composition. Some members were lost, other young members were gained. Gradually, as the snows build and winter winds howl, our deer begin their annual movement toward the wintering grounds. It's a fact that many will never return. The worse the winter, the higher the loss—bet on it.

Slowly at first, a small trickle, a few deer from any given area begin their trek to traditional yards. Gradually, over

Starving Deer. Late February and especially March are very hard on our deer, particularly those in the north. This one didn't make it. Note the gaunt pelvic area and the protruding front shoulder blades. The general maturation of northern Michigan forests is going to mean an even greater decline in deer herds in the future. Of particular concern are northern conifer swamps; they're decreasing in size, number, and productivity. Deer cannot survive without them. New technologies give hope that conifers can be successfully replanted in the future. Without adequate deer harvests in the meantime, starvation is a certainty.

the next two weeks or so, this living tide will swell. In some places, virtual highways will form leading from summer farms and uplands into the lowland cedars or higher-ground hemlocks. In the case of a doe, it will be the same yard that her mother and her mother's mother used; in the case of a buck, it will be whatever yard his bachelor group uses—it may or may not be the one in which he spent his first winter. By mid-to-late January, some 5 percent to 10 percent of the available range will hold more than 95 percent of all the deer. During a series of especially mild winters some deer fail to migrate to yarding areas and instead choose to winter in what is more traditionally summer range. When a severe winter strikes, such as the winter of 1985–86, nearly all these animals succumb.

Deer throughout the northern Lower, meanwhile, are following much the same pattern, but their average travel distances will be less. Quantifying the wintertime movement of our southern Michigan herds is a much more unpredictable proposition, as is true, actually, of all of our farmland whitetails, be they in the U.P., the northern Lower, or southern Michigan. If, and when, our farmers harvest their crops, it makes a tremendous difference upon the movements and aggregational patterns these animals exhibit. It is known, for example, that the deer in central to northern Huron County in the Thumb will, in bad winters, move south as far as thirty-five to forty miles if the crops are down. If, however, as in the fall of 1985, '86 and again in '92, the fields are too wet for harvest, the deer are then far less likely to move. Harsh weather forces the movement of all animals. For deer this movement will be for a much shorter period of time, beginning later and ending sooner, than that of other forest animals. Nonetheless, when winter weather is at its worst, deer will get down into the thicker, more protective areas where wind chills and heat loss will be lessened.

Although so many deer are now forced to share a common range, they still maintain their much smaller family and bachelor groupings. Matriarch does still control their offspring and their movements, and dominant males still linger in the shadows with their more cautious brethren.

The critical factors for the deer at this time are to minimize heat loss and to maintain as much caloric intake as possible. For deer in the north the second factor translates into minimizing the degree of negative nutritional balance; there is no way they are going to take in as much nutritional energy as they're going to burn, they simply try to minimize the deficiency. For southern Michigan's cropland deer, this is much less of a problem.

The larger and more aggressive the individual animal, the better its chances of surviving this period. Prime-age individuals—both bucks and does—are seldom at high risk; it's the young, the old, and the weak that suffer the most. (In the winter of 1985–86, 85 percent of our losses were fawns—as is almost always the case.) That nine-year-old, heavily beamed twelve-point that was the very essence of buckdom last October is frail and weary by mid-March. He had gone into December's snows and cold weighing fully 25 percent less than at his peak in early October; it's been steadily downhill since then. His shoulder blades now jut ominously four inches above his back as he plods wearily along. His pelvic girdle is clearly etched against his skin. On the morning of March 18 it begins to snow, and a heavy, wet blanket six inches thick finally settles by two that afternoon. The winds shift to the north and temperatures plummet—zero degrees by ten that night and windchills of thirty below. By five o'clock the following morning, the buck cannot stand; by seven the monarch is dead.

The facts are immutable, and at times such as the winter of 1985–86 they're harshly demonstrated; the habitat can only support so many deer per square mile. If you attempt to build the population above those levels, you inflict irreparable damage upon that habitat, and it will thereafter support fewer deer. For both hunter and nonhunter alike it's high time we understood the message: if wild fluctuations in whitetail numbers are to be avoided two things must happen. First, the habitat must be managed more wisely; second, deer numbers must be kept in check.

The critical factor for the deer at this time is the reduction of heat loss. Their heavy winter coats act as such magnificent insulators that snow falling on them will not melt. Nonetheless, it's vital that the animals reduce their exposure to windchill and stay within the warmer portions of their habitat. Our coniferous stands—the so-called thermal cover—are so absolutely vital in the north. Left in the hardwoods, more open swales, and the pines, our northernmost herds would succumb. While ambient air temperatures will only differ by a couple degrees in the conifers, windchill differences are often more pronounced, and the real benefits are reductions in radiant and convective heat loss.

Over the course of one or two days, such differences would be insignificant, but over the course of two or three months they're absolutely critical. To further conserve vital calories, by late January the deer's metabolic rate will be diminished by as much as 30 percent and their activity levels by 50 percent. Fat deposits, which within adequate summer range were built up earlier, are now burned to help subsidize the meager rations imposed.

It's not the sudden blast of January's arctic air that kills; it's not the foot and a half of snow that falls on that cold early February night; it's not even the windchills of forty to fifty below for three straight nights in mid-March. Instead it's the cumulative effect of all three factors—and more—delivered relentlessly day after day. If the snows aren't too deep, if the yards are young enough, if we've managed the herds wisely, and if winter's icy grip loosens early enough, all is well with our deer herd despite the inevitable individual losses. Spring will come and life's cycle will quickly be renewed for yet another year.

2

Whitetail Management

On Sunday, March 2, 1986, DNR District Biologist James H. Hammill addressed a meeting of the Metropolitan Farmers' Union of Dickinson County. Thanks to association president Henry DeGroot, I was invited to tag along. As I sat there listening to Jim explain just where we are in terms of deer numbers within his district, it began to dawn on me that he is in a no-win situation. His is the proverbial position between the rock and the hard place. Let's examine some of the pressures that the DNR must contend with in this Upper Peninsula district.

Jim Hammill is the District Biologist for Wildlife District II in the U.P. This area is composed of Iron, Dickinson and Menominee counties. Within Jim's district lie fully 50 percent of all the deer in the U.P. Failure, should it ever occur, to manage this herd properly could well mean failure of the fabulous deer hunting for which this area of the U.P. has long been noted. Additionally, it's clear that such a failure would have severe economic impact upon many of the local merchants. Towns such as Iron Mountain and Crystal Falls rely heavily upon the infusion of tourist-related dollars as a part of their annual income; for many businesses, the hunting season is the height of that tourist trade. It has been calculated that if the deer population per square mile were reduced by half in northern Menominee County alone, a yearly reduction of one hundred thousand dollars in hunter-generated income for the area would be a direct result.

About 88 percent of the land mass in this district consists of forest lands, while almost 12 percent is agricultural. The southern half of Menominee County is heavily cultivated and grows mostly high-energy grains for the thriving dairy herds found here. Found here also are the highest deer densities anywhere in Michigan—sixty to seventy per square mile. This is the area that has the highest buck-hunter success rates of any place in the state, more than 35 percent, more than twice the statewide average. Southern Dickinson County also supports a thriving agricultural community. The main crops are potatoes, alfalfa, and corn. Deer densities are high as well, running at forty-five per square mile throughout much of the area. Farmers within both of these areas are incurring lots of crop damage; they are justifiably concerned about their future, and they want some relief. The DNR is well aware of, and in sympathy with, their plight.

One of the things that Jim Hammill told this farmers' gathering was that the following week he had a meeting scheduled with a local sportsmen's group. He said he knew that this group was prepared to present him with a petition, containing at least two hundred signatures, opposing any kind of a doe season or cropping plan for Dickinson County. (As it turned out, this meeting never materialized—but that's immaterial to the point I'm making.) "Based upon the assessments the DNR has been conducting in this area, I'd like to see the herd in southern Dickinson brought down to roughly thirty to thirty-five deer per square mile," he said. "This cannot be done without some sort of an antlerless kill, and I can't get an antlerless season in southern Dickinson County to fly unless we can sell it in Iron Mountain." In other words, Jim was saying that he can't give the farmers any kind of meaningful relief unless he can sell the idea to the hunters who live outside of the immediate problem area.

This is a situation common throughout all of Michigan— hunters from outside the problem areas heavily influence the decisions being made. We, as sportsmen, must become more sensitive to the farmers on whom we rely so heavily; we cannot afford to alienate these folks, and there's no reason for us to do so. We cannot expect them to continue to carry the economic burden of our ever increasing farmland deer herds. As explained later, this need to compromise with the farmer is becoming more important all the time.

To complicate the situation even further, what Jim Hammill said that night was only partly true—and he more than anyone else was painfully aware of it. It's not that Jim was misleading anyone, it's just that a lot of what may happen in that district could well be beyond his—or anyone's in the DNR—control. Two days before that meeting I'd traveled with Jim to a major wintering area, and what we saw was not a pretty sight—starving deer never are. The particular yard we visited was in northern Menominee County and it is not just another yard. It is the major yard in District II and carries deer from much of southern Marquette County, a major percentage of Dickinson County, nearly all of northern Menominee, and even some from the extreme western reaches of Delta County. This one yarding area is thus responsible for wintering deer from more than seven hundred square miles of uplands from one year to the next. The thermal cover within the yard is mature and, in its present age structure, it carries too many deer. As a result, with each year that passes, the yard is capable of carrying fewer and fewer deer.

"This yard is slowly losing its ability to hold deer, it needs to be managed," Jim explained. "The problems arise when we consider how it should be cut, and how the forest stands should then be regenerated. In large measure, my hands are tied in just how all of this progresses. This land is owned by a corporate timber company, and while it falls under the category of CFR land, the landowners up to now have taken the hard-nosed attitude that this is their land and they'll do with it as they damn well please."

CFR is the acronym for Commercial Forest Reserve. Land thus classified is enrolled in a program whereby it's open to the public as recreational land; in compensation for this the owner then receives a very sizable tax break. It's a program frequently used by large land-holding corporations as well as by private landowners, and it benefits us all. But what this means is that the citizens of Michigan are footing a large percentage of the tax burden on such lands. Shouldn't we then have a say in how they will be managed? The people of Michigan have a substantial vested interest in this land and, if challenged legally, I believe, the courts would agree. Meanwhile, Jim Hammill and the DNR are trying very hard to keep things from getting out-of-hand.

Succinctly put, the problem is this: some corporate landowners are managing their lands for maximum profit without regard to the impact that their management practices are having on other resources—especially wildlife. One of the most controversial practices is that of "conversion." Timber types that are productive of wildlife are typically clear cut and the site is then "converted" by planting a species more desirable to the corporation. Most commonly that species is red pine, and it's typically planted in large monocultural stands that offer little to wildlife. When this practice is undertaken in deer yard areas, the impact is greatly magnified. In this particular case, the habitat of literally tens of thousands of deer hangs upon these corporate decisions.

The situation described above has changed since March 1986, but unfortunately it has not been improved for the deer. In 1990, the DNR signed an agreement with the Mead Corporation regarding this land. The Lansing politicians thereby sold out Michigan, both its deer and its citizens. The agreement had many clauses, only a couple of which affected this yard. The rate at which the yard will be cut in the future was to slow down, not stop, and secondly, conversion would not occur in this particular area. Hemlock and cedar were to be replanted, thereby attempting to protect the future ability of this area to hold wintering deer. This, in itself, doesn't sound too bad; essentially that's what this yard needed. The rub came when the state agreed to tie the yard issue in with pollution issues that, so far as local DNR people knew, had until 1990 been treated as a separate problem. Nonetheless, the state agreed to back off on the pollution questions, which has not made our Wisconsin and Ontario neighbors real happy. One heck of a compromise is all I can say. Apparently both the corporation and the state have a common attitude: "If we can't starve the deer out, we'll poison them, the fish, and everything else, people included!" Somehow, I don't believe we've heard the end of this deer yard issue.

According to the DNR, the yard continues to be harvested at the rate of roughly three hundred acres per winter, while the replanting of seedling hemlock is only one hundred acres per year. The seedlings thus far planted are, as yet, still below the snowline, so it's too soon to tell if they'll be successful. The acid test will come when they creep above the snowline. Then the deer will either leave them to grow or nip them back, thus stunting and eventually killing them. The push of the timber industry for "conversion" continues unabated. We've not heard the end of this; this yard, as well as others throughout the entire northern two-thirds of Michigan, will dictate the future of our northern deer and, right now, things don't look good.

The course that the management of our deer herds in Michigan should follow is never clear cut; it is a complex process that is never the same day to day, let alone year to year. It is not the same in one region as it is in the next; it can even vary tremendously within the same region. It must, generally, be accomplished over a land area, much of which is either privately owned or in the form of federal holdings; the state currently has no control over the habitat conditions on either. Even where the state owns a large percentage of the land involved, it certainly has no control over the market demands for the land's timber products. Harvesting (habitat manipulation) cannot occur on a large scale without a buyer at the other end of the process. I believe it is important that sportsmen gain a little insight, and historical perspective, about the problems, as well as where we are today.

We must first realize that until 1933, when Aldo Leopold published his textbook *Game Management*, there was no such thing as "wildlife management." Scattered events occurring here and there for many years, such as the court

Buck in Autumn Woods. Controlled sports hunting is one of the most powerful management tools available to us. By the careful regulation of the annual kill, a herd can be kept within the carrying capacity of the habitat and the normal boom-to-bust cycle of "natural" populations can be avoided.

case of *Geer v. Connecticut* in 1896, had firmly thrust the management of nonmigratory game onto the various states, but there was no scientific basis upon which to build such management. Management, what little there was, was always a haphazard, trial-and-error, scattergun type of process, geared mostly toward the timber industry, and to limiting the number of animals taken. Leopold, by combining the science of ecology with the theories of management, quickly changed all that.

In Michigan, both preceding and coincident with this new scientific field, a raft of sweeping environmental changes set the stage for practically everything that has since happened to our deer herd. In a very real sense, it is only now that we finally have both the knowledge and the potential (through habitat manipulation made possible by a thriving timber industry) to alter our wildlife habitat in a truly desirable manner.

When the first Europeans came to Michigan, deer were found throughout our state, but populations were extremely low compared with today. This was particularly true in the northern two-thirds of the state. As our southern hardwood stands fell before the ax and plow, the deer largely disappeared. The overwhelming desire of the settlers was to tame a harsh and uncontrolled land. In 1875, only 200,000 people lived within our boundaries, and by far the majority of them lived south of Saginaw; they quickly changed forever the wilderness they had found. No one dreamed that the resources of this state—deer included—could ever be depleted. There were no hunting seasons, no bag limits, no hunting licenses, no restraints whatsoever. Game was shot as game was needed.

In an attempt to fulfill insatiable demands from ever growing eastern cities, market hunters scoured the land. In 1878, 70,000 whitetail carcasses were shipped east from the Lower Peninsula; by 1880 that number had grown to 100,000, and even more animals taken were taken for use in Michigan. Records do not reflect the total kill of that era, but it obviously exceeded the animal's ability to reproduce itself. By 1885, the southern lands of Michigan were under tillage, and the once-expansive stands of virgin hardwoods were gone. So too in vast areas were the whitetails. A good many southern counties would not have white-tailed deer again until the early 1960s.

By the 1870s, humanity was pushing the frontier north. The unbroken stands of pine in the northern Lower were beginning to fall; by the 1880s they were rapidly disappearing. For more than a decade, from the 1880s to the 1890s, Michigan led the nation in timber production, at times cutting more than one billion board feet of timber per year. The term "clear cutting" took on a horrible new meaning as everything in the lumberjack's path fell. Terrible brush fires followed, setting the stage for a deer explosion that was without equal.

Finally, in 1900, the state began a feeble reforestation program. Concurrent with this came a successful campaign to prevent further fires. As marginal farms and clear-cut lands reverted to the state for nonpayment of taxes, state land reserves flourished, especially in the north. At the same time, hundreds of thousands of acres in northern Michigan were being gathered under federal control as the national forest system came into being. As conditions changed and second growth timber took over, the once marginal north country became a new mecca for deer. With historically low deer densities, the early stage successional growth had the opportunity to flourish unimpeded. Aspen and birch responded at once, and so did hemlock and cedar. Once the fires died out and reseeding began, new growth rapidly took over.

The northern timber surge continued, and even before the northern Lower Peninsula was denuded, the butchery had begun in the Upper. The results were the same: the land was plundered, but when given the chance to reseed, both the vegetation and the highly adaptable whitetail flourished. Whereas the mature, largely unbroken pine and northern hardwood forests of the north supported few deer, the new second growth was ideal habitat. By 1930, our northern Michigan deer herds had exploded.

In the forty years or so it took for these changes to occur, our environmental consciousness awakened. Rules and regulations had been sporadic, while early enforcement and acceptance were nil; but efforts were underway to control the wanton slaughter of our game. State sportsmen's clubs, through their mother organization the Michigan Sportsmen's Association, had earlier fought hard for laws regulating how, when, where, and for what purposes game could be taken. But the state was reluctant to get involved and chose instead to leave the enforcement of these laws up to the various county sheriffs and local prosecutors. The result was no enforcement at all.

Finally, in 1887, the state caved in to sportsmen's pressure and created the office of State Game Warden. Even so, funding was woefully inadequate, and no effective enforcement campaign could ever be mounted. There were simply too many loopholes in state-based game laws, and too few men to try and enforce them. Because these problems were pervasive and not unique to Michigan, a new law at the federal level in 1900 came into being; it was known as the *Lacey Act*.

Undoubtedly, the *Lacey Act* was the biggest single advancement along the road to protecting our game up to that point. Overnight, it became a federal offense to transport illegally taken wildlife across state lines. This accomplished what various state laws had been unable to do in more than twenty years; it put an end, once and for all, to market hunting. It came too late for the passenger pigeon. It was almost too late for the whitetail, the wood duck, the bison, the turkey and many other species.

Keep in mind what I've described up to this point has had nothing whatsoever to do with the science of wildlife management—there was no such thing. We had obviously been "managing" our game in a very negative sense, but such management invariably was an effect of the manipulation of the environment, not the result of wildlife management per se. There was no state agency, or department, charged with the responsibility of management until 1921. Finally, all the various conservation-related activities of separate agencies and offices were brought together under one new department: the Department of Conservation. Because the system was hampered by political interference, it was deemed by sportsmen to be flawed, but it at least consolidated functions so decisions and policies could be more effectively coordinated.

At roughly the same time, there was a new impetus in

our higher education system to produce well-trained professional specialists to oversee our environment, our forests, our water, and our wildlife. As beneficial as these courses of study were, the ones geared toward wildlife still had to wait for Leopold, and his creative genius, to separate them from forestry and fundamental biological theory.

By the 1930s, whitetail numbers throughout the north were at historical highs, and every year their ranks grew. As the new second-growth timber spread, whitetails flourished. The spreading economic affluence of the 1920s, along with the much improved automobile of the day and paved roads, allowed many southern Michigan hunters for the first time ever to head north in search of game. Your grandfather, or your father, has undoubtedly told you about the fabulous hunting that greeted him, deer aplenty and lots of big bucks! This situation improved throughout the 1930s and '40s. It's believed that the Michigan deer herd numbered as high as 1.5 million animals by the early 1940s, with almost all of them in the northern two-thirds of the state.

Deer populations throughout the southern counties were so low that the entire area had been closed to all deer hunting from 1926 until 1948. Prior to '26, a smattering of southern, and several northern Lower counties, had been closed off-and-on since 1891. (No counties have been closed to deer hunting since 1948.) The geographical distribution of our herd continues to change even today, and it has changed markedly since 1960. In 1960, it was believed that 30 percent of our deer lived in the U.P., 65 percent in the northern half of the Lower, and only 5 percent in southern Michigan.

When I was just a kid I well remember going north with my folks, and how I'd anxiously wait until we got north of Pinconning so I could see all the deer—and boy did I ever! You'd get into that area and farther north, and it was as if someone had thrown a switch. There were deer everywhere, whereas just a few miles south there seemingly were none at all. At night we'd go out riding and it was nothing to see fifty or even a hundred deer. Not anymore. Now I hear people say, "The damn DNR, we don't have any deer left and they're still saying that we've got over a million—where the hell are they?" Well, they have moved. As habitats shift, adjust and mature, deer populations follow. It's not the DNR's fault; it's simply a natural progression as the result of environmental and social changes.

I mentioned earlier that by 1885 nearly all of southern Michigan had been timbered and was then under tillage, and that's much the way it remained until the mid-1920s. At that point, industrialization, spurred on by the thriving auto industry, swept through Michigan. Most major towns including Detroit, Pontiac, Flint, Saginaw, Midland, Kalamazoo, Grand Rapids and others gave new life to struggling rural folks who had been trying to eke out a living on marginal farmlands. There was a massive population shift to the cities, which lasted until the 1960s. Those southern Michigan lands that were too sandy, or too wet, or too contoured to provide good farming were abandoned. Thousands and thousands of acres were left untended, to revert to brush-filled fields, thickets, and reclaimed swales. Such lands in southern Michigan, with our generally mild winters and surrounded by high-energy crop fields, have proven a boon for our deer. In a dramatic reversal of the trends found forty to fifty years earlier, our deer herd has now shifted markedly to the southern counties.

By 1989, the distribution of our deer had changed radically; more than 30 percent now live in southern Michigan, while somewhat less than 20 percent live in the U.P., and roughly 50 percent live in the northern Lower. For the first time since deer-kill records have been tallied, more bucks were harvested in 1985 from the southern Lower Peninsula than from the U.P. This pattern will probably be with us for quite some time. As I point out in Chapter 6, the whitetail has an uncanny ability to live right under our noses. Not only can it survive, it'll thrive as well—providing it has adequate habitat.

Way back in the early 1940s, when all those deer lived in northern Michigan, trouble was on the horizon for them, and the Department of Conservation knew it.

Habitats have an insidious way of developing to maturity. There's a natural and orderly progression from grasses and forbs to brambles and brush and from aspen and birch to oaks and maples. The changes—"succession" as it's called—

are never-ending until final maturity or the "climax" stage is reached. It was obvious to many as early as the late 1930s that this was the direction in which we were headed, and it was known for a long time—just as it is today—that mature habitats carry far fewer deer. Knowing full well what the overall feelings of the sportsmen of Michigan were, the Department of Conservation was very reluctant to propose widespread doe seasons, and yet it knew that was exactly what was needed.

Throughout many areas of both the northern Lower and the Upper, we lost deer through starvation nearly every winter during the late 1940s and early '50s. Even in the years when we didn't, too many deer, yarding in areas too small for them, caused such serious overbrowsing that the area was capable of holding even fewer deer. In such areas, deer have two factors working against them: (1) the habitat continues to mature, the trees grow a little larger and more of the lower limbs die off, and even without deer browsing on them, there's going to be less browse the following year; (2) by over-browsing, the deer actually eat an even higher number of limbs leaving less browse for the following winter (see *Figure 2.1)*. It takes a range several years to regenerate after over-browsing occurs. This was happening over large areas of northern Michigan all through the 1940s and early '50s.

Finally the Department of Conservation began making some inroads into the sportsmen's resistance to shooting does. In 1949 the state of Michigan had its first liberal antlerless season in almost thirty years. (There had been some very restricted antlerless deer seasons in Allegan and Van Buren counties, which ran annually from 1941 to '48, but on average only fifty deer per year were harvested during these hunts.) Hunters saw from this first hunt that disaster did not strike, the deer did not disappear, and the department was able to hold a larger hunt in 1952. Still, department biologists knew it was not enough—more does had to be taken if starvation losses were to be lessened. What has followed from that time to today has been a public relations nightmare, and no one is free from blame: not the Department of Conservation (which became the Department of Natural Resources [DNR] in 1969),

Figure 2.1
Deer are dependent on their essential habitat

The viability of our deer herd is totally dependent upon the condition of its habitat. Habitat undergoes continual change in at least two ways. First, the change is through the process of maturation, illustrated by the schematic drawing presented here. Insidious and unrelenting, it is easy to overlook maturation changes, but they are no less real or damaging. The second is through the sudden and dramatic alteration of habitat, be it man-made (logging, conversion to agricultural lands, the spreading of urban areas) or natural disasters, such as fire or tornado damage.

The key to maintaining our herd is to replace their essential habitat. This is especially important in the northern two-thirds of the state where the so-called thermal cover is the deer's only protection from certain death. (Drawing by Roger Miller) and not the sportsmen of our state.

The state did a credible job of selling us on the need for a doe harvest, but it failed miserably in educating the average sportsman as to why it was needed. The typical hunter got only half the message: "They want us to thin the herd." As a result, our state's hunters have become polarized, and unfortunately this still plagues us today. Some have developed the flippant attitude, "OK, they want the damn does shot, I'll shoot 'em," and they shoot everything they see. (Poaching is a serious problem and, according to some estimates, may equal or exceed our legal kill.) Others have taken the attitude that no matter what, they wouldn't shoot a doe, and they won't associate with anyone who would! Fortunately, the vast majority of us are somewhere in between these two radical positions; we're willing to agree that a doe season is probably a necessary evil, but we don't really understand why. The DNR, to be honest, still has not done a very good job in educating us.

Whitetail management is not an easily understood subject. It has a lot of wrinkles and even today a lot of unknowns, but it's important that we do understand it. Perhaps if we do, we'll then all be able to pull more effectively for the purpose of attaining our desired, and common, goal: the finest habitats possible, with the healthiest herds.

Let's examine the issue of doe seasons: the reasons for having them, their effects, and their benefits. By statute, the DNR can only recommend an antlerless season for one or more of the following reasons: (1) the herd is beyond the carrying capacity of the winter range, (2) there's been excessive crop damage, or (3) there are excessive highway kills.

Once it's been decided that a doe season is appropriate, the ideal deer density for that area is calculated based on field data and past studies. Such calculations are always given in terms of deer per square mile and they are based, as much as is humanly possible, upon sound data and facts. In reality, the only time a doe season in some form is not appropriate is when an attempt is made to build up a herd's numbers, and the only time that is a prudent option is when the habitat can adequately carry more animals. Unfortunately, it is frequently public sentiment, rather than scientific fact, that dictates the DNR's final recommendations.

The benefits of balancing a herd with its habitat are many. The most important is that those animals that remain will be healthier and more fit. When populations are such that artificial feeding programs are necessary to get them through most winters, or when we routinely lose animals through starvation even in average winters, then we're carrying too many, and no amount of hunter satisfaction can justify such a situation. Another benefit of a balanced herd is that healthier animals will produce more viable offspring. A higher percentage of animals will be bucks, and each buck's antler development will be enhanced as well.

The disadvantages? There are none—not in the long run. A failing (maturing) habitat is going to carry fewer deer—period. It's not a question of whether or not we want it to, it's simply a question of whether we let nature take its course, with starvation and loss of reproductive ability, or do we intervene in a sensible, controlled and timely manner? This is precisely the situation we currently have (and have had for many years now) in many areas of the north, i.e., the western end of the U.P. and Crawford County (among others) in the Lower.

When Leopold created the science of wildlife management, he did so on purely theoretical grounds. He argued brilliantly that wildlife populations could be successfully managed or manipulated in desired directions if we but understood the various factors that control them. As is the case with any new area of study, his theory lacked sound supporting data, but he showed us the direction we needed and he gave us the principles to follow.

Leopold spent the latter part of his life teaching and gathering the data that he earlier lacked. By the late 1930s, many of his students were doing the same, and the search for this data goes on today. Despite this lack of information, our wildlife managers still had the responsibility to manage, and that we have as many whitetails (not to mention turkeys, wood ducks and others) today as we do is testimony to the type of job they've performed. They've done remarkably well, but understandably they've made mistakes—and

Deer in Winter Yard. The fortunes of our northernmost herds are entirely dependent upon how we manage their habitat in the next few years. If habitats are left to mature, or manipulated for timber production only, then our herds will decline. Of primary concern is how to handle, preserve, and improve the winter range.

they'll make mistakes in the future as well.

As mentioned, wildlife managers have often neglected to argue their needs in a clear, logical and understandable manner to the laymen whose support they needed. Also, there have been a few glaring cases of miscalculations. There's no denying that at times, such as in the early 1970s, we overharvested our does in certain areas of the state. But as sportsmen we must realize too that this entire process— and it's only been fifty years—has been a learning process. Management principles are not written in stone. The data and the technology sorely needed simply didn't exist, and on top of that, our wildlife people (no more than the rest of us) cannot predict the future. Is next winter going to be typical, less severe than average, or very harsh? What is the demand for lumber products likely to be in 1999, or tougher yet, in the year 2010? Is our nation going to need more hardwood or pulp? What use is such knowledge, even with a correct forecast, if you don't have the industrial base with which to produce it? What's the next major societal, technological or recreational advance that's going to affect our deer?

As sportsmen we must realize our wildlife people are faced with a multitude of variables that are totally beyond their control. It is too easy for us to sit back, as we so often do, and blame the DNR for every blip that occurs in our deer population. We'd be much further ahead if we continued to demand accountability from the DNR, to make sure we have the best-trained personnel possible in our wildlife division, and to push for the required continuing research. Even today there remain many unanswered questions about our whitetails and their environment, and it's to the benefit of us all that we continue searching for the answers.

We've long had a superb research program in Michigan, one of the most respected in the nation. Cusino, in the U.P., and both Houghton and Rose Lake research areas in the Lower have produced a wealth of management-related research data that has greatly helped our field managers. It is vital that we continue with these efforts in the future.

Another tremendous influence over our state's deer herd is the federal government through the national forests. Beyond any doubt the national forests have done a far less adequate job of maintaining deer habitat than has the state. In every area under federal control, deer populations have dwindled more than they have on adjoining lands, and there's no arrest in sight for these declining figures.

In 1985, all the national forests issued proposals for the future management of their lands, and in every single case they have left our wildlife wanting. The national forests' major emphasis, despite their denials to the contrary, has always been and continues to be on timber production. They care little about wildlife, and with each proposal that has been advanced, wildlife numbers are bound to decline even further.

With almost one-third of the land mass in the U.P. falling under national stewardship, what the Feds do here will obviously impact intensely upon this area. They do little to convince me that they are serious in their proposals "to maintain population (1980) of 22,000 deer (estimated)" when they insist on describing "balsam fir—jack-pine types" as

Fawn and Iron Mule. Unrelenting hunger takes precedence over the fear of humans. By late winter the sounds of screaming chain saws and revving motors act as attractants instead of deterrents, as the deer come in to feed on the fallen tops (white cedar in this case).

winter thermal cover suitable to the extreme western U.P. (These quotes are taken from page IV-34 of the *Proposed Land and Management Plan* for the Ottawa National Forest, November 1985.) Every single major reference available for the northern Midwest climes suggests fir and pine as inadequate thermal cover. Equally well documented is the fact that white cedar and hemlock are the only northern trees capable of satisfying the whitetails' winter needs. The proposals call for maintaining these species at their current levels—too few and too mature. With these proposals, the U.S. Forest Service seems intent upon fulfilling the prediction it has promulgated: that wildlife recreation days will remain essentially static on its lands through 2035.

The problems we're facing in the management of our deer will not disappear. Northern Michigan forest lands will continue to mature, and our northern conifer swamps will continue to deteriorate and dwindle, if we don't somehow arrest this progression. Deer will continue to plague our farmers. But now, more than ever before, we have the opportunity to mitigate these problems. New technologies and knowledge have given us the ability to do many things we could not have done just a few years ago. A rapidly expanding forest industry, particularly in the Upper Peninsula, now gives us the "clout" to renew habitat, provided it's used wisely.

The Mead and Champion corporations alone now have a combined capability in the U.P of processing more than one million cords of timber products per year. Such capacity allows for a lot of "tinkering" with the habitat. Let's be certain it's done wisely. Perhaps Leopold said it best: "the first step in intelligent tinkering is not to lose any of the pieces."

There is simply too much at stake—and it's not with the narrow focus of the deer hunter that I say this—for us to mismanage what is now within our grasp. The economy of the U.P.—the economy of Michigan—needs a vibrant, healthy timber industry. But the other pieces we need to keep track of include the tourist industry, the lakes, rivers, natural flora, and the lifestyle so important to the people of the U.P.

We've come a long way, and it seems clear to me that the path we're following points to a bright future for the white-tailed deer in Michigan. Their populations will obviously continue to shift and adjust in the future, but they are secure.

Part II

Special Deer— Select Places

3

Big Bucks
Are Different

It was October 1, many years ago. A high school buddy and I were partridge hunting. We were in a very dense swale, northeast of Gladwin, in the northern Lower Peninsula. All of a sudden there was a commotion in the windfall right beside me. Believing, momentarily, it was a partridge trying to explode from cover, I began to swing my 20-gauge pump in that direction.

What came out of that windfall was not a pat, but the largest white-tailed buck I'd ever seen! He broke cover, took about ten paces, stopped, and stared at me. For what seemed an eternity, that buck just stood there in all his magnificent glory, staring at me.

If there is one thing that ignited an inextinguishable desire for big white-tailed bucks, it had to be that instant in time. I'll never forget it. Even today, all whitetails are compared with my memory of that long-ago buck.

As a kid who had yet to tag his first deer, that buck awed me. More than anything else, I wanted to hunt bucks like that. "But how?" I wondered. Not knowing anyone who had ever taken a whitetail like that, it was not an easy question.

Now, after more than twenty-five years of deer hunting experience, I believe I've gained some insight into the complexity of that simple question, and solved some of the riddles regarding big bucks.

The real key to successfully hunting any animal is in the understanding of the creature; this is especially true in the case of trophy whitetails.

It is important to make the distinction between whitetails and trophy whitetails. Trophy whitetails are by all accounts among the rarest of big game animals. There are an estimated thirteen million white-tailed deer in the continental United States. Roughly 60 percent of these are believed to be does, so there are five million bucks. It is believed that four or possibly five bucks out of every million would qualify for "the book," or a listing in Boone and Crockett.

If even ten times this number would qualify as "big" for our purposes here, we're still talking about only 250 animals spread across all of the United States. That comes out to one animal for every 14,400 square miles!

One thing is certain: no matter how you define "big" or

Mature Buck . A fully developed buck such as this one is a sight to behold.

"trophy" in terms of mature white-tailed bucks, they're few and far between.

Why Are They Different?

As a biologist, I'm intrigued with the question of whether big bucks are different because they live longer and therefore are wiser, or whether they start out different and therefore live longer. The jury is still convened on that one. As a hunter, I'm just satisfied to know that they *are* different, and in order to pursue them intelligently I must understand those differences. I must know the nature of those differences, and how they translate into the behavior exhibited by big deer.

Big Bucks Are Loners

White-tailed deer are for the most part gregarious animals, living in a principally matriarchal society. They live in small family units of three to five or more individuals. These units generally consist of a mature doe, her offspring of the previous spring, and sometimes her offspring from the year before. The majority of the time, two or more of these basic family units will come together and form even larger groups. Small bucks up to a year-and-a-half old will frequently be found within, or at least associated with, these groups.

However, older (and hence bigger) bucks will seldom be seen among the does. In fact, they'll actively avoid association with them for most of the year. When large bucks are found in close association with other deer, it's generally with other large bucks. It's not uncommon for two, three, or even four big bucks to live together in an all-male unit. These groups will be quite permanent, except during the rut when the bucks become irritable with one another and drift apart for a time.

They Are Secretive

If your aim is simply to shoot a whitetail, hunt the fringe or edge of cover. Hunt openings in heavy cover; hunt crop fields in farm areas; and hunt runways leading from feeding to heavily used bedding areas. Hunt areas that show a lot of

Buck in Velvet. For the nimrod, serious in his quest for a truly outstanding trophy, it's never too early to start. Study and quiet, persistent observation, along with never being satisfied that you know enough, are the keys to success.

deer sign and a high incidence of deer usage. If, however, you desire to shoot a trophy whitetail then you'll want to avoid such areas like the plague!

Big bucks, if they use openings at all, only do so when forced. Or they use openings under the complete cover of darkness. Several years ago I hunted a farm in southern Michigan. On the fourth day of the season I shot a superb eight-point, with a twenty-three-inch spread, and twenty-nine-inch main beams. As I sat admiring him, the farmer's twenty-two-year-old son came along a nearby creek checking his rat traps. For several seconds he just stood there with his mouth open. "Man, I've been watching the deer around here all my life; I've never seen one that big. I never dreamed one like that lived here!" As I said, truly big bucks are seldom seen.

Long before the first rays of daylight, big bucks will abandon crop fields, orchards, and open woodlots and head for dense and/or isolated cover—their natural haunts. They won't leave this cover again until long after nightfall. Because of such behavioral traits, big bucks often live almost under your nose and you'll never know they are there. This cannot be overemphasized. For this reason, a high percentage of white-tailed bucks that live four and a half years or longer die of natural causes.

I'd be willing to bet that within ten miles of the area I normally hunt in southern Michigan at least three, and perhaps five, bucks die of old age each year! I believe the major reason for this is most hunters use tactics that are ineffective for taking mature bucks.

On opening day a few years ago, I thought, rather naively, that I might actually catch a big buck in the open. There were two dense tangles of cover in my hunting area, separated by an opening roughly one hundred yards wide. From the sign present, I had every reason to believe there was a big buck freely using both areas to hole up during the day. I thought if I covered the opening, perhaps I'd catch him pussyfooting between the two.

Shortly after daybreak I heard a deer moving to my left and in front of me, approaching the opening. Moments later a doe stepped cautiously out and slowly followed the runway that cut between the two pockets of cover. Shortly after that, I again heard a deer approaching, just like the first one. Once more a doe nervously broke cover, slowly following the run. A couple hours passed and nothing moved. I had seen no other hunters and had heard only a couple shots, far off in the distance. Just before eleven I again heard a deer approaching.

The cover was so thick that in the earlier cases I could not see the does until they stepped out. This time it was the same. The deer approached the opening, just as the others had done, and stopped. This time, however, the deer bolted across the opening in a flat-out run. From the instant he hit the open until he disappeared on the other side, he never broke stride, he never slowed down. I can still see the sunlight glinting off his massive rack! Big bucks are smart, and that fellow was nobody's fool; he wasn't about to get waylaid in the open. I left that night feeling pretty foolish. I should have known better.

They Move in Slow Motion

This is not a contradiction to the anecdote above. When exposed, a big buck will get back into cover as quickly and directly as he possibly can. The thing to remember is that he'll seldom expose himself.

Move through good deer country, and you'll see deer scattering in front of you, running off in all directions as you approach them. Watch deer feed; they're nervous, anxious, and at the first detection of danger they'll bound off, flags flying. Big bucks are skulkers and much craftier at avoiding detection. They much prefer to walk away from danger or, even better, they'll let danger walk away from them. Since they're seldom caught in the open, this is often possible. They'll frequently lie where they are and let danger—you—pass them by.

Big bucks are far less inclined than most deer to retreat at the first hint of danger. Even when they are disturbed enough to exit, big bucks generally do so slowly, unnoticed. Seldom will they flush, flags flying—more likely they'll sneak off.

The seasoned hunter will take advantage of this trait by hunting in slow motion. Use your eyes and ears, instead of your feet.

When I believe there's a big buck in the vicinity, I sit tight. To the uninitiated this sounds easy, but it is very demanding and crucial to the trophy hunter. My wife, who is a nonhunter, cannot understand why I'm so exhausted by the end of a day in the woods. But a hunter who from daybreak to dark is constantly on the alert for any sound or movement, no matter how subtle, is worn out by day's end. If he's not, then he's doing something wrong! Deer hunting for big bucks is hard work.

The Significance of the Rut

The latest research in relation to the rut holds tremendous significance for trophy hunters. It has been discovered that the significance of scrapes is the identification by other deer—both bucks and does—of the most dominant bucks in the area. It is not, as formerly thought, where the dominant buck actually meets most of the estrous does. It is, however, the dominant buck in any given area that makes the majority of the scrapes.

Research shows that all deer within the area will visit and investigate scrapes. The dominant buck will, in all probability, visit and renew them only after dark. Therefore, bucks actually shot over scrapes are most likely subordinate to—smaller than—the bucks that made them. How then do we get to the real big boys, the ones we desire? The answer to this question involves a lot of hard work and a thorough knowledge of the deer in your hunting area.

The entire purpose of the scrapes a buck makes is to identify himself as a dominant animal. This communication is accomplished by the rubbing of the overhanging tree limbs with head glands, and by urinating on the scrapes. This lets all the deer in the area know who he is; it tells the does that when they're ready, he'll be available. When the does are ready to breed they will then seek him out. The does do this by increasing their levels of activity. During the twenty-four hours or so when a doe is in estrus, she will be as much as twenty-eight times more active than usual. This heightened activity level guarantees her encounter with a suitable buck.

Since the buck wants all the deer to get the message that he is ready and willing to serve, he makes his scrapes in the area with the highest rate of deer usage at that time. Your job then, in scouting, is to locate that area. You must answer specific questions. Where are the deer feeding? Where are the majority bedding? Where, given the above, is the densest cover available for old "mossyhorns," since he demands isolation and protection yet must be available?

The accompanying sketch (see *Figure 3.1*) is specific for farm country, but analogous layouts could be made for any area. The most remote corner of our Upper Peninsula, with its big woods habitat, will have cover meeting the above requirements and located near the area used by most deer. That's precisely the place to look for signs of Mr. Big. Look for particularly large scrapes—three feet or more in diameter (remember, bigger bucks, generally speaking, make bigger scrapes). Look for outsize tracks sunk deeply into the earth, which indicate extreme weight. Look also for the oversized droppings typical of big bucks.

Effective Hunting Strategies

If you hunt in a group and are willing to share your opportunity at a trophy, drives can be very effective, but only when done correctly. Two hunters are most effective with this technique. The dense cover to which a big buck retreats is often totally isolated, and unless absolutely forced to do so, he will not leave it. With one hunter on stand, the other can slowly and as quietly as possible move through the area. The driver stands almost no chance of a shot (those monstrous racks don't grow over pea-size brains), but if he's persistent enough, the blocker will eventually get his chance. Of course, the hunters should switch roles at agreed upon intervals.

Drives, when you know a trophy is utilizing an area, may be the most effective hunting strategy possible.

The only other effective method for hunting really big bucks is to take a stand and stay put. Big bucks will not forsake their havens during daylight hours, but they will move about within their confines, usually quite freely. To be most effective, the hunter should be on his post a half hour before daylight each day and should not leave until after dark—period! Once the buck senses your presence (he will if you're moving about during the day) the jig is up and you might as well move on.

It has been my experience that the middle portion of the day is actually the best bet for really big bucks. I've seen

Figure 3.1
Farm country sketch, showing scrapes of dominant buck

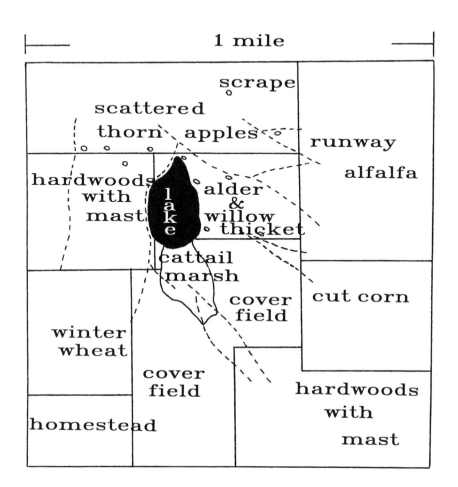

more big bucks between 11:00 A.M. and 3:00 P.M. than any other time period. I believe that by midday these big boys are hungry, stiff and perhaps cold. They get up off their beds, wander about within cover for an hour or so, and then lie down again. That's why it's critical to get into the cover early and stay put.

Hunting a stand for trophy deer, done correctly (which means in the right cover), offers the hunter very little chance of seeing deer, since very few deer inhabit such cover. But, paradoxically, your chances of seeing the trophy of a lifetime are excellent. Such hunting takes discipline and a tremendous desire, but the results, for the hunter who can stand the strain, are very often worth it!

Referring to the schematic diagram, the majority of the deer will feed more actively in the alfalfa field (upper right corner) and on the mast in the hardwoods to the left. They are bedding among the thorn apples along the upper boundary. The most dominant buck in the area has created a line of scrapes along the broken edge extending from the hardwoods to the corner of the alder/willow tangle just to the right of the lake. The scrapes identify him to the herd and allow the does to know he's willing. He'll then bed within the alder/willow thicket with access to all his biological requirements and also the solitude and protection he requires.

Just where a hunter might position himself for a hunt would be dependent upon several factors. Early season bowhunters, in an area with little hunting pressure, might choose a stand near where the lake, thorn apples and willow thicket meet. With little human intrusion, a big buck might well wander to the edge of the thicket before dark or perhaps linger near the edge even after daybreak.

A midseason rifle hunter should find an avenue leading into the interior of the thicket and plan to remain the whole season, if need be. By then the buck he's after will have seen (and heard) enough hunting action to know he wants no part of it. Locate yourself between a major runway (such as the one leading from the thorn apples) and the lake, or between the runway and a favorite bedding area. Do not attempt to sneak into a bedding area. This will only alert the buck and

Bucks in Fall. While it's true that a truly big buck could be caught almost anywhere, it's equally true that the vast majority of them are to be found in heavy cover. This is then the place to concentrate your efforts.

change his pattern, reducing your chances to near zero.

A late season muzzle-loader or archer should concentrate on southerly exposures within the dense cover. On particularly sunny yet cold days, he should take a stand along the boundary area between the willow thicket and the cover field, or perhaps along the edge of the cattail marsh. Here the buck can garner the warmth of the sun and still have an easy and rapid retreat to cover. *Remember that cover is always the critical component of any hunting strategy designed to tag a big white-tailed buck.*

One Last Thought

Now that I've said all I have about hunting "big" or "trophy" bucks, I want to add that I believe in some ways our emphasis on trophy hunting is exaggerated, and totally out of line. I strongly believe that all the emphasis we have with huge, outsize racks places an extremely unfair burden on most

Figure 3.2
Where the big bucks are tagged

Ever wonder where Michigan's biggest bucks come from? Prior to 1981, the answer was the subject of pure speculation. But then *Commemorative Bucks of Michigan* came into existence and now we have a very good idea of just where our biggest bucks are tagged. The accompanying map records bucks officially scored by CBM. The numbers in bold for each county are the number of bucks that have met CBM's minimum standards (140 Boone & Crockett points), which have been taken regardless of the year. The outline numbers listed in some of the counties are the number of bucks taken in the various 1985 seasons (archery, rifle and muzzle-loader), which met the minimum CBM standards.

Note that the vast majority of our biggest animals today come from two main regions: the extreme southernmost counties in the Lower Peninsula, or the U.P. Very few "trophy" animals today are taken from the northern Lower Peninsula. Kalkaska County is a good example: of the fifteen heads that meet CBM's minimum standards, only five were taken in the 1980s and two others in the late 1970s! Of the 132 registered from Iron County in the U.P., forty were taken in the 1980s and fully half of them have been taken since 1970.

hunters, especially our younger hunters. I further believe that this fascination we perpetuate has two very adverse effects: (1) it increases poaching and illicit activities via peer pressure among the young, and (2) it greatly decreases the sense of satisfaction and accomplishment young and/or inexperienced hunters should feel when they tag a smaller buck.

In the fall of 1984, I was hunting on a farm in the Thumb region. The farmer had three sons, all very nice young men and, from what I could tell, all good sportsmen. As is typical of my deer hunting efforts, I was out and about the farm and the immediate area at least six weeks prior to the actual season. Over time, I got to know the farmer and his family, and they became accustomed to my presence. The normally quiet and reserved boys gradually warmed up, and we began to talk at length. Finally, about a week before the season actually opened, the oldest boy, "Joe," told me that he'd taken his very first buck the year before on the farm. "But it's only a small four-point, not much to brag about," he said, almost apologetically.

Trophy hunting, especially trophy hunting for white-tailed bucks, is just like any other aspiration in life. Every high school freshman on a junior varsity football team must, at some time or another, have visions of becoming the next Barry Sanders or Dick Butkus. Of course, few will. For every state college freshman, how many dream of becoming a doctor or a nuclear physicist? Again, few will.

Trophy hunting is no different; it's a goal many strive for, but the limitations of time, patience, aptitude, skill and money will restrict it to few hunters. I firmly believe trophy hunting to be the pinnacle of the sport, the ultimate goal attained by just a few, following many years of study and hard work. It is not a realistic, overnight goal for the young hunter or for the man who casually approaches the sport of hunting. For us to promote "Big Buck" contests and then look down our noses at the smaller heads is a foolish, snobbish, and painfully unfair attitude to bestow on our younger hunters like my friend Joe. I hope you read this, Joe, and I sincerely hope that someday you finally feel the sense of accomplishment you deserve from that "small four-point."

You see, Joe, that buck may have only carried four points, but he was a whitetail—in my mind the finest of all big game animals anywhere. Don't ever apologize, you took him as a true sportsman would.

Whitetails In the Farmland

Midmorning in mid-November found me alertly skirting a cedar swamp on one side, and a standing cornfield on the other. I moseyed along a step at a time, looking for sign and, hopefully, for deer. During the previous two hours I'd seen plenty of sign, but no deer. Finally I worked my way up a long incline; here the corn had been cut and the cedars gradually gave way, first to a dense alder thicket, and then to a thick stand of hardwoods.

A couple scrapes along the wood's edge, which I'd found a week earlier, were still evident, but no longer fresh. The rut was far from over, but the checking of scrapes was obviously a thing of the past. When I reached the crest of the hill, the land fell away in front of me and I sat down to rest. Still hunting, if properly done, is mentally but not physically taxing, and I sat down, more to rest my mind than my body.

Nestled at the base of the hill was a farmhouse and its adjacent outbuildings. A couple hundred yards beyond the barn was a patch of standing corn, and adjoining its western end was a twenty-acre woodlot. I told my friends at the farmhouse that I would probably drop in and help them drive the area late that morning, but as I sat watching I saw a bustle of activity as the house quickly emptied and the drive began. I decided it would be more fun just to watch. Moreover, I thought, they have plenty of hunters already.

From what I saw through my binoculars over the next hour, plus what my buddies told me later, this is what transpired.

Eleven hunters took part in the drive. It was intended to roust deer out of the woodlot on the west, pushing them past blockers as they moved to the east on their way to another woodlot several hundred yards distant. From past experience, the hunters (mostly local farmhands) knew that deer normally would leave the woodlot via the standing corn, then traverse the corn to a fencerow on the east, and follow the fencerow to the next woodlot south.

Eight drivers started through the woodlot coming from the west. Two blockers were posted at the northeast corner of the woodlot, each slightly back from the corner itself. A third blocker was posted at the southeast corner of the standing corn. As the drivers neared the woodlot's eastern edge, three deer—two does and a moderate-size buck—escaped into the corn too quickly for anyone to fire a shot, although three of the hunters saw them. The men posted on the woodlot said the deer never came out of the corn. The hunter posted on the corn said they never came out. I was elevated enough to know that deer never came out of the east, north, or south sides of the corn.

Quickly, two hunters were posted at the eastern end of the corn. The cornfield was no more than one hundred yards by two hundred yards in size. Nine drivers went abreast through the standing corn. When they were roughly halfway through, the does broke cover, running down the fencerow as expected to the next woodlot. The buck was never seen again!

I believe that the buck somehow slipped back through the advancing hunters, despite the fact that each man could see the two men adjacent to him during the drive, and then retreated to the original woodlot. Regardless, that buck escaped without a shot having been fired in his direction. Almost any other whitetail, in any other location, in such circumstances would panic and then be tagged, yet such experiences are not uncommon while hunting farmlands.

I believe the overwhelming reason for this seemingly phenomenal savvy in farmland whitetails is their familiarity with humans—both hunters and nonhunters. Farmland deer are exposed to humans on a daily basis. In large measure, they live in a fishbowl environment, continually bombarded by the sight, sounds and smell of humans. They cannot afford to panic every time a human gets too close—so they simply adapt. The farmland whitetail's armor, then, is his escape cover, but it is not without flaw. More than any other whitetail, he is inexorably tied to it. This is true because cover in farmland is only a small percentage of the available land area.

For the farmland whitetail hunter, cover is a two-edged sword. For those unprepared to work it correctly and not understanding all its nuances, it's their nemesis; for those understanding how it's used and the whitetails' ways, it's their staunchest ally. It matters little where you happen to hunt in Michigan's farm country. It may be in southern Michigan or the U.P.'s southern Menominee County; it could

Hunter Dragging Buck. The author took this little four-point from a semiopen woodlot surrounded by crop fields in northern Oakland County.

be Cheboygan County or perhaps Benzie—the whitetails' habits are basically the same. They're absolute masters at utilizing available cover to their optimum benefit. They'll often confound the hunter who pursues them. Those same deer, who feed so brazenly in open fields throughout the early fall, seem to vaporize when the redcoats go afield. Of course, they do not vaporize, they simply adjust their schedules, seek out protective cover, and avoid exposing themselves to the danger from hunters.

I spent much of our gun season about five years ago in a dense woodlot on a heavily hunted farm in the Thumb region. Yet, in more than ten days of hunting, I saw no other hunters. I believe this is a perfect example of how farmland hunters underestimate the importance of cover, and how to work that cover to their maximum benefit.

Unlike their western cousins, the mule deer, whitetails are essentially creatures of the forest. This is where they evolved, where their senses were honed, and where their basic instincts still lie. Pressure of any kind causes them to seek cover and, especially for bigger white-tailed bucks, the heavier the cover, the better they like it. Once these deer get into comfortable cover, they're extremely reluctant to leave it. Clearly, to them it's far better to sit tight and let danger pass than to expose themselves prematurely.

I've seen this demonstrated often, but one instance is particularly memorable. Six or seven years ago I hunted a large farm whose north side was essentially undeveloped. There was a two-hundred-acre woodlot of mixed hardwoods and brushy bottoms on the east of this area. On the west was an equally large area of brushy bottoms and thorn apple-filled hills. Two weeks earlier I'd found three large scrapes among the thorn apple trees, which were now abandoned. I was convinced that the buck who'd made those scrapes was still around. From the size of the scrapes and the damage he inflicted on some nearby hardwoods, I knew he was a real brute. I knew further he hadn't yet been tagged, for in a small community like this, word would have spread quickly and I'd have heard about it.

The third or fourth afternoon of the season, I took a stand

overlooking a brushy draw that led from the woodlot into the thorn apples. A well-worn run traversed the draw, and led to within fifty yards or so of the first scrape in the series. I knew the buck wouldn't check his scrapes. I believed the reason he originally planted them where he had was because the herd routinely used that corridor as its gateway between the woodlot, the thorn apples, and an abandoned orchard still farther west. From evidence I saw that morning, the deer were feeding heavily in the orchard.

I'd been on my stand for roughly two hours when another hunter ambled over a rise and headed my way. When he reached me, we stood and talked quietly for at least ten minutes; he then continued on. The wind was in my face the entire time and now the other hunter walked downwind away from me. When he was forty yards or so away, from out of a dense tangle covering all of a hundred square feet emerged the biggest buck I ever saw in the area—not twenty feet from the other hunter. By the time I heard the commotion and turned, all I saw was the buck jumping a four-foot fence. As he ran straight away, I could see antlers on either side of his wide rump!

I never had a chance to shoot, and my comrade-in-arms was so flustered—as was I—that he never got his gun out of port position. That wily old boy had been lying holed-up right there all day (I later looked at his bed). He obviously had winded me long before, but it was equally obvious that he was content to stay in his bed as long as he knew where I was. Had the other hunter not wandered along, that buck would have either slipped out the back door whenever he chose to do so, or he'd have waited until I left. Bucks like that are hard to tag, but they're not infallible.

Three or four years ago, about six weeks before the season opened, I found signs of an enormous buck roaming between two farms that I routinely hunt. I spent the next six weeks trying to pinpoint his activities. I was in the area almost daily, and spent my time both scouting for deer and chasing partridge. I found some absolutely massive buck rubs in a thicket of tag alders and willows, which grew along the southern edge of the area. In addition, I located enormous tracks in the cornfields to the north of this thicket and on the runways between the two. Without giving away the information thus gleaned, and my fondest hopes as well, I discreetly questioned the farmers and their sons about the various bucks seen in the area. No such buck had been seen—yet I was convinced that he existed.

When the rut came in early November, I found a great many scrapes in the area. Along the edges of the woodlots to the north I found scrapes two to three feet in diameter. I found sparring rubs where the bushes and trees had been bent and broken as well. In the thicket to the south I found scrapes four feet or more in diameter; some bushes and trees were completely destroyed. Now, more convinced than ever that one big buck lived there, I began to postulate a behavior pattern for this critter.

The "boss," as I was beginning to think of him, lived in the thicket year-round; it was his core range. The thicket was extremely dense and covered perhaps eighty acres. He hid and slept there during the daylight hours, venturing north into the nearby crop fields and adjacent woodlots only under the protective cover of total darkness. He was clearly the dominant buck in the area, and he seldom, if ever, left this daytime retreat during daylight hours. I decided the only realistic hope of tagging this fellow was to go into the thicket each morning before daylight and stay there until dark.

Little happened during the first four days of the season. I saw a few deer, including one small buck, and on several occasions I heard others, but the cover always prevented me from seeing them. From all the shooting, the sounds of all the traffic in the background, and the occasional yelling, I knew that the surrounding areas were being hunted quite intensely, yet I saw no other hunters. Midmorning of the fifth day I saw the "boss" and my season was complete. A massive eight-point, with a nineteen inch inside spread, was my reward for seven intense weeks of activity. The key to the entire hunt was the cover, and how both the buck and I had used it.

Before someone jumps up and down and tells me how all that scouting and tramping prior to the season will spook the deer, let me explain why it's not always so. Too much scouting, or too much activity of any kind—logging, for example—will in most cases severely affect a deer herd and its behavior, but not with farmland deer. Dubious? Here's a good example of what I mean.

The Department of Natural Resources in southern Michigan has, as I'm sure you know, a program known as "the hunter access program" in which the state leases hunting rights on certain farmlands. The farmer is paid so much per acre each year to enroll his land in this program. In turn, he then allows so many hunters per day access to his lands. Only a relatively small percentage of lands are enrolled in this program and most are heavily hunted.

Some years ago I hunted two farms adjacent to each other that were in the access program. Throughout the upland bird season, and then the waterfowl season, these farms were hopping. The farmers were actively harvesting their crops, and the hunters were constantly tramping through every acre of both farms for at least five weeks prior to the general gun deer season. Partridge and woodcock hunters, myself included, hit the woodlots, planted pines, and tag alders hard. Waterfowlers worked both the marshes and the fields, as the farmers brought in their crops. Squirrel hunters thoroughly hunted the hardwoods for weeks, and rabbit hunters with their hounds had punished the brush. Even the nights were busy, as coon hunters worked the corn and adjacent woodlots.

Two days before our gun season, I was down to serious scouting. I cruised through a woodlot to check on some scrapes found earlier. I then moved to the edge, intent on checking one more place before dark. As I broke cover, I looked to the far end of the harvested bean field and there stood three deer. At better than five hundred yards, I did not need field glasses; there was no mistaking that glinting sunlight—one of those deer had one heck of a rack! I hunkered down in the fencerow to watch the show.

Intent on sexual matters, every few minutes that big bruiser would lower his head almost to the ground, sway it from side to side, then give chase. The two does would run a short ways, then stop; in a few minutes the process would be repeated. At four o'clock in the afternoon, with the sun still high in the sky, that buck couldn't care less about the three rabbit hunters working the brushy field immediately to the north of him. Only the does, disappearing into the woodlot, finally took him into cover.

Much to my amazement, the very next day (the day before the gun season opened!) nearly the same scenario was repeated, but by a different buck. The first buck had extremely wide horns, set low on his head. The second buck's horns were very high, heavy, and not nearly as wide.

Opening morning of the deer season, I ran into three young men about a half hour before daylight. They explained how they'd been hunting rabbits a couple days before and had seen a monster of a buck in the open. They told me they were going to hunt the perimeter of the bean field. I moved off into a nearby woodlot and took a stand. At daybreak four shots rang out from the bean field—then total silence. That night I discovered one of the young hunters had taken a nice little eight-point early, but no more deer had been seen. I'd seen seven deer, but no horns.

Off and on through the remainder of the season, I kept encountering two of the young hunters. Falsely believing that if their friend had taken one buck from that open field, others must follow, they continued to hunt the field exclusively. When I last saw them, near the tag end of the season, they'd only seen two other deer, both does, despite twelve days of hunting between them. In the meantime, I'd seen more than seventy deer, including two small bucks and others I couldn't identify with certainty, while hunting in thick cover.

The point is simple. Although I'm not sure how, it's obvious that deer know when they're the object of a hunter's pursuit. Hunt birds or scout for deer in farm country, and the deer will pretty much ignore you. Hunt deer in farm country, and you'll drive them into cover every time.

Farmland cover does not have to be overly heavy to hold deer; it simply must provide them with needed relief from hunting pressure, the escape routes they require, and therefore a sense of security. Thick fencerows, particularly those leading into larger tracts of cover, often harbor farmland

Old Farmhouse.. Abandoned farmlands dot our state. The second growth on these lands supports large numbers of deer and creates beautiful hunting opportunities.

deer, as will any fingerlike projection of cover extending from larger tracts. Bramble thickets, thickets of olive or multiflora rose, as well as cattail marshes and patches of thorn apples, will all provide deer with suitable escape cover.

What does all this mean? Because of the whitetail's natural tendency to seek cover, large expanses of farmland can be safely ignored by hunters, especially those intent on tagging a buck. With the possible exception of opening day, it is highly unlikely that a mature white-tailed buck, anywhere in farm country, is going to be taken in the open, unless forcefully driven from cover. Therefore, concentrate your efforts on hunting within available cover, not on hunting its perimeter or in open areas.

Whitetails everywhere depend on their senses—particularly their sense of smell—but what causes a reaction in a wilderness whitetail will generally trigger a completely different response in a farmland deer. For example, let a wilderness whitetail scent you and you can almost always color him gone. Not so a farmland deer. Farmland whitetails have learned to separate the activities of humans into at least two categories, neutral or threatening. The reasons for this are quite simple.

A farmer, perusing his fields or mending his fences, walks and behaves in a completely different manner than a hunter. To the whitetail, the farmer doing his work signals no danger or fear, while the hunter is a definite threat. The difference in deer is that the farmland whitetail will not react to the sight, smell or sound of a human until it has made that differentiation, while the wilderness whitetail will. The wilderness whitetail never encounters many humans, and it's far safer to assume that all threaten his well-being than to make any distinctions.

Often the farmland hunter can use this learned behavior to his advantage. One way, especially in lightly hunted areas, is to intentionally move deer, then cut them off or simply out-maneuver them. Many years ago I was hunting some heavy brush, a quarter of a mile or so north of an active farm. I knew that some out-of-town relatives of the landowner had been intently hunting the crop fields and nearby woodlots, but they hadn't ventured into my area. While changing stands at midday, I jumped five or six deer. I heard them crashing out in front of me, but all I could see were a few flags flying as they bounded away. I heard them running for fifty yards or so, and then silence. Figuring they wouldn't go far, I thought if I moved steadily on, they would then slowly circle back to the same area just vacated. I moved steadily for a hundred yards, making plenty of noise as I went. At that point I began to quietly, but quickly, circle back down-wind to the place from which I had originally come.

About forty yards from where I'd first seen them, I stopped and leaned against a tree. Twenty minutes went by and I heard brush popping. Moments later, I heard more brush, then the rustling of leaves. Four does and a nice six-point ambled into view, slowly feeding on their way back to their beds.

By continuing to move steadily away—not showing any interest whatsoever—the deer felt so secure that I'd simply passed them by, just as the farmer does every single day while doing his chores. Ambushes like that can be routinely effective for the farmland hunter familiar with the land and the deer. The factor to keep in mind is that farmland white-tails have less effective cover than other deer. Knowing that there were hunters and a lot of activity surrounding them, it was a safe bet on my part that the deer wouldn't leave that woodlot just because I'd passed through. When hunting farm-land whitetails, learn the cover, then make it work for you.

At times, whitetails seem to have an almost cavalier atti-tude about their proximity to humans, their homes, domes-tic animals, and so on. This is especially true of farmland deer. I've lived in rural farming areas for most of my life, and it still amazes me just how comfortable whitetails are in this environment. Last spring I awoke early one morning to find a deer grazing in my backyard—while my bird dogs dozed in their kennel, not twenty feet from where he fed!

A couple years ago I dropped a nice little eight-point buck in the latter part of the season, after I observed every hunter in the area was moving deep into cover. Each morning as I hiked to my various stands, I'd see guys walking in ahead of me or some would pass me by after I'd reach my spot. Finally it occurred to me that no one was covering that little thicket immediately west of the barn. That afternoon I tested the area and sure enough, nobody had been hunting it.

It wasn't much: four or five acres separated from a much larger woodlot by a hundred-yard swath of cover field. Everyone had been walking around it, heading for the wood-lot or the crop fields even farther. Next morning I arrived a little earlier than usual and was on a stand about one hun-dred feet from the barn, before anyone else arrived.

Soon a parade of hunters drifted past, through the field behind me, heading for more distant stands. Shortly after daylight I heard something move in front and upwind of me but saw nothing; then for a time everything was still. Just before eleven, I again heard faint rustlings. I then saw a deer's flank as my little buck complacently fed not fifty yards from the roadway! Don't overlook the obvious—frequently the very best hunting is right under your nose.

Hunting tactics in farmland areas should be dependent on personal preferences and an honest and realistic appraisal of hunting abilities. Still hunting possibilities are usually excellent, provided you have the patience and required skills. S–L–O–W is the key ingredient to this deer hunting approach. You must learn to let your eyes, much more than your feet, explore the cover. Anticipate where the deer are likely to be. To a certain extent, this is the result of years of experience, but an important and often overlooked element is in knowing where most hunters are, or more correctly, in knowing where most hunters are not. Cover too thick, or too wet, or too far off, or too near the road—cover that demands either much effort or is too obvious—is exactly where you should be. Often, something as simple as a pair of hip boots will get you into areas where other hunters seldom go. Even in the most heavily hunted farm areas, there are at least some places, for whatever reason, that few hunters use. Search these out to increase your odds, and keep in mind that the majority of farmland hunters are found in open areas almost exclusively.

Stand hunting is another productive tactic for farmland whitetails. Choose stand locations with great care—truly the key to a successful season—and do so well in advance of the season. Always get to your stand at least a half hour before daylight. Whenever possible, plan on spending the entire day on the same stand. Generally, farmland cover is found in small segments and, if you move from one stand to another, the deer will detect your presence and simply slip away unnoticed. Do not use the same stand more than once or twice a week; human odors will accumulate (in areas where deer do not normally encounter them), and deer will simply avoid the area altogether.

Prior to opening day, you should have selected at least a half dozen stand sites, preferably more. Concentrate the majority of your sites in bedding areas, rather than feeding areas, because farmland whitetails quickly revert to night-time feeding schedules during the deer season. Always keep track of your quarry through their sign. Recheck your stands as the season progresses on the basis of fresh sign. It makes little sense to spend precious hunting time in a location if the deer have changed their activities. The harvest of crops, or the disappearance of hardwood mast, will often prompt such movements, as will hunting pressure. You must be alert to such changes.

You'll probably find as the season progresses, especially with heavy hunting pressure, that deer will move farther back in the cover. You should also adapt. The deer will be getting into these areas earlier and staying later. So should you. Because of its optical capabilities, a good-quality scope—even if you hunt with a shotgun—will add a few additional minutes of effective hunting time at both ends of the day. Those few minutes could spell the difference in your season.

Farmland areas provide unequaled opportunities for well-organized deer drives; in some areas it's essentially the only approach that will work. It is imperative, however, that a critical element of deer driving be always in mind: safety must be the priority!

Deer drives can be productive with as few as two hunters, and probably should never include more than ten or twelve, and then only if the hunters are highly experienced. There should always be a drive master in complete

Buck on the Edge of Field. The author took this photograph just two days before our gun season opened. This is the kind of buck that won't be found in winter wheat fields when the redcoats are afield!

control of every drive. The drive master assigns positions, directs the tempo of the drive, chooses the routes for each member, and coordinates timing.

In order to accomplish this, the drive master must be intimately familiar with the areas hunted and, in addition, he must have a detailed map of each area. This must be a map developed by himself, preferably with the assistance of members of the drive party; commercially available maps do not have the details essential. Every major feature of the area must be included: crop fields, favored fence crossings, major and minor deer runs, stand sites, creek and river crossing areas, everything of importance regarding the deer and their possible movement. With the aid of such maps, locations for each member are clearly assigned and their roles are delineated.

As you can see, being a drive master is a tremendous responsibility; it should be decided by the group who is best qualified. The assignment must be made far in advance of the season so all the necessary preparations can be completed.

All participants, drivers and standers alike, should wear as much blaze orange as possible; blaze orange snowmobile suits are probably the best choice. At the very least, blaze orange coats, hats and gloves are essential for everyone involved. It is important that everyone on stand have some sort of concealment as well. Break up your silhouette by employing blinds, brush, trees, whatever. Remember that a drive's success or failure can hinge on your actions. Your hunting partners, especially the drive master, have put a lot of time and effort into this operation—follow directions and stay alert at all times.

Any whitetail, in any environment, is an admirable and worthy quarry, but to my mind farmland whitetails are the most challenging. With nerves of steel, they possess the senses and instincts that are perfectly suited to dupe the best woodsman on any given day.

5

Wilderness Whitetails

In the early 1970s, I was chasing whitetails in our U.P.'s Ontonagon County. As I pulled into a restaurant late one evening, a car pulled in beside me. I got out and stared in disbelief at the two bucks draped across the hood; they were huge by any standard. Two of the most beautiful ten-point racks I'd ever seen! What struck me as utterly amazing at that time was that they'd both been taken from the same stand, in essentially the same spot, one in the morning, the other that afternoon!

Having dropped his deer first, the gentleman driving the car suggested that his wife sit on his stand, since she'd had no activity on hers, and he had seen several other deer. Repeating the scene in every detail, an almost identical buck wandered down the same runway within minutes of her arrival.

After congratulating the happy couple, I passed the whole affair off as nothing more than chance and put it out of my mind—at least I tried to. But it just kept nagging at me. How was it possible, in all that wide expanse of country, that those two bucks would be found in such proximity? It was only several years later, after I had gained more insight into wilderness whitetails, that I realized this event represented a lot more than mere chance. Those bucks were tagged in that manner for some very basic reasons, and if I could figure out what they were, I'd undoubtedly be much more successful in my own hunting efforts.

Ontonagon County is about as wild and remote as any piece of real estate you'll find in whitetail country. About half of its three-quarter-million-plus acres lies in state and national forests. By far, the majority of the county is a tractless expanse. There are many square miles where no motorized vehicles, ATVs included, can penetrate. There are a good many square miles that never see a hunter year in and out. The few local hunters fare pretty well, but the success rate among nonlocals is quite low.

The terrain in Ontonagon County varies from the ruggedness of the Porcupine Mountains in the extreme north, along the Lake Superior shoreline, to a flat or gently rolling landscape in the south. The habitat varies from solid stands of mature mast-bearing hardwoods that tower to eighty-foot heights, to hemlock stands so dense that even sunlight has difficulty working its way through. There are tag alder swales that defy negotiation, and clear cuts that once sported poplars and birch, and will again in a few years.

There's another fact about Ontonagon and similar wilderness areas anywhere in the whitetail's range; this is big buck country! Deer densities are invariably low, about six to eight per square mile over most of the range. With very few hunters, those who hunt here do so for the mystique of the country as well as a very realistic hope of tagging the buck of a lifetime.

In a state where the average buck taken is eighteen months old and carries spike horns, Ontonagon's bucks average two-and-a-half years of age and sport eight-point racks. There's a real solid opportunity for hunters to tag bucks of four-and-a-half or even five-and-a-half years of age here, and that means trophy-size racks as well.

From the wilderness of Ontonagon to the wilderness of Marquette County, from the isolation of northern Iron County to the pines of western Chippewa County, the whitetail is king—our number one big game animal. Today, more than ever before, the whitetail is now pursued in wilderness areas. Whitetails thrive in such environs, and today's hunters cherish the solitude, thrill and challenge of hunting these areas.

Since the vast majority of today's hunters come from city or suburban areas, they're frequently more than just a little bewildered by a deep woods or true wilderness area. The problem confronted by these hunters is where and how to hunt, in all that sprawling expanse, in order to maximize their potential for success?

That's a mighty difficult but important question to answer, unless you're quite familiar with wilderness regions, understand the habitat, and are knowledgeable regarding the biological needs of whitetails. We'll certainly have a solid beginning, however, by realizing all that vastness in any wilderness region is not created equally.

I well remember the frustration experienced the first several years that I hunted the remote Upper Peninsula. I wandered for miles, seeing little sign and even fewer deer. I was overwhelmed by the immensity of the land and density of

Deer Camp. This group of hunters from Saginaw has a beautifully designed and well-built setup that keeps them more than comfortable and gives them the flexibility of making camp any place their four-wheel drives will take them. Such freedom is very beneficial to the serious wilderness whitetailer. For such hunters the camaraderie of camp life is an important part of the hunt.

the habitat. Without an experienced wilderness hunter to guide me, I was forced to slowly learn the ways of these whitetails on my own. It took me five years to tag my first U.P. buck, but I learned a lot during that time, and now the sightings are much more common, the opportunities more frequent. Here are a few things I've learned over the years.

Narrow a Wilderness Region to Manageable Size

Take a good hard look at any wilderness area and you will soon see, in both small and large spaces, that the habitat is rarely uniform. The cover along the creek bed is much different from that along the ridge to the east. The mixed woods are vastly different from the cedars in the bottoms. The oak thicket varies greatly from the midgrasses a little ways north.

In addition, within each area the habitat is vastly different at various times of the year. Mature hardwoods serve as strong whitetail magnets when they drop their mast crop. As high as 50 percent, or more, of a whitetail's diet will consist of acorns if and when they're available, but these same hardwoods offer precious little any other time of the year. Due to the total absence of any understory, there's neither food nor shelter there for the greater part of the year, and consequently very few whitetails.

The cedar/balsam, hemlock, and spruce/balsam swamps of our north are the habitats that allow our whitetails to survive the extreme harshness of our winters. The cedar is the only known tree in those areas that completely fulfills the whitetails' winter needs, both nutritionally and also as protection from the elements. Yet the cedar, so critical to winter survival, is practically ignored throughout the rest of the year.

More than anything else, it's understanding factors such as these and their effects on the deer that separates successful from unsuccessful nimrods afield in wilderness areas. While it's vitally important to know where deer are most likely to be, the main benefit to this understanding is how much area it eliminates from consideration. The vast sprawling wilderness effectively becomes much smaller. The real key to wilderness whitetails is an understanding of their ways relative to their environment at any given point in time. You must force yourself to see the trees rather than the forest. You must mentally dissect the habitat, and then work the most productive areas.

That was precisely what I did to tag a nice buck some years ago. It was the latter part of the season and the snow was already beginning to pile up. While I knew it was far too soon for the deer to be yarded up, I also knew they'd be moving into close proximity of the cedars in the area. Bird hunting a month earlier, I'd seen a lot of sign in and around the hardwood ridges in the area.

The mast was now gone, and since there was no browse in the hardwoods, I knew the deer had moved on. Their yarding area was an immense concentration of bogs and cedars four miles or so to the east. In between and along the western fringe of the swamps were thickets of lowland willows. Since this is a favorite whitetail food, it was there I headed.

Almost at first light I knew I hit pay dirt. Fresh tracks crisscrossed the willows everywhere, and late that morning my hunt ended when I connected with a nice six-point. You must learn to read the habitat.

Search for Variety in the Habitat

Monocultural areas never sustain large whitetail populations. Whether we're discussing a large red pine plantation, a mature climax forest, or even an extensive expanse of brush, it doesn't matter, such uniformity cannot fulfill the whitetails' basic survival needs.

I've never hunted whitetails anywhere, nor have I ever heard of an area where habitat variation didn't produce a great many more deer. I eagerly seek out areas with a lot of "edge" and avoid unbroken forested regions, whether they're mixed or not. A great many of the more desirable foods of the whitetail are intolerant of shade and grow only in open or semiopen areas: clear cuts and natural meadows are very attractive to deer.

Ontonagon County provides a good case in point. The Michigan DNR deer data are very misleading (not intentionally so, it's simply a question of the DNR's needs compared with the hunter's) since they're listed in a countywide or even regionwide basis. As a result, the average deer density is six to eight deer per square mile. There are other, much smaller areas that may support thirty or forty deer per square mile during selected times of the year. In fact, throughout the winter months, there are areas within the hemlocks where there will be several hundred deer per square mile!

Areas with the highest deer densities will be those with plenty of brush, a good age mix to the timber, sufficient hemlocks to winter the herd, and plenty of openings. They also will have a water source nearby, and they'll be in the more southerly portion of the county, away from the deeper snows and the energetic, brutal winter winds coming off Lake Superior.

Know Their Favorite Foods

Biologists rank the whitetails' food sources according to primary and secondary foods. Primary foods are those most preferred, sought after and highly nutritious. Secondary foods are sought only when primary sources are depleted, and are generally nutritionally inadequate as well. (See *Table 10.2*, in Chapter 10, for a list of the most extensively used whitetail foods in this region.) Areas deficient in these vegetation types will, quite naturally, support fewer deer.

In addition to the essential browse plants, there must be an adequate amount of summer grazing and forage food stuffs. This category includes the various fruits, forbs, mushrooms, and grasses, as well as the greenery of shrubs and saplings. These foods, both in quality and quantity, are important to fatten deer so they enter the harsh snow period in optimum condition.

Can you go out, right now, into the areas where you hunt and identify what the deer are feeding on? Can you list even four or five of the whitetails' preferred foods in your hunting area? A great many hunters cannot. If you can't, you are fighting against the odds all the way. Turn things around; as a deer hunter your biggest challenge is to make every single facet of the whitetails' life cycle work for you. Learn the deer's food preferences and be able to identify each one; you'll then stack the deer hunting odds in your favor.

Know the Limiting Factor

A limiting factor is a parameter in the environment that most effectively controls the size of the deer herd. We want to identify those factors over which we have some control. Once identified, they can either be sought out or avoided, depending upon their influence.

For example, throughout the extreme northern portion of the whitetails' range (the northern two-thirds of Michigan included), cedars, hemlocks, spruce and balsam are crucial wherever deer yard up to survive the winters. Snow depths outside of these swamps and lowlands may reach three to five feet, maybe more. When this occurs there may be unlimited browse literally one hundred yards outside of the swamps and it won't do the deer one bit of good; it might as well be on the moon. With snow of such depths, the deer cannot feed outside their swamps; if the food supply inside falls short, they'll perish.

When snow depths are so great, these retreats become the limiting factor in that environment. There's no other habitat where the deer can successfully winter. Therefore, large expanses of the extreme north that lack such cover, or areas in which such cover is too mature to offer adequate browse, should be avoided. (Hunting within swamps is normally not very productive in a true wilderness area—see Chapter 8 for an explanation of their importance in heavily hunted "middle Michigan.") This is true no matter how perfect the rest of the habitat is in that area.

You can have an area otherwise perfect except for one critical element, which will determine the upper limit of the deer population; determine that element in your hunting

Buck in Woods. Ever alert, wilderness whitetails are quick to react to any kind of intrusion into their world. Remember, they're not accustomed to humans; you have to make this work to your advantage.

area and you will be way ahead of the game. It may be free-standing water, or winter browse; it may be extreme maturity of the habitat, or lack of variety; whatever it is, you should be aware of it and plan your hunt accordingly.

Avoid Maturity in the Habitat

We have had for years a tremendous feud raging in parts of Michigan over the culling of does. Sound familiar? A great many people—hunters and nonhunters alike—feel that the Department of Natural Resources is trying to wipe out the deer herd by shooting all the does. This past summer I found myself in the line of fire on this issue. While scouting the habitat in our Upper Peninsula, I pulled into a gas station one day. Trying to make small talk, I asked the young man filling my tank how the deer hunting was in that area.

"Sure as hell ain't what it used to be! Not since the DNR killed off all the damn does!"

Stupidly, I tried to get to the real issue: "You think this habitat can support more deer? I've just spent the better part of three days going over every inch of the area north of here, and the habitat is terrible—much too mature to support deer at all." Sometimes I amaze myself! Stupid! Having said that to the young fellow, he then raised such a ruckus that his dad wandered out to see what was going on. Backing off—way off—I paid my bill and left.

I don't blame the young man or his dad, for I'm convinced they genuinely believe that particular habitat can support a great many more deer than it currently does. After all, back in the 1950s, when the young man was just a glimmer in his daddy's eye, his dad had good deer hunting nearby. Those twenty-year-old hardwoods had probably rendered many a nice buck to his group, as did the poplar thicket just north, and the planted pines next to them. The young man had grown up hearing about all those hunts, all those bucks, and all those good times. Then the DNR issued all those doe permits and, overnight it seemed, all the deer were gone.

The maturation and succession of habitat—whether helped by human hands or not—is an insidious thing; it never stops changing and generally it's so slow and subtle we're not even aware of it. (See Chapter 2 as well as *Figure 2.1*.) But change it does, and when that change is maturation, it's almost never good for the deer. Those twenty-year-old hardwoods where the man took his first buck are now sixty years old. The poplar thicket is now a poplar forest with its canopy forty feet above the open ground below. The planted pines that had provided both food and cover to those deer, those many years ago, are now completely open to a height of twenty feet.

With such changes occurring in the habitat, the DNR generally encourages the thinning of the herd in order to ease them into the increasing constraints of the environment, and to prevent the needless starvation that surely would follow otherwise. With or without doe permits, deer herds in maturing habitats are going to decline, and that's a fact we cannot change.

It's much easier to find a scapegoat to vent our frustrations, like the DNR and the culling of does, than to deal with, or even be aware of, the nebulous, changing complexity of habitat. It doesn't do deer any good though, and the resulting rift between the hunters and the DNR doesn't do us any good either. The rule is simple enough. Avoid maturity in any habitat for improved deer hunting. A corollary to this is it's highly unlikely that one area, over a prolonged period of time, is going to offer the best hunting.

As habitats in one area mature and deer hunting quality declines, other areas are timbered, burned, grazed, and hence improved. Too many of us become complacent and hunt the same places year after year, without regard to the changes that surround us. The most successful hunters are going to be those who adjust to a maturing environment. If you need to hunt in an area that is too mature, then search out the naturally occurring edge areas, natural glades, openings around swamps, lake shores, and creek and river banks. You'll find improved food sources in such areas and hence increased deer usage.

One of the most productive counties in all of Michigan is Dickinson County, again in our U.P. Dickinson is remote, with a very low human population; it has few roads, and is covered with a good mix of habitat types and age. There's a very active timber pulp industry, which assures an excellent supply of browse as well as lush forest openings for a wide array of soft plant types. Deer populations, as a result, are very high. To increase your deer hunting odds, such areas should be sought out, no matter where you hunt. Remember, the critical height for deer browse is less than six feet, anything higher than that and the deer simply cannot reach it. In snowbound areas, the browse ideally should be between two feet and six feet high.

Strategies For Hunting Wilderness Whitetails

After you've narrowed down your hunting area, and you are confident that deer are working that area, how best do you hunt it? Depending upon the area itself, the number of deer working it, and your own personal preferences and abilities, any of the traditional approaches will work, if you employ them in the proper manner, at the proper times.

Before discussing actual hunting strategies, I think it's important to highlight a couple other points first: runways and when to hunt.

Runways

Some runways, from a hunter's point of view, are sure-fire winners and should be hunted heavily. Others are meaningless and should seldom if ever be hunted. Runways in cedar swamps and in wilderness areas where there are few hunters per square mile are the result of massive winter use. There are few deer in these areas until the snows pile up, so hunting here is futile. (This is not true in rural areas where there is heavy hunting pressure; in these areas, the cedars are often very productive as the deer seek shelter and isolation—again, see Chapter 8.) Deer feeding in open areas—hardwoods with no understory, for example, or in abandoned orchards—wander at will; hence, runways traversing these areas are not important when the deer are feeding here.

In other cases, some runways are certain winners. I've hunted brush-choked areas in northern Michigan and in southern Texas that were so dense there was no other way through them except on runways. When deer are in these areas, the runways are heavily used, and they should be hunted. Runways around boggy ground areas are sure bets as well. When traveling around watercourses or marshy areas, the deer use runways—you should be watching them.

When to Hunt

Michigan's wilderness areas are managed as multiple-use lands. Generally they're forested and their primary products are the timber resources. As a result the habitat is rarely ideal for whitetails, and deer populations, while healthy, are seldom high. (The nice thing about such circumstances is that buck-doe ratios are invariably high, and although you won't see a lot of deer, your chances of seeing a buck are excellent.)

Persistence thus becomes a cornerstone to deer hunting success in these areas. The most successful wilderness deer hunter I've known was a gentleman who hunted in my father's hunting camp for many years. Every year Tracy got his buck—every year, that is, for more than thirty years! The secret to Tracy's success? He made arrangements to hunt the entire season every year—if that's what it took—and he never left the woods from daylight to dark, day after day.

Very often in farmland and rural hunting situations, the buck kill is extremely high and most are claimed relatively early in the season. In Michigan, as I point out in Chapter 7, more than 80 percent of our legal bucks in southern Michigan are taken each year, and fully one-third of these fall on opening day. Clearly, if you don't score early, the odds are increasingly stacked against you. This is not the case in wilderness areas where only a low percentage of the bucks are taken, and your odds at the tag end of the season are about the same as they were in the beginning. The bottom line then is to hunt whenever you can.

Drives

Contrary to popular opinion, deer drives can be very successful in wilderness areas, but the key lies in the choice of areas to be driven. Generally these drives work best with just two or three hunters. Once harassed, hounded or stirred up, whitetails are likely to vacate small areas; if this has not occurred they're far more likely to simply skulk about within cover. With but two hunters you can post one and have the other move about slowly and quietly.

For the moving hunter, this should be nothing more than a still hunting exercise. Beginning deep within the cover, the hunter should start still hunting in ever increasing circles; or beginning on one edge, the hunter should start casting back and forth slowly, as he advances through the cover. In either case, the posted hunter should be overlooking a well-used runway, or preferably more than one.

A technique I've employed on many occasions is excellent for cover in the form of bands or strips, such as along creek beds or hillsides. The hunter who will post up goes on ahead three or four hundred yards. While advancing, he stays well back from the cover to be hunted, and he moves quietly down or crosswind. When he reaches a predetermined location, he settles into the cover itself overlooking a run and at least one of the edges. Once a prescribed amount of time has elapsed, the other hunter or hunters advance, again quietly and slowly. The hunters can take turns, switch roles, and move forward again. Very often it's the moving hunter in this type of drive who sees the game. Drives such as these can be effective at any time of the day, but frequently work best early and late, when the deer are more prone to be moving on their own. When executing middle of the day drives, do so through known or likely bedding areas.

Still Hunting

For those having the necessary skills and patience, still hunting is highly productive in wilderness areas. It allows the hunter to continue scouting his area while hunting at the same time. Any shifts in deer activity, or any signs of deer concentration missed in preseason scouting are far more likely to be picked up by a still hunter than by a hunter on stand.

Whitetails in wilderness areas are generally far less spooky, initially, than whitetails closer to human populations. A good still hunter will often be able to stalk within easy range of these animals without putting them to flight. Concentrate your efforts more on known feeding areas, or areas between feeding and bedding sites early and late in the day. During the middle hours of the day, you should hunt resting areas in the hope of catching the deer feeding within the cover. It's unlikely that you'll successfully roust deer from their beds and get a decent shot.

Wilderness areas are rarely hunted hard and, for this reason, these deer do not normally retreat to the real heavy cover that a lot of whitetails do. Hunt the edges of dense cover and avoid the jungles themselves. If you have reason to believe that a big buck is sticking to the heavy cover, then hunt the runways in these areas.

Stand Hunting

Provided that the hunter selects his stand in those areas we've discussed as having the greatest potential, stand hunting is probably the most successful approach to pursuing wilderness whitetails. Because these deer encounter so little human intrusion, they are far less nocturnally oriented than a lot of their nonwilderness brethren. They are thus more active during daylight hours; they browse later and begin routine evening activity earlier in the day. They will move freely to watering areas, and feed placidly even in the middle of the day.

Good stand selections are those overlooking feeding areas and along runways on the edges of bedding areas. Several stand sites should be selected, and never hunt the same stand on consecutive days. This reduces the buildup of human odor in the area; nothing spooks wilderness whitetails quicker.

I'm a great believer in hunting all day, every day, no matter where I hunt, but when hunting wilderness whitetails, I simply refuse to leave the woods. Research has shown whitetails to be far more diurnal, and this is particularly true in remote areas.

Dress comfortably, narrow the vast expanse of your immediate area down to manageable proportions, and place yourself in the most advantageous spot you can. Carry a snack or lunch, hunt the whole day through, and you'll find that solving the riddle of wilderness whitetails is not that difficult.

6

Deer in the Backyard

I just have to tell you about a fella who used to live in my neighborhood. My introduction took place on a Sunday afternoon in April a few years ago, and right then and there I knew this guy was something to behold!

There was a rap at the door. "I'll get it," I said.

"Hi, I'm————, my wife and I just bought the ten acres down the road." That in itself wouldn't endear the man to me; I had hoped that that vacant piece would sit undeveloped for a long time. Oh well, a slight inconvenience.

"I wanted to see what the back of the property looked like and I managed to get my truck stuck. Think you could pull me out with your jeep? I'm just a little ways off the road."

Not overly thrilled with the idea of turning my jeep into a part-time wrecker, I nonetheless didn't want to be rude.

"Hang on a second, I'll put some shoes on."

To make a long story short, when I got to where he was, I discovered he'd grossly understated his predicament. He was not, as he had said, "stuck." Mired and submerged would have been a more apt description of his plight. A swamp ran through the middle of his ten acres. I mean a true, honest-to-goodness swamp, with standing water, muck, cattails—the whole shot. There, sitting about thirty feet in from the swamp's roadside edge, his truck was in serious jeopardy of sliding completely out of sight!

"There's no way my jeep could get you out of that. You've got to be kidding. Just what did you think was in there?" Undaunted by my sarcasm, he asked if he could use my telephone, and added, "My cousin will get me out."

Back we went to use the phone. When we arrived, my wife met us at the door. Introductions made, I said, "The phone is next to the TV—help yourself," gesturing to the opposite end of the living room. Without hesitation, this klutz then proceeded to tramp across my living room carpet, muddy boots and all, to the telephone. The call completed, he hung up and looked at three of my deer heads hanging on the wall.

"Nice, just a little smaller than the one I got down in Georgia a few years back," he said. "Take it right around here?" he asked, pointing at a mule that has a twenty-five inch inside spread, and whose rack sits some twenty-nine inches high!

If you haven't gathered as much by now, I didn't care for my new neighbor. But what's pertinent to this discussion is that he was definitely not the man I'd turn to in need of some insight into whitetails, their ways, or how to hunt them.

After he built his house and moved in, this gentleman was the talk of the community. It seems his introduction to nearly everyone in the area has paralleled my own experience. I often thought he meant well. He devoted himself, for a couple years, to putting in a yard and fixing up his house. He was constantly out there puttering around, and he roamed his ten acres, proud as a peacock.

In November a couple years later, I was in the Upper Peninsula in search of deer and called home to say hello, and see how everything was.

My wife answered the phone. "Will you accept a collect call from John Williams?" the operator asked.

"Yes."

"Go ahead, sir." Before I had a chance to say anything, my wife said, "Honey, you're not gonna believe this! Guess who killed a twelve-point right behind the house on opening day?"

Yes, it was my neighbor. The same one who didn't know a mule from a whitetail. The same one who didn't know better than to drive a truck through a Michigan swamp in April. The same one who didn't have the common sense to take off his muddy boots before he tramped across my front room carpet!

At first I was dismayed. It then dawned on me: something that's been foggy and slightly out-of-focus, but in the back of my mind for years, suddenly became very clear. When it comes to deer hunting, local hunters have a very decided edge!

I'd known that for years. I'd even paid lip service to the idea, yet I'd never fully comprehended its truth until that moment.

Immediately south of my neighbor's acreage was an alfalfa field. South of that was a dense thicket that lead directly to a hardwood woodlot and farther, a variety of other cover types. Immediately north, and on the opposite side of the road, was a large field, usually planted with corn. The swamp on his property was actually formed from the overflow of a small feeder creek that flowed north and south just east of his property.

Deer routinely used the resulting north-south cover as an avenue to move from the cornfield on the north to the cover to the south, and vice versa. It was a natural avenue of travel for them, and yet it is one that wouldn't necessarily be apparent to anyone unfamiliar with the area and the local herd.

Puttering around the yard, getting up early every day, my neighbor could hardly have missed the significance of this corridor over a two-year period. On opening morning he sat right on the southern point and, sure enough, along came the twelve-point slowly ambling from his dining room to his bedroom, just as he probably had done every day for two months or more. To all the guys who hunted hard the whole season on the surrounding accessible land, my apologies; you never had a chance right from the beginning!

Travel patterns, normal escape routes, favored feeding and bedding areas, scrape lines, and more, all so evident to local residents of an area, require hours and hours of intense scouting activity from the nonlocal hunter. The local nimrod, with little or no effort on his part, has an almost insurmountable lead over the competition long before the season ever starts.

Buck in Velvet. The result of Michigan's ever-expanding deer herd is that whitetails are often found in our backyards. Off-season observation is not only very pleasurable for the serious whitetailer, it's educational as well.

A case in point involved the four deer taken during the 1985 season in the area immediately surrounding my home. The biggest landowner in the area is a dairy farmer, and he had more than six hundred acres of his lands enrolled in our Michigan "hunter access program."

The farmer and his son, however, head north to do their

hunting each year (as does practically every other local in the area). They hunt northern Michigan for the first week or so of the season, and normally head north again over Thanksgiving. In between, and after chores, they'll conduct a few drives on their lands here at home, with an assist by some of the other local hunters who might be around. By far and away, the majority of the hunting hours spent on their lands, however, are by nonlocal hunters. Although I'm never around, my wife tells me that the hunting activity is intense the first several days of the season, and then picks up again on the weekends and, of course, over Thanksgiving.

Despite all of this lopsided activity and effort by the non-locals, all four deer taken in my immediate neighborhood in 1985 were tagged by local hunters! A neighbor claimed a nice ten-point, while another neighbor west of the dairy farm took an eight-point. Two does were tagged by the dairy farmer and other drive members.

It's not that my neighbors are all hotshot deer special-ists—they're not. They're guys, just like you and I, who enjoy white-tailed deer and their ways. Whenever they happen to be out and about they're simply alert to whatever the deer in the area are doing. As the farmer works his fields, he's alert to the deer he sees. I don't know how many times in the last ten years he's told me that while haying a few years ago he killed a fawn in his combine. It made an indelible impression on my friend. He'll never forget it, and he'll never forget pre-cisely where that fawn was lying at the time.

Deer, generation after generation, tend to do things exactly the same way, for whatever reason. Where one deer lies down, others are sure to follow, perhaps not today but tomorrow, or next week, or next year. With a series of first-hand encounters such as my neighbors have had—as with all locals in deer country—pretty soon, without even a con-scious effort to do so, you know the local herd and most of its nuances. Hunting becomes almost as simple as going out and perusing your land.

Even the effects of habitat change are readily apparent to local residents; not so for those unfamiliar with the area. In agricultural areas, for example, the rotation of crops has a

Doe Lying Down.　Due to the everyday exposure of our neighborhood deer herds, local hunters have a tremendous head start in understanding the behavior patterns of nearby animals. Success rates for local hunters, in all areas of our state, are significantly higher than those for outsiders. Don't overlook the deer right in your own backyard!

tremendous impact on deer movements. A nonlocal hunter, who devoted his entire season last fall to pinpointing the areas of intense deer activity, could very well be starting from scratch this year with just a few routine rotations. An uncut bean field this year instead of last year's wheat stubble, a cut cornfield instead of one still standing, or even a dry summer as opposed to an average one, can all significantly alter deer patterns and throw a nonlocal hunter into fits of despair; the locals have it all laid out for them long before first light on opening day.

Such advantages do not belong only to the local hunter in agricultural areas. They assist locals in any environment. Last fall I hunted in a remote forested section of the Upper Peninsula. The day before the season opener I hiked all the way to the end of the two-track off of which I planned to hunt. Near its end I came to a large camp with several vehicles parked nearby. Wanting to be sure of where everyone was going to be the next morning, I stopped and introduced myself. The camp itself was temporary home to five hunters from downstate, all of whom had hunted the area for years and seemingly knew it quite well.

In addition to these five, I discovered that there'd be four other hunters in the area, besides myself. Two of the guys were locals, and the other two were out-of-state residents from Ohio. The season opened on Friday. On Monday the five fellows from downstate broke camp and headed home sans deer, although one of the guys had an opportunity at a small buck and missed. The two guys from Ohio hunted hard until Wednesday when they too had to leave. The day before the season opened, by his own admission, one of the two local guys told me that he was more of "a social hunter" than anything, and I never saw him again after opening day. I don't believe it to be insignificant that the only deer taken out of the area the first week was taken on opening morning by the other local hunter. Shortly after daybreak he nailed a fine eight-point as the deer ambled within fifty yards of the man's stand.

So important is the insight of local hunters, that even in areas with significantly lower deer densities, the local hunter is probably better off hunting near home. I well remember a little story from years ago that highlighted this. A farmer and his son from Tuscola County planned to hunt somewhere in the northern portion of the state. Prior to the season, the old man had gone out and supplied his son with everything the young man would need to get him off on the right foot.

A new woolen hunting outfit was purchased, along with new boots, gloves, hat, compass and, above all else, a sporting new gun. The young man was ready—no expense had been spared. With high hopes they "headed north," just as most hunters do. Once there they hunted hard. They tramped the brush; they assisted each other with two-man drives; and they sat quietly for endless hours. But it was all for naught, and one week later they returned home empty-handed.

What they didn't know until their return, however, was that the Mrs. had awakened on opening morning and, while puttering around the kitchen, she chanced to look out at the abandoned orchard behind the house. There, contentedly nibbling away at her apples, was an eight-point buck! After she poleaxed him with a shotgun, a neighbor was kind enough to hang him in the barn for her, and that's the sight that greeted the "hunters" upon their return.

"Luck" you say and, yes, you're absolutely right. For someone just to look out a window and see a buck feeding contentedly in her yard would have to be considered luck. But for a local resident to waylay a deer with just a minimal amount of effort and hunting savvy is quite common.

A year ago or so, I was in the Upper Peninsula, poking around, and went into a restaurant in the town of Iron Mountain. My waitress and I began talking, and I explained that I was scouting for deer.

"Got quite a few deer right around here ya' know," she said, "but nobody hunts 'em. Everybody feels they got to head out into the countryside. My two sons live downstate and they hunt up in an area thirty miles north of town here every year. Last year they came over one night for dinner, really disgusted; they'd hunted hard for a week and hadn't seen anything. I suggested that they hunt right around the house my husband and I live in, right on the edge of town, but they said they thought it would be better out at the camp so they left." She continued, laughing, "Next morning, I was driving in here and saw a real big buck not two hundred yards from the house!" Her boys returned to the Detroit area empty-handed.

Of course it's easy to say that the "boys" should have

taken their mother's advice—20/20 hindsight. The truth of the matter is that one should give serious thought to what a local resident says, especially when he knows that the local really is trying to be helpful, as this mother obviously was.

As proof positive of the tremendous advantage a local hunter has, consider this. For years I lived in a small, agriculturally based community, thirty miles north of Detroit. Deer densities in the immediate area were always low, running I'd guess from four to six per square mile, perhaps even less. Despite this, I managed to take six bucks in seven seasons there and passed on several others in the process. What's really astounding though is that I generally knew of two or three other deer that were taken in the area every year and every single one, without fail, was claimed by another local hunter!

Just as where I now live, nearly everyone who hunted in that small community headed north for our season's opening. They would hunt for a few days or perhaps a week, and then return home. The remainder of the season, they'd hunt weekends and odd hours around home. Meanwhile, hunters from the greater Detroit area had been intensely combing the area since opening day. Nonetheless, the locals stole the show year after year.

A classic example occurred the year before I moved. One of our local school bus drivers always reached a certain railroad crossing each morning at approximately the same time (fortunately for him, always with an empty bus), and for weeks saw a big old buck along the tracks. Day after day, that old boy was in roughly the same spot, at the same time. On opening day, the driver made arrangements for someone else to drive his bus, and sure enough, as he waited just down from the crossing he tagged his buck.

Obviously, it was only after the big twelve-point hung safely in the bus driver's garage that the rest of us even heard of the buck's existence. But that's all right. I wouldn't have let anyone in on such a secret either!

Another example of what a local hunter can accomplish is illustrated by the only white-tailed buck I've ever tagged in his bed. For years I hunted the area directly in front of my home. This area was two full sections in size and consisted of broken agricultural lands, swales, woodlots and thickets. The only homes in the entire area were spread thinly around its periphery, and no roads bisected its interior. It was the same area in which I ran my dog. It was my retreat when I needed to think, and all through the early fall that year I hunted birds and squirrels in there as well. In addition, for the two weeks prior to our deer season, I ran a string of fox traps through the area, so I spent hours every single day in there.

For weeks I watched one particular buck; in fact, he was the only buck I saw in the area, and I learned his habits well. It's funny, the learning process was almost incidental to everything else I was doing. I don't for a minute mean to imply that I didn't care—I most certainly did. It's just that it all happened so naturally, I'd be hunting squirrels and see him. I'd take an evening stroll, and see him. Even driving home from work, I would see him. It got to the point where it was ridiculous. I felt like that buck was literally mine, and there was absolutely no doubt in my mind that his nine-point rack was going to hang on my wall as soon as the season arrived.

A week before the season opened, I located a string of scrapes that ran through some mast-bearing hardwoods, and several times I had found the buck in the immediate vicinity as well. His tracks indicated a lot of early morning activity in the area; I was then certain of where he was bedding for the day.

Opening morning, convinced I would have him on the meat pole by breakfast time, I took up a stand well before daylight, downwind of the most active of the scrapes, and settled in. By nine o'clock I was getting a little fidgety. I felt something was wrong. I should have seen him by then, but I sat tight. By noon I'd seen three other hunters, but no deer and I knew something foul was afoot.

The buck somehow must have sensed his danger and changed his ways, but still I sat. All day I was the picture of patience; I knew I had that buck figured out and I was determined not to let him slip away from me!

The second day was a carbon copy of the first. Again, I watched a few hunters drift through the area—but no deer. By nightfall I decided if I hadn't connected early on the next day, Friday, I would take matters into my own hands and go find the buck on his own turf. I was worried that otherwise a beefed-up weekend crowd might beat me to it, or at least so alert the buck as to severely confuse the situation.

By nine o'clock of the third morning I hadn't seen my buck, so I headed the quarter of a mile north to where I thought his bed was. In the northwest corner of a large cover field there was a dense thicket of brush, no more than fifty feet across. On one occasion, probably three weeks before, I'd actually watched the buck come out late one afternoon, and on numerous other occasions I'd found beds in different spots within the thicket. For weeks there had also been a number of beds along the length of a thick fencerow just west of the thicket which divided that field from the next one over. I figured that where he might bed down on any given day was probably dependent on the wind as much as anything. I also felt on that particular day he was probably out in the thicket where he'd have good vision of the surrounding area and a good breeze coming from the next field to the west, an area that most of the other hunters had been working heavily.

The field had some contour to it, so I slipped down along its eastern edge and headed north until I was directly downwind, being careful not to expose myself. Slowly and quietly I then turned west and uphill toward the brush two hundred yards ahead. I inched my way through the dried goldenrod, stopping often and always keeping to the lowest lying land. By the time I saw the thicket, I was no more than fifty yards from it. I then slowed down even more and began crouching. I could hear the voices and the hammering of a carpentry crew building a house not more than four or five hundred yards behind me.

Ever so slowly I moved, a step at a time, followed by a long period of staring intently at the cover. I saw nothing, yet somehow I never felt unsure of the eventual outcome of my quest. I lost track of time and, looking back now, it seems as if I almost glided into that thicket. I'm not really sure how I did it, but suddenly I was actually in amongst the brush itself, and still I saw nothing. I then moved a foot, leaned into it and saw something different: a small patch of brown that didn't quite match what surrounded it. Leaning forward a little farther, it got bigger and I realized that it was indeed a deer. But was it my buck?

I literally inched ahead, not moving my foot more than two inches at the most. Again I leaned forward and stared, puzzled at what I saw. Finally I made out the curve of an antler, and then a shoulder. The buck was curled up in his bed lying down, just as my dog might, his head flat on the ground, completely unaware of my presence not twenty feet away! Silently I slipped the safety and shouldered the gun. At the sound of the shot, he involuntarily straightened his hind legs and that was it. I had my buck and my greatest whitetail hunt ever.

The satisfaction of such a hunt must be experienced; it cannot be described. The entire key to it was in knowing that particular animal and the lands where he lived. Such knowledge cannot be garnered in just a few days of preseason scouting, or even by hunting the same area for several years. Such knowledge is obtained only by a local resident by virtue of continued exposure over prolonged periods of time.

This illustrates yet another benefit of a local deer herd to the serious whitetail enthusiast: the deer as an object of study. I have a good friend who lives in a southern Michigan township where all hunting is banned because of high human population. Jim nonetheless studies the deer in the area intently. Because of this study, he has become very good at understanding and predicting the ways of whitetails in agricultural areas. He intuitively knows the deer's reactions in relation to the lay of the land, the cutting of crops, weather, and so on, simply because he capitalized on his opportunity to observe them. Such observations have made him a much better deer hunter.

With their unbelievable growth in our southern counties over the past two decades, whitetails are now found in nearly every nook and cranny in Michigan. Most hunters today have at least some deer right in their immediate neighborhood. I won't suggest that old hunting camps and longed-for trips be abandoned, but I do suggest that you try putting some of that in-depth knowledge you already hold to use, right in your own backyard!

7

Late Season Trophies

A couple years ago, the opening day of our general firearms season found me sitting in a woodlot, roughly one hundred yards from its northern edge. According to my routine, I'd gotten to my stand at least a half-hour before daylight. At dawn, four shots rang out directly behind and north of me. "The stubble field's edge," I thought, and momentarily kicked myself for not having picked that location.

When I returned to my friend's farmhouse, I discovered the four shots I'd heard at daybreak had been fired at a nice eight-point as he drifted toward the security of the woodlot from the open stubble. Unfortunately for me, he never made it.

I'd hunted the same area three years before. On the eighth day of our sixteen-day gun season, I was in a dense tangle of brush about a half mile south of the woodlot. About 1 P.M., I dropped a fat little four-point as he followed behind two does that passed within twenty yards of my stand.

You might be inclined to say: different seasons, with totally unrelated events having no connection to each other—and let it go at that. Perhaps, but I believe these unrelated events highlight some very fundamental differences in deer behavior as the season progresses each year. I believe further that to hunt intelligently after the opening day salvos of gunfire have died away, a hunter must fully comprehend the nature of these changes, for they most assuredly affect your chances of success quite dramatically.

According to George Burgoyne, a former woodlands wildlife specialist and now the Chief of Wildlife with our DNR, Michigan's deer hunters harvest our legally antlered bucks very heavily, particularly in the Lower Peninsula. Consider the consequences of the following statistics: fully 60 percent of our total annual buck kill is claimed by the end of the third day of our season, and 75 percent is taken by the end of the first week. Consider further: of the total legally antlered population (those with at least three-inch spikes), 80 percent of them is tagged annually in Michigan's southern third, 70 percent is taken in the northern lower, and 50 percent is claimed throughout the breadth of the U.P. Clearly the hunter who does not score early in the season in Michigan has his work cut out for him. The situation, however, is not hopeless. What you need, as a hunter, is some insight into the behavior of late season bucks. You also need an ample dose of patience in pursuing them.

Further discussion about the two scenarios mentioned earlier will shed some light on this whole issue. While scouting a couple years ago, I often saw deer feeding in that open stubble field where the eight-point was taken. Although many bird hunters had been working the area, the deer, including some very large bucks, were using the field with regularity. The farmer and his sons told me they saw deer in both that field and in the adjoining winter wheat field each morning and evening throughout the fall. Just two days before the season opened, I saw a massive buck and two does in the open field, fully two to three hundred yards from the nearest cover, at least one-and-a-half hours before dark. The next afternoon, I saw a different buck in the field, again long before dark.

Assuming the deer would continue to use the field throughout the night, I thought an excellent location to hunt on opening day would be a stand overlooking a major runway leading into the nearby woodlot. Had it not been for the young man who waylaid that buck just before he reached the woodlot, I may have been correct in my analysis. It is not unusual to see white-tailed bucks in the open prior to opening day of the gun season. Even on the second or third day of the season, you may catch a love-struck buck or a youngster in the open, unknowledgeable in the ways of human hunters. However, those that survive beyond this early period of vulnerability wise up in a hurry. Even smaller bucks (such as my little four-point three years earlier) will retreat quickly to cover and seek isolation, if they're to survive.

Success in the late season is possible, and in fact this may well be the best time to score a big buck; if you're to do so, you must adjust, just as the deer. To optimize your chances, however, this adjustment must be more than simply heading to thicker cover. Depending upon what part of the state we're talking about, I prefer to separate the deer season into different periods. (Although the following is specific to the general gun season, similar arguments are pertinent to our archers and late season muzzle-loaders. See Chapters 11 and 12 for more specific suggestions found there.)

For the lucky few, there may be only one period to the hunting season. If you're fortunate enough to hunt a very large tract of private land, with essentially zero hunting pressure, you'll probably not have to make any major adjustments during the course of the season. Except for the natural and normal changes—the succession of the rut, the cutting of crop fields, the natural disappearance of the mast, and so on—there will be nothing to alter the deer's normal patterns, and nothing to alarm them. You'll simply proceed through the course of the hunting season without change. Few of us are so blessed!

Hunters throughout much of our state, however, are going to be confronted with what I consider to be a two-part season, and an adjustment for the late season is most critical. For usually a very brief period in the early season, the deer *may* respond much as they did preseason; from then on their behavior is altered quite dramatically. If you were scouting an area during the preseason, on opening morning it *may* be wise to hunt in those areas showing abundant

Doe with Fawns. In the latter parts of the season, does and fawns still linger along the edges and sometimes even in the open. Bucks seldom do. The bigger the buck and the heavier the hunting pressure, the less likely it is you'll ever see him in the open.

sign. In other words, it *may* be wise to hunt in areas that hunters traditionally hunt. In farm country, areas such as crop fields, cover near crop fields, orchards, runways leading to active bedding areas, hardwoods with mast, and so forth, are all likely locations. For nonagricultural areas, hardwoods bearing mast, cover fields, the forest edges, abandoned orchards and heavily used runways could all prove productive. Succinctly, these are the areas where you're accustomed to seeing deer.

It is impossible to say how long this initial period of the season will last; it is entirely dependent upon hunter density and the subsequent disruptions. That is why I say it *may* be a good idea to hunt the traditional areas. *Even on opening morning*, traditional hunting tactics are very suspect in areas with extremely heavy hunting pressure. For example, I would say that the young man who took that eight-point behind me a couple years ago would not see another deer all day long had he not connected. The disruption in many deer hunting areas in Michigan is so severe prior to first light on opening morning that many deer, especially the bigger, wiser bucks, are so disturbed that they forsake their earlier routines. This is what I counted on when I went into thick cover on opening morning that year. I took a calculated risk; I gambled that the deer wouldn't be in the field at daybreak, that they'd have detected the hunters' presence, and they'd be in thicker cover. I was wrong that time, but I believe it was a good bet. And I believe I would win that gamble most of the time in similar situations.

In areas I have hunted in the Thumb region the past few years, I've seen tremendous changes in hunting pressure. Several years ago, I hunted every day of the season, heard few shots—none close by—and saw only one other hunter. I really don't believe the deer ever abandoned their preseason routines; they never knew the deer season was on. This has since changed, as more and more hunters use the area. A couple years ago, we experienced a three-part season in this area. The first part was opening day, or perhaps more properly the first few hours. As many hunters invaded the deer's territory on opening morning, the deer quickly retreated to heavy cover. They lay low, abandoned their normal bedding areas, and avoided open areas.

Once the opening day rush diminished, and fewer hunters were afield, the deer began to calm down. After the fourth or fifth day, I never saw another hunter. Slowly the deer began showing up more in the openings again, almost as they had during the preseason period. On the fourteenth day of the regular gun season, at one o'clock, I saw a massive buck materialize out of the fog in front of me. He'd come out of a cattail marsh, walked across an old beaver meadow, and was slowly meandering toward a cedar thicket.

Two years ago the hunting pressure—where I hunt—was more constant throughout the season; consequently, we had a two-part season in that area. After the opening few hours, the deer were in the thicker cover areas. They abandoned entirely their preseason routines and never reverted to them until long after the regular season had ended. Such a situation is common in many areas—most areas, I believe, at least in the Lower Peninsula.

Sign is your most important clue to where the deer are and what they're up to at this time. Chances are excellent that they will not abandon all that's familiar to them, although they might for a day or two. More likely they'll simply adjust their timetables. They'll leave feeding areas earlier in the mornings, and arrive at them later than usual in the evenings. These are the kinds of changes that require increased efforts on the hunter's part, if he hopes to connect.

You should plan on getting to your stand a little earlier each morning, and on staying deep in cover a little later each evening. The deer are not only coming and going sooner than usual; they are also more alert to danger. Your objective is to short-circuit their detection mechanisms. With few exceptions, this is a poor time for still hunting. Unless you have great abilities as a still hunter, and proper areas in which to do so, your best bet is a stand. Several stand sites should have been selected prior to the season, and now is the time to use them (see Chapter 12 for a detailed discussion of stand selection).

Every effort must be made to minimize all motion and noise while on stand. I strongly recommend a seat of some sort, with adequate padding, to be comfortable. Few hunters are able to stand without fidgeting for prolonged periods, and this can spell the difference between scoring and spending the remainder of the season in vain. An added layer of clothing can go a long way toward insuring comfort and minimizing movement as well. Good quality boots, gloves, and a hat are all essential. I also recommend moving to a different stand each day, since the area will quickly become laden with your scent.

A key ingredient to success in the late season is to remain alert. This is much more easily done if you are confident about the area. Confidence to a large degree goes hand in hand with experience, but young or inexperienced hunters can be much more confident if they've done their homework. There's nothing like spending time afield to learn the art of deer hunting and the ways of whitetails. Time should be spent before, during, and after the season studying deer. If possible, you should do so in the area where you hunt.

During this part of the season, the cover you should be hunting is where the deer retreat whenever they feel threat-

Buck in Autumn Cover. Even in the most heavily hunted regions of Michigan there remain legally antlered bucks in the latter parts of our seasons. To connect on these animals it is crucial that you concentrate all of your efforts within heavier cover, hunt from daylight to dark, and whenever possible, use whatever hunting pressure there is to your advantage.

ened. In northern Michigan, it can be cedar swamps, or planted pines, or perhaps areas that were logged more than ten or fifteen years ago and are now covered by dense stands of young growth. In southern Michigan, it can be cattail marshes that contain a little high ground (deer won't lie down in standing water), or brushy creek bottoms, or thorn apple thickets. The precise spots must be selected by studying the sign present *after* the season opens. This is where experience within the area is a big help, as it will save both time and leg work when you really should be concentrating on the hunt itself.

Once the season is underway, look for changes in the use of runways, and then hunt accordingly. Some runways, seldom used during the preseason, should now show heightened activity, while others heavily used will show less. Pay particular attention to corridors of cover that lead from one area to another. Some years ago, I was hunting an area in the U.P. that had partially burned over. The burn covered four or five hundred acres and was covered with grasses and brambles two feet high or so, and the deer loved it. They'd forage freely each night over the entire space, but were careful to slip into cover before daylight, following the opening day barrage of gunfire. There was a small creek flowing through one corner of the burned area, and on the fifth morning of the season I took a stand in the dense cover along its banks.

The creek's moisture allowed a lush undergrowth to spring up, spreading about twenty feet wide on each side of the two-foot-wide watercourse. There were no runways, and few tracks were evident, but I felt this would be an excellent avenue for any deer that lingered late in his feeding or was trying to move from the cover in the north to that in the west.

In front of me, for at least a half mile, there was nothing over three feet tall. To my left and right there were thick brush, some scattered pines, and dense brambles all along the waterway. About noon I heard something moving to my left, but saw nothing. A half hour went by. I'd almost put the noise out of my mind, when I heard it again. I turned slowly to face that way, and within five minutes I saw movement about forty yards away. I dropped a nice six-point that had

Trophy Rack. The big bucks are still out there in late season. To find one such as this takes persistence and hard work—and luck.

probably been there for much of the morning. As I did so, three other deer exploded from the creek's cover and headed upstream. I found numerous beds and trampled areas right in the immediate vicinity, but really no sign anywhere else. I was lucky, yes, but it's not uncommon to find deer utilizing such areas at that time of the season. They'll use them to move from one area to another, and for bedding in. Such corridors are seldom worked by hunters, even though they provide an excellent escape route for the deer if they are pushed from either direction.

This incident points out another truth about late-season whitetail hunting. They're frequently taken in midday. Hunting pressure cuts into the deer's normal feeding times, and although all deer commonly feed for short periods several times during the day, these periods become even more important; they are more extensive in mid and late seasons. The difference is that the deer feed totally within cover at this time. It's, therefore, particularly important later in the season to hunt the entire day.

Another frequently overlooked strategy is to look for isolated areas of cover after opening day. Several years ago, I took a buck the first day of the season and then resumed running my fox traps. For several days I kept cutting a huge deer track, always leading away from a woodlot of oaks toward a cut cornfield, and always on the same runway. It puzzled me, because I never saw the track running the other way. The morning before Thanksgiving, I took a fox from one of my traps nearby and rested for a moment. As I sat there, I kept looking at the little patch of brush that surrounded a pond on the far side of the cornfield. The longer I sat the more I wondered if that deer could be hiding there. It seemed ridiculous. I was very familiar with the spot as I'd often hunted ducks there just weeks before. I knew the cover was thick, but very narrow—maybe ten feet wide at the most around the pond's perimeter.

Leaving my trapping basket in the middle of the winter wheat field, I walked to the cover. I'd gotten to within thirty yards or so of the pond when I heard a deer crashing through the brush and back up the fencerow toward the woodlot to the north—the same woodlot from which his tracks had always led.

That night I called a friend and explained what happened. He hadn't filled his tag yet, and I suggested he go out with me. The next morning, well before daylight, I placed my buddy on the side of the runway leading from the woodlot. I told him I'd jumped the buck (I assumed from the size of the tracks and his behavior that it had to be a buck) the morning before from his hideout, but I explained I didn't think I'd frightened him since I hadn't shot nor even trailed him, but immediately left the area.

I told him I expected the buck to come straight at him from the base of the little hill and walk within thirty yards of his position, and that he should be ready. The wind was perfect, as it was blowing straight away from the woodlot. Quickly I left him on his own and proceeded to run my traps. I checked my nearby trap and was on my way to the next one when I heard my friend shoot. I was really excited; boy, I had that deer pegged, and there's something special to me about outsmarting a late season buck!

Another important consideration is that a much higher percentage of deer movement later in the season is slower, and seemingly more calculated than what you're used to. Whereas prior to the hunting season, deer tend to move rather uninhibitedly, and during the early period of the season they tend to move quickly away from danger, in mid- and late-season periods they will often slink from danger and move almost in slow motion. Watch more carefully. Watch for very minute movements associated with noise—the crackling of dried or frosty leaves, the snap of a twig—and watch for pieces of a deer, such as an ear, or the swish of a tail, rather than the whole animal. Such a practice will pay big dividends. At the very tag end of the season, in those areas where few hunters remain, I've found still hunting a very satisfying and productive method (this is one of the exceptions mentioned earlier) among small pockets of broken cover. Areas such as this are common. I had an experience many years ago that now highlights an important point about such hunting.

I'd been pussyfooting through an area of scattered thorn apple thickets and old brushy fencerows in Oakland County. It was a cool, sunny afternoon at the tail end of the season. I had seen nothing in four hours of combing this two-hundred-acre plot. Moments before, I stopped and enjoyed a cup of coffee. I then moved downhill and through a swale lying in an old creek bed. On exiting the opposite side, I remembered my gloves, which I'd left where I had my coffee. Turning back, I slowly made my way through the swale. Midway through, a small buck jumped up no more than fifteen feet in front of me, and about thirty feet or so from where I'd passed just moments before. Had I not turned back, he'd have been perfectly content to lie there and let danger pass him by. Patience, determination and a slow, thorough approach are the keys to hunting late season whitetails.

8

The Mid-Michigan Whitetail

Somewhere between the majority of the farms of our southern counties and the bulk of the wilderness regions of our Upper Peninsula, we have what I refer to (for the lack of a better term) as "middle Michigan." By middle Michigan, I mean to describe more a condition than a region. Within middle Michigan this condition exists most frequently. The condition is very heavy hunting pressure.

The counties that comprise Region II (the northern half of the Lower Peninsula), while having roughly one-sixth of our state's land mass, carry more than 50 percent of our deer hunting pressure. This relationship holds true for all our various deer hunting seasons: archery, gun and muzzleloader. But this is not to say that the hunting pressure found in parts of Region II does not occur in other areas as well. The pressure in Region II is not uniform by any means, and in fact, less than half of these counties carries more than 65 percent of Region II's total hunting pressure. Our state lands throughout southern Michigan fall under these conditions, as does much of Calhoun County, parts of Jackson, Montcalm and Kent counties in southern Michigan, and

Figure 8.1
Michigan's most heavily hunted counties

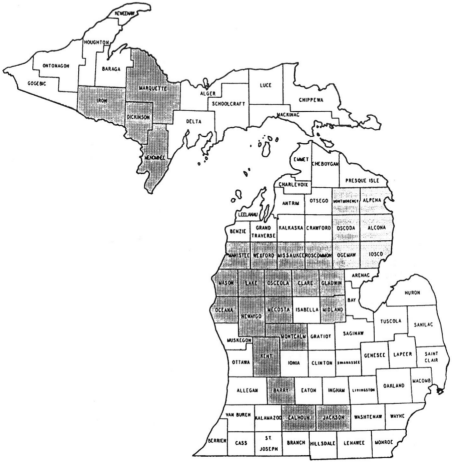

The shaded band of counties pictured here represents a land area of less than one-third of Michigan, yet it bears more than 60 percent of our total deer hunting pressure. In the rural forested areas of Region II, the wilderness regions of southern Marquette County and the farmlands of Jackson County, traditional deer hunting techniques discussed in Chapters 4 and 5 will not consistently work. Rather, we must learn to use the resulting hunting pressures in "middle Michigan" to our advantage by hunting the escape routes the deer utilize, as well as their retreat cover.

parts of Marquette, Iron and Dickinson counties in the U.P.

We will discuss the methods that should be used when hunter densities reach roughly fifteen hunters, or more, per square mile. We've already discussed hunting techniques and tactics that are most effective for taking both farmland whitetails and wilderness whitetails. But when hunting pressure attains the proportions we're addressing here, then all bets are off—those strategies won't work, or at least they won't work consistently. So we must alter our approach. Here are some tactics that will work under these conditions.

The most important thing to remember is that somehow we must use all the disruptions caused by intense hunting pressure in such a way that they work to our advantage. Research shows that deer—yes, even the bucks—seldom forsake home ranges when hunters make their lives chaotic. What they will do, however, is decrease their active range, turn more nocturnal, and become much more cautious. They'll also develop nerves of steel, and will often lie literally within feet of a passing hunter without bolting. Intense preseason scouting, or an intimate familiarity with your chosen hunting area, is the real key to success here. Exit or escape runways, the heaviest cover in the area, and those areas avoided by most other hunters—for whatever reasons—are crucial to the deer's survival and are places you must learn about.

Throughout the whitetails' range we find at least two types of runways. One is the type used by the deer in their normal day-to-day travel. These runs most commonly lead from bedding to feeding areas and vice-versa. The other primary type of run is the escape or exit runway. Invariably these runs lead from one stretch of bedding cover to another. They do not meander around, they lead directly from one pocket of cover to another. They may show heavy usage, and most frequently the bigger, wiser bucks will use the least conspicuous ones—so search the area thoroughly. These are the runs you'll want to concentrate on throughout middle Michigan.

Hunting escape runs will be most profitable the first couple days of the season while the deer remain unsettled, and again in the tag end of the season when many hunters are attempting to drive the thicker cover, or when hunting pres-

Deer Lying in Snow. Whitetails throughout their range are more comfortable when they're near or in cover. The deer in "middle Michigan" have an absolute penchant for it.

sure has thinned considerably. In our heavily hunted agricultural areas, it will be most profitable to locate where a lot of feeding activity is taking place, and then figure out where these animals are bedding. Once that is done, the sides of the bedding area(s) away from the food source(s) should be searched for escape runs. It is along these runs that I'd hunt during the early season because a lot of the hunting pressure will undoubtedly be directed to the bedding areas. As the deer attempt to flee to more distant coverts, you'll be in position to poleax them.

Throughout our forested areas such a strategy will be more difficult to implement. Feeding here is going to be far more widespread, but it can still be done. Search intently for the most concentrated active feeding areas—mast-bearing white oaks, heavy stands of favored browse species such as willow, honeysuckle, poplar, and others (see the food list for forest whitetails in Chapter 10). Then, just as in the agricultural situations, determine the bedding area(s) associated with this feeding. Once this is done, then locate the escape runs on the distant perimeters.

At best, for general gun season hunters, this is the one kind of hunting where the usual knowledge, garnered by preseason scouting, will be of minimal value. It will do you no good to learn, even intimately, what the deer here are doing two days before the season opens because they won't be doing it by opening morning. The commotion of all those vehicles, all those hunters setting up camp, making blinds, taking preseason forays—whatever—serves only to alert every deer in the woods, dramatically altering their behavior patterns long before the first light of opening morning.

I've mentioned it earlier, but it deserves reiteration: just like humans, deer prioritize their needs, and when all those redcoats go afield the number one priority—and for a time the only one that counts—is safety. Invariably, for the buck at least, this means cover. Generally, the thicker and more impenetrable, the better. Once an animal reaches cover like this it's virtually impossible to make him leave it. We're not talking about bedding areas, but much thicker, nastier, escape cover. The solution is either to beat him to it and thereby waylay him as he approaches his sanctuary, or to actually penetrate his sanctum and simply wait him out. Both methods will work, although the second one, if you've several days to hunt, is much more certain. The problem with the first method is that you're gambling he hasn't yet entered his sanctuary either prior to your arrival or first light. If you're wrong, you end up waiting for a buck that will never show.

Deer Licking Herself. Midday movement in really dense escape cover is quite common and safe. Since most hunters will not penetrate such areas, you should. This will increase your chances of success.

Buck Next to Sun-Splattered. Tree This "middle Michigan" buck, quite easily captured on film in August, will be much more elusive come November. Don't insult his intelligence by altering the environment he knows so well. Minimize your body odors, employ only the natural surroundings and materials—no artificial blinds here.

Waiting within the cover itself is far more effective. Research also shows, in addition to the behavior already noted, that deer within sanctuary cover will actually increase their activity. However, the "core" area of safety is very small, probably in the neighborhood of five acres or less. Miss it by as little as one hundred feet and you'll wait in vain. The solution is to move your stand site daily, minimize movement, minimize your bodily odors and eliminate noise. Still hunting is generally futile here unless you possess remarkable stalking abilities.

While difficult, all these can be accomplished. Your stand for any given day should be chosen with several factors in mind (see Chapter 12); regardless, it's important to move it within the general area you believe the animal you are after is residing.

Dressing appropriately, for comfort will go a long way toward eliminating unnecessary movement. A warm, comfortable hunter is far less likely to be fidgeting than one who's shivering with cold. In addition to adequate clothing, a good woolen hat (not a cotton cap), quality gloves and the best boots you can buy are mandatory for the serious nimrod.

If your guess was correct about where the animal is—at any given time during your hunting day you're probably within one to two hundred feet of him—it is extremely important to minimize odors. Errant odors, and failure to neutralize easily eliminated odors, will again leave you waiting in vain. Don't smoke, don't consume strong smelling foods or beverages, and don't urinate nearby. It's easy to carry a urine bottle, emptying it somewhere outside of your immediate hunting area. Do not wear talc, aftershave or cologne. Daily bathing, good personal hygiene, and the washing of all of your clothing in an unscented detergent are also important.

Avoid heavy cover and this type of hunting on those days when the wind is either absent, or when it wafts unpredictably. All you'll succeed in doing on such days is to alert the animal, making him just that much tougher to tag later on. The elimination of noise is accomplished by again ensuring your comfort by dressing appropriately, with a comfortable seat. Do not build blinds. The animal you are after will be intimately familiar with this small piece of real estate and the presence of anything new will alert him instantly. Sit still and remain alert at all times and hunt from daylight to dark whenever possible.

No matter how heavily hunted an area is, there is almost always cover somewhere within that is barely, if ever, hunted. Finding such spots generally takes several years of hunting experience in the area, but it's something you should always be looking for. Pay attention to where and how other hunters work the area, and then put that knowledge to work for yourself. Ask yourself repeatedly throughout the season, "If I were a deer where would I go to find safety?" It could easily be argued that the most successful deer hunters are recognized not necessarily by the knowledge they possess, but rather by the questions they ask. Keep your mind alert in pressure-packed deer hunting areas, and search out the isolated or impenetrable stretches of cover. You'll be far more likely to score.

Part III

Hunting Tips and Secrets

9

Tools
of the Trade

I'd like to tell you a story about bear hunting. What it has to do with deer hunting will become clear. I was planning a Quebec bear hunt a few years ago and one of the fellows who was going along had never hunted bear before. I carefully explained the setup, the baits used, type of cover, the average distance between bait and stand (less than fifteen yards), and so on. I further explained that the average black bear taken in that area weighed in at about 250 pounds live weight, and that although a black bear was not terribly difficult to bring down, in the type of cover we'd be hunting my companion would want a bullet design that would flatten considerably upon impact with muscle tissue. He'd want to put in two or preferably three rounds before the bear escaped into cover—a distance, in most cases, of roughly ten or fifteen feet in any direction. I'd been in on numerous searches for wounded bear over the years, in both Ontario and Quebec, and explained that I had no desire to be included in any more. Believe me, they are never fun, and I've yet to see a successful one. The cover these animals stick to will swallow them up and they're never found.

Imagine then my surprise, while setting up camp, when this man, who is an experienced hunter, pulled from his gun case a Remington Model 700, bolt action, chambered in .30/06 and topped with a 3X–9X powered variable scope! Predictably enough, two days later when a good-size bruin walked directly beneath his tree stand, he succeeded only in getting off one shot before the animal escaped into cover. Worse yet, he wasn't even sure what part of the animal he'd hit because all he could see through the scope when he fired was fur. Not only did he put himself, and the rest of us who helped him search, into an extremely dangerous situation, he also ruined his whole trip and came home empty-handed. The unforgivable upshot of all this, however, was what he'd done to the bear!

No matter what game you're hunting, matching your weapon, its sights, and the ammunition used to the game and its environment is critical. A mismatch, as illustrated above, deprives you of a successful hunt and possibly a trophy. More importantly, it subjects the animal to unnecessary suffering. The hunter's objective must always be to obtain the most humane and swiftest kill possible once the decision to shoot has been made.

How specifically does this apply to Michigan deer hunters? To begin with, for gun hunters, we can speculate on the conditions under which the "typical" deer taken in Michigan is bagged. It is going to be taken, on average, at fairly short range, under fifty yards in all probability. It's going to be shot in cover of some sort. The cover can range from sparse hardwoods or even crop fields, to dense cedars or thick tag alders. In addition, there's a very good likelihood that the animal will be moving when shot, perhaps even running. And, the majority of the animals will be taken in low light situations, either early or late in the day. Given all of this as typical, let's now grapple with the meaning of it all in terms of the weapon we choose: its action, caliber, sights, and bullet design.

Figure 9.1
Vital areas of the deer's anatomy

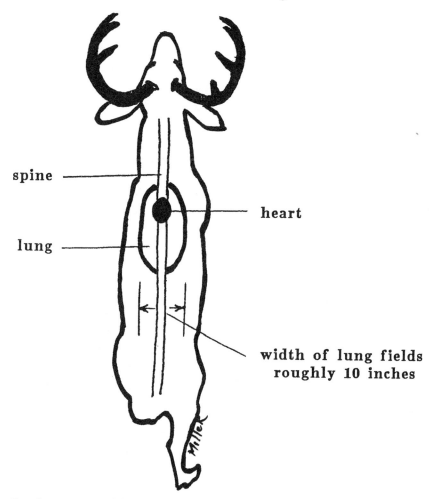

spine

heart

lung

width of lung fields
roughly 10 inches

Gun hunters in Michigan aren't presented with the overhead shot often, but for archers it's quite common. Notice the nonvital spaces to each side of the lung fields. A shot slipped in here may well lead to a mortally wounded but untagged animal. A midline shot (or near the midline, four to five inches to either side) is what you should aim for. "Spine" the animal and you probably won't kill it outright, but you'll completely immobilize it. (Drawing by Roger Miller)

The Bolt Action

For the serious rifleman this is unquestionably the most popular rifle action in use today. Its positive attributes: it

Figure 9.2A

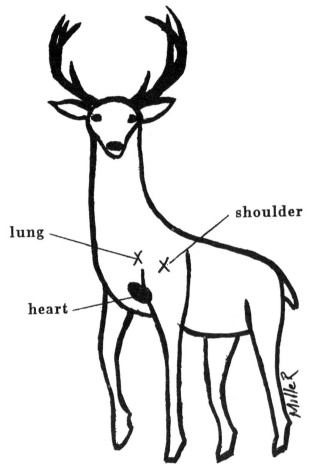

Some variation of the broadside shot—from the animal quartering to you, to the animal quartering away—is by far the most common shot. The heart-lung-shoulder region offers all hunters their largest target area. Don't be lackadaisical, however. Concentrate on a particular spot and be certain of your shot. (Figures 9.2A, 9.2B and 9.2C drawn by Roger Miller)

readily accepts and digests reloads and hot handloads without jamming; it is capable of better accuracy than most other types of actions; it will accept any type of sight aperture desired; and it is available in any imaginable caliber.

However, for the average Michigan deer hunter, the bolt action has a couple of major drawbacks that to my mind far

Figure 9.2B

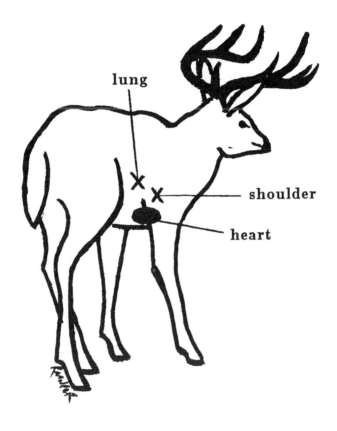

outweigh its pluses. First, it is a difficult action for a left-handed shooter to operate unless it's a left-handed gun; second, it is extremely slow in getting off repeat shots in the hands of the average shooter. A sloppy or carelessly executed first shot is never justified, but the hunter should always be in a position where he can get off repeat shots if needed. I don't believe the average hunter, in the type of habitat generally found in Michigan, can do this with a bolt action gun. Such facility with a bolt action is not difficult to achieve, but

Figure 9.2C

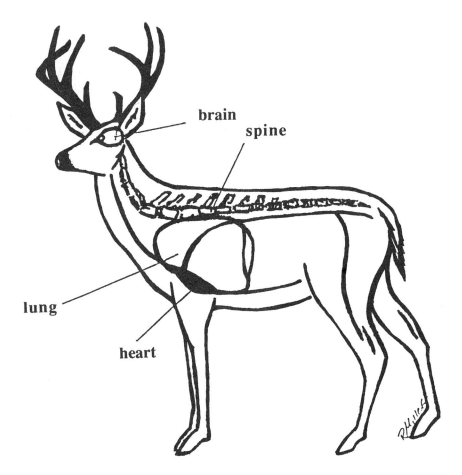

given that the "average" Michigan hunter makes one trip per year to the range, I don't believe he can adequately perfect those skills. Also, there are better options available for him.

The Lever Action

With Winchester's development of the smokeless-powder .30/30 cartridge in 1895, its Model 94 lever action soon became the sporting rifle to have. Even today it remains the world's all-time number-one seller among sporting rifles, and with good reason.

Perhaps its biggest advantage is its speed. The short, lightweight construction and hammer cocking mechanism provide speed and easy handling in the tight cover that is so typical of much of Michigan's hunting. Repeat shots are fast also. These guns are chambered today for a wide variety of cartridges in addition to the classic .30/30, which remains a very good round for the Michigan hunter, since his average shot will be far less than the 150-yard mark where the .30/30's ballistics tend to deteriorate. Its accuracy is more than adequate at these ranges, and most models can be fitted with any type of optics desired. Another important consideration is the overall economy and durability of the gun. Winchester's Model 94, .30/30, is clearly the leader. You can still get one out of the door, taxes and all, for roughly two hundred dollars. With that investment you'll have a gun that, if taken care of, will last forever, and probably be trouble free. And, of course, ammunition for the .30/30 is readily available, even in the smallest, most out-of-the-way Michigan hamlet.

The only negative point of the lever action involves its spent cartridge extraction capabilities. Should a casing swell after firing, prying it loose can be a real chore. Still, this seldom occurs, and with the use of factory ammo I don't believe it's a real concern.

The Pump Gun

Christmas morning of my ninth year is a day I'll never forget. Under the tree lay a box all wrapped in brilliant color with a large bow and my name on it. As I tore the paper loose I saw the name REMINGTON in its traditional bold green type. The gun was a 20-gauge Model 870, and a love affair began that gets sweeter all the time. To this day I'd rather have a pump in my hands than any other gun, whether I'm heading into the fields, woods, or onto a skeet field.

Shooting the shuck gun is as natural to me as breathing. They make excellent brush guns, and are popular with Michigan hunters. They are fast, lightweight, can be chambered in almost any caliber a deer hunter could desire, and they are capable of good accuracy at ranges up to two hundred yards. They'll also accept whatever sights you might desire.

Their minuses include a lack of camming power, so that hot handloads should be avoided and care must be taken to keep the chamber clean and dry.

Semiautomatics

Semiautoloaders are very popular here in Michigan, and with good reason. They are quick handling and very quick shooting, offering repeat shots as needed. They come chambered in a wide variety of good deer hunting loads. They readily accept most any sight you might desire to use, and they posses fair to good accuracy at Michigan deer hunting ranges. For the man (or woman) who shoots only a few times a year, semiautomatics are very easy to handle, and the self-cocking action helps to soak up the recoil that is so distasteful to most shooters.

The disadvantage is that they are quite finicky about the ammo they eat. Handloaders in particular want to be careful in their resizing operations, and they'll want to avoid hot loads where casings tend to swell. Factory loads seldom present a problem, however, and the average nimrod, with moderate care and quality ammunition, should never experience a problem.

Deer Cartridge Requirements

Before embarking on the question of what is a suitable cartridge for deer in our state we must first decide what minimum criteria we want that cartridge to meet. For the sake of the animals we hunt, we owe it to them to do all within our power to ensure clean, consistent kills, under a variety of circumstances that are often less than idea.

With this as our goal, many cartridges can be automatically eliminated from consideration. Unquestionably, any of the .22 centerfires have taken their share of deer, but with the energy that these bullets pack they cannot satisfy our basic requirements. Even those juiced up by handloaders won't fulfill the need. On the opposite side of the coin there is such a thing as overkill. Undoubtedly, deer have fallen to such giant slayers as the .375 Holland & Holland; but dead is dead, and the average hunter in the woods cannot handle such guns, nor does he need to in order to assure consistent kills on whitetails.

The ideal cartridge then would lie somewhere between these two extremes. It should give the oomph that's needed (most ballistics experts say for whitetails that's around 1,000 foot-pounds of energy at the point of impact), and it should be in a package (gun plus sights) that's both comfortable to shoot and comfortable to carry for a day in the field. Too many Michigan deer hunters go afield each year with too much gun. These men, women and children are toting .30/06s, 7mms, or other guns that they're afraid of. My first deer rifle was a bolt action, .280 Remington. I shot it poorly, to say the least, because I was afraid of it. When I pulled the trigger on that gun, I knew it was going to hurt. Bless my father's heart, he was trying to make "a man" out of me, and every time I'd tell him that it hurt, he'd tell me I was a sissy! He said I'd get used to it. With all due respect to my father—I never did.

I hope times have changed enough from when I was a kid for us to have grown beyond that kind of mentality. I'm 6'5" tall and weigh 205 pounds; I'm lean, fit, athletic and in very good physical shape, but to this day I don't like a gun to beat me around. When I was a kid it hurt, and it still hurts today!

Fathers and husbands who are considering a gun for sons, daughters, wives, or for yourselves, keep this in mind: nobody shoots a gun well that hurts. If you're overly conscious of the recoil, you're going to squint your eyes, tense your muscles, and jerk the trigger instead of squeezing it. You'll soon flinch, and then be left wondering about those nine-inch patterns at fifty yards, or why the paper is missed altogether!

To this day the diminutive .30/30 is still the front runner in terms of the number of deer it has killed; it makes a beautiful cartridge for our state. Standard factory ammo comes in 150 and 170 grain weights, and at one hundred yards it still packs 1,296 foot-pounds of energy. I consider it a reliable load both in energy and accuracy out to 150 yards. The Winchester .243, and the nearly identical 6mm Remington, are two more

Mature Doe. A properly executed shot is far more crucial than tremendous shocking power. Keep in mind that whitetails are not big animals. This is a fully mature, seven- or eight-year-old doe. Mature whitetail does stand roughly 30 inches high at the shoulder and, while exceptional specimens may run upwards of 200 pounds, the average Michigan doe weighs roughly 110 pounds. Bucks run a bit larger (32 inches at the shoulder and 130 pounds) on average.

excellent choices for those who might be recoil shy. With the standard 100 grain factory ammo, they will do an excellent job on deer out to two hundred yards. Jumping up a notch—in terms of power, better trajectory, and more recoil—we have the .270 Winchester. With standard factory loads in either 130 or 150 grain bullets, the hunter has more than adequate ballistics out to three hundred yards—farther than a Michigan hunter would likely need in a lifetime of hunting.

The list of potential deer cartridges goes on and on: the .280 Remington, .30/06, .303 British, and .308 Winchester being some of the more popular, just to name a few. The truly important factor, once minimum ballistic and trajectory requirements are accounted for, is the comfort and effectiveness with the caliber of choice. Long before any gun is taken into the woods the hunter must be intimately familiar with it. He or she needs to be able to obtain consistent groupings at one hundred yards, of say four inches or better. Further, the shooter must be familiar with the sights, be they open iron sights, peep sights or telescopic. One also needs to be adept at handling the action of the gun in order to get off those sometimes critical second or third shots.

The Southern Michigan Deer Hunter

Deer hunters hunting south of a line drawn roughly from Au Gres on the east to Muskegon on the west must do their hunting with shotguns, and this requires special discussion (check the *Annual Hunting and Trapping Guide* for exact details). Shotguns shoot two kinds of ammunition that are designed for use on deer: slugs and buckshot. Both are legal in Michigan and, depending upon where you hunt, you may have a need for one or the other, or perhaps both.

Buckshot comes in a variety of sizes ranging from Number 000 Buckshot, the largest, to Number 4 Buck, the smallest. The standard two and three-quarter inch, 12-gauge No. 000 Buck load carries just eight pellets, while the two and three-quarter inch No. 4 holds twenty-seven pellets. Standard factory buckshot loads are made for 12-, 16-, 20- and .410-gauge shotguns. For reasons I'll explain later, I'm limiting this discussion of shotguns for deer hunting to 12-gauge guns.

Shotgun slugs are a single piece of lead. Some brands have "riflings" along the sides, and hence the misnomer that's often applied—"rifled slug." Most slugs are not a solid mass, but rather they're cast hollowed in the rear. It is this weight-forward design that helps lend stability in flight— not the riflings found along the sides of some slugs.

When it comes to the throwing of deer loads, be they buckshot or slugs, shotguns are notoriously inaccurate. Ballistics, trajectory and the pattern of these loads make it clear that unless the constraints inherent in their use are clearly understood by the hunter, they make a very poor weapon for deer. Be that as it may, in our state it is the law because of safety reasons. The southern portion of Michigan is simply too heavily populated to risk the firing of long-range projectiles. That's a fact any hunter heading afield in the south must live with. If the hunter understands the limitations imposed by these guns, however, shotguns can be extremely effective. I've hunted southern Michigan for many years and have taken several deer with shotguns, both with slugs and with buckshot, and have not experienced any difficulties.

Most autoloading and pump guns on the market today can be fitted with special "slug barrels." I highly recommend that anyone thinking of shotgunning for deer makes the investment in one of these barrels. There are also specially packaged "slug guns" marketed by almost all the major shotgun manufacturers; Ithaca's Deerslayer, for example, is one such model. All the slug barrels and slug guns are fitted with a straight tube: that is, a bored-improved cylinder. This eliminates the deflection encountered in most other barrels as the slug passes through the choked section of the tube. They also come equipped with standard open rifle sights, compared with the front bead sight on most scatterguns. This greatly improves the shooter's sighting plane. A quality slug barrel should be able to deliver six-inch groups at fifty yards. I've personally seen two scatterguns that could deliver groupings that tight at one hundred yards, but that is unusual. If you have a shotgun that can do that, hang on to it!

Author with Eight-Point Buck. The author took this big eight-point down instantly with one load of 12-gauge No. 00 Buckshot at twenty-three paces. Twelve-gauge Buckshot, within thirty yards, is a devastating load.

One thing to try for improved accuracy in slug guns is to switch the brand of shell you shoot. Due to slight differences in each manufacturer's tolerances, some brands will just naturally perform better in a particular gun than will others. The gun that shoots just so-so with Remington slugs may excel with Federal or Winchester, or vice-versa. A German-made slug manufactured by Brenneke is highly recommended by many shooters today. The best approach is to try several different brands and see which one your gun throws most accurately.

Another major problem with all shotguns, and that's why I limit this discussion to the 12-gauge, is the tremendous drop in oomph that these guns deliver beyond the fifty-yard mark. A 12-gauge slug at fifty yards packs 1,340 foot-pounds of energy, but that figure drops to just 875 foot-pounds at one hundred yards. The 16-gauge delivers 1,070 foot-pounds at fifty yards and only 700 foot-pounds at one hundred yards. If you have an extremely accurate 16-gauge it could suffice for hunting in tight cover. Just to show why the other gauges don't merit consideration: the 20-gauge has only 840 foot-pounds of energy at fifty yards and 550 at one hundred, the .410 only 345 at fifty and 205 at one hundred. If the hunter remembers the range limitations of the 12-gauge slug and is familiar with his gun, it's a deadly combination. With careful shooting he should have no problems.

The load of choice in typical southern Michigan cover is a slug. In very dense cover, however, where you're certain the animal is going to be within a maximum of thirty yards, buckshot is highly effective. When I load buckshot I always back it up with slugs. I carry a Remington 870 with a slug barrel; my chambered load will be buckshot (my personal choice is No. 00 Buck) backed up by slugs whenever I'm in dense cover. Otherwise I stick with slugs entirely.

Again, the most important thing to remember is the severe limitations this combination gives you in terms of range. Beyond thirty-five yards, both buckshot patterns and energy levels deteriorate horribly. Don't risk injury to that animal—if you can't kill him cleanly, don't shoot!

Sights

Basically, there are three types of rifle sights: iron (or open) sights, peep sights and scopes. Iron sights are standard equipment on most any rifle as sold by the manufacturer. Many hunters complain of inaccuracy with iron sights, particularly when shooting at moderate to long distances. Certainly for long distances they are inferior to other sights. However, I believe the average Michigan hunter would be well advised that if he attains three- to four-inch groups at one hundred yards from his rifle with iron sights to stick with them; he needs nothing more. The hunter who shoots his deer rifle once or twice a year at a range and then goes afield during the season is, in my opinion, better off with iron sights than with the more precise, but demanding, scope sight.

Peep sights are a puzzle to me—I've never understood their lack of popularity. They're very fast when installed properly (which means the rear sight or "peep" is close to the eye), and unquestionably more accurate than iron sights. Most peep sights come equipped with an inner disc screwed into the peep. Once the peep is installed, the shooter would be well advised to unscrew the disc, and throw it away. The larger aperture facilitates quickness and results in a much improved field-of-vision. Once the shooter is familiar with it, the peep sight will be as accurate as the iron sight since his eye will instinctively center the front bead in the opening. For the shooter who puts in just a little extra practice, these sights are a tremendous improvement over open iron sights. I highly recommend them.

For the serious rifleman, there is no question about the sight of choice—the scope wins hands down. Anyone who shoots enough to become comfortable and proficient with the use of a scope has a tremendous advantage over those with more primitive sights. The problem is that scopes do take getting used to: they require practice and repetitive usage. For those who plan to use a scope, I'd highly recommend a fixed-power model of 1.5X to 2.5X. Scopes of higher magnification will be a handicap on close shots at running game since they reduce the width-of-field. A 1.5X scope gives a wide field-of-view, centers the target quickly, and allows good light. For Michigan hunters there are several advantages of fixed- over variable-powered scopes. Generally speaking, fixed-powered scopes are lighter in weight and they are more durable than the variables. The hunter won't get caught in tight cover with them set on maximum magnification either, and they are considerably cheaper than variables of equal quality. The most important consideration in the purchase of a scope is quality. A good rule of thumb is to stick with brand names and buy the best you can afford.

Once the decision is made to go with a scope, there are a couple of other considerations. One is the type of mount to get. My personal opinion is that if you carry a scope, you should plan on becoming proficient and comfortable with it. This means getting it mounted low to the barrel and doing away with the iron sight entirely. I do not like the "over the iron sight" type of mount; you have to lift your cheek from the stock or cant your head with this mount. Hence you'll never really become proficient. The other consideration involves the type of reticle or aiming element. Any of the thicker types of elements give better visibility in Michigan's typically wooded and brushy environments than the thinner-style cross hairs.

One final suggestion regarding scopes is to have a competent gunsmith do the installation, unless you really know what you're doing. It has been estimated that at least half of all scopes in use are improperly mounted. A poorly mounted scope, or one that's loosely fitted, could cost you dearly.

Bullet Design

There are several things to keep in mind when considering bullet design. Remember that the animal we hunt is not really large; the average whitetail in our state weighs roughly 110 pounds. Although they're not exactly pushovers, whitetails are not easy to kill either. Moreover, bullets kill by virtue of their shocking power. The way to maximize that power is to design the bullet so that it expands—"mushrooms"—on impact. This expansion, however, must happen in a controlled manner. You want a bullet that can buck its way through some brush intact, and yet expand when needed.

This controlled expansion is nicely obtained with the partially jacketed bullet designs on the market today. Remington's "Core-Lokt" design is an excellent load for whitetails, as is Winchester's "Power-Point," and Federal's "Boat-tail S.P." To be avoided are fully jacketed bullets that offer no expansion in an animal the size of a whitetail, and those designed with extremely high velocity and lightweight construction, which disintegrate on impact.

One final observation. All rifle and shotgun hunters will greatly benefit from a good sling. A sling frees both hands for other purposes when needed, and it serves as an excellent brace whenever the hunter's forced to take quick off-hand shots.

All the above pretty well covers the needs of most Michigan riflemen, but there will be those who hunt in selected areas of the north whose needs will differ. Those hunters working the farming areas of Montmorency or Chippewa counties, for example, may well be offered shots more typical of our western states; for them, bolt-action rifles with scopes of three- or four-power and flat trajectories will more likely define the gun of choice.

Other Weapons

In the last fifteen years or so, Michigan deer hunters have become increasingly enamored with our "primitive weapons." While most muzzle-loaders and archers enjoy seasons in their own right, they've also offered us the opportunity to greatly extend our hunting season. No longer is the Michigan sportsman confined to the traditional sixteen-day November season. Handgunning, too, has become increasingly popular, and while not having a separate season (handgunners are limited to the regular gun season), their sport received a significant boost in 1985 when the legislature voted to permit the use of these weapons statewide rather than confining them to the north, as had earlier been the case. Let's discuss each of these weapons and try to settle on some minimal requirements for each.

Archery

No sport in Michigan (or nationwide for that matter) has enjoyed more rapid growth in the past twenty years than

archery. The first year that Michigan held an archery season, in 1937, 180 hunters laid claim to just four deer. In
1965, over 50,000 bowmen headed afield, and that year they
brought back 2,170 animals. Our bowhunters today exceed
250,000 in number, and annually claim somewhere in the
vicinity of 70,000 animals.

Bows

Unpalatable to some purists, there is no doubt that improve-
ments in archery equipment, particularly the compound bow,
have been most responsible for this phenomenal growth.
When I began bowhunting in the mid-1960s, nearly everyone
in the woods was toting a recurve bow; today, well over 80 percent of all archers use the compound. This love affair with the
compound is far more than just a mindless fad; it's soundly
based on some very real advantages that the compound has to
offer. Chief among these is the "let-off," or reduction in draw-
weight, as the bow is drawn. Compounds also shoot much flatter and faster than other bows of equal draw-weights.

It is generally felt that the minimum standard for deer is
a forty-five- to fifty-pound draw-weight bow. With a "let-off"
of anywhere from 15 percent to 50 percent (depending upon
the manufacturer and model) of this weight with the compound, it's easy to see why these bows are so popular.
Instead of pulling the full fifty pounds, the user of a compound is actually only pulling between twenty-five and forty
pounds, again depending upon the brand of bow used—one
heck of a lot easier than pulling and holding the full fifty
pounds required with either a long bow or a recurve.
Because of this, accuracy is greatly enhanced with the use of
a compound; the compound thus has actually allowed a good
many archers the opportunity to hunt big game who could
not otherwise. The most popular brands on the market today
are Hoyt/Easton, PSE, Golden Eagle, Ben Pearson, Darton,
Bear-Jennings, TSS, American Archery, Martin Archery,
and Browning.

Arrows and Broadheads

Every bit as important to the archer as his bow is the arrow he throws. Arrows do not kill by virtue of their shocking power, but rather by virtue of their hemorrhagic capability. Dropping the animal is totally dependent upon his losing large quantities of blood—the quicker the better. To accomplish this requires the sharpest broadhead possible. Moreover, the arrow must be correctly matched to the bow. A precise matchup is best left to the experts; most archery shops will give you solid advice on the arrow length and weight required for your particular bow and draw length.

In terms of terminal tackle—the actual broadhead itself—there are a great many on the market more than capable of doing the job. Personal choice dictates; you'll simply have to experiment a bit to see what suits your tastes and average hunting conditions. There is at least one manufacturer, Muzzy, that makes interchangeable heads for the same shaft, all with the same weight. These heads include the broadhead, Turkey Thumper, field point, and Judo practice point.

Archery is a demanding sport, much more so than rifle hunting. It requires constant practice to keep sharp. Follow the advice of an accomplished friend or knowledgeable, respected dealers. When you've acquired your basic equipment—practice, practice, practice!

Actual hunting tactics and techniques for archers are the same as for riflemen. The differences are in degree, not kind. Archers must work over a shorter distance; again, the compound has changed archery in this respect as well. Back in the 1960s, the average Michigan whitetail was arrowed at roughly twelve yards; today that average has increased to about twenty yards, and shots out to forty yards (depending upon the individual's capability) are not unheard of. Though still hunting is the ultimate challenge for any archer, and properly executed drives are productive, the vast majority of deer are taken by hunters off stands.

Accessories

In addition to the weapon, there are a few essentials for the archer that warrant mention. Portable tree stands (archers are allowed to hunt from elevated stands) are now considered a must. There are many brands on the market, including the Baker stand, the Quick and Quiet Seat Climber, and the Golden Eagle. The most important consideration with tree stands is safety; a significant number of hunters are seriously injured and even killed each year as a result of their use. I consider a safety belt essential whenever I'm elevated in a stand. String silencers are another essential. These are bowstring add-ons that help deaden the thud or whack from released bowstrings. Again, there are several different kinds on the market. A hunting quiver that protects both you and your broadheads is important. Most archers today also use a sight of one kind or another. These devices fasten to the bow's facing and greatly assist the shooter to obtain a consistent degree of elevation, time and time again. This list could go on and on, but in your practice on a range you'll quickly determine what's vital to you and what's expendable. For anyone new to archery, I'd highly recommend joining an archery club where, in the presence of more accomplished shooters, you'll quickly learn the fundamentals of the sport.

Muzzle-loaders

Like archers, Michigan muzzle-loaders have come of age. In 1975, Michigan became one of a handful of states to begin offering sportsmen the option of a separate "primitive" weapons season. It was always legal to hunt with the muzzle-loader, but it had to be done during the regular rifle season only. How times have changed! In the initial season, 8,500 hunters took to the field, to claim just 150 antlered animals. In 1989 (preliminary estimate), more than 100,000 front-end loaders went afield and claimed 11,000 animals!

The .45-caliber is normally considered the minimum

standard for deer, and most popular are the .50- or .54-caliber models. These rifles come in a variety of forms; there are both flintlock and percussion models, and a variety of manufacturers and models. Some are preassembled (off-the-rack), and there are a variety of kits for those who enjoy putting their own together. By far, the percussion style kits are the most popular. Off-the-rack prices range from $175 to $225, with kits running $30 to $50 less.

Muzzle-loaders may hunt with these weapons during the regular November gun season if they wish, but they also have their own separate season, which generally runs for eleven days in early December. Muzzle-loaders are limited to antlered bucks only, unless they possess an unfilled doe permit.

Properly sighted-in and loaded, these guns are perfectly capable of reaching out to one hundred yards with good-to-excellent accuracy. Certain precautions must be taken to keep both the gun's charge and the firing cap dry, and repeat shots if necessary are, of course, rather slow (forty-five seconds with practice). Muzzle-loaders, however, are certainly capable of doing the job.

Handguns

Michigan does not have a separate handgun season; nonetheless, more and more handgunners are in the field each year attempting to fill their tag. They must hunt during the regular gun season, and they must take only legally antlered animals, unless they possess an antlerless permit.

Handgunners, like archers, face a severe limitation upon their effective shooting range. Like archery, handgunning requires a great deal of practice in order to realize the full potential of the weapon. While hundred-yard shots are possible in the hands of some experts, most handgunners limit their shots to about the fifty-yard mark. State law requires at least a .35-caliber gun, although most handgunners prefer a .41- or .44-caliber, with the .44 being the most popular.

Double-action weapons rather than single-action are the most popular, and while a few of the smaller manufacturers do turn out automatics chambered large enough for use on deer, few Michigan sportsmen are using them. Barrel length for hunting handguns is usually in the neighborhood of six to ten inches, since these offer the greatest accuracy. Roughly half of our handgunners today are using the relatively new long-eye relief scopes.

With sufficient forethought—matching your arrow weight with your particular draw length, your bullet design with your chosen caliber—as well as mastery of your weapon, few animals should suffer the fate of my friend's bear.

10

Scouting

Pick up any book on deer hunting or practically any article on the subject and you will find the word "scout" or "scouting." Everyone talks about it. Everyone says it's important, but just what is scouting and how is it accomplished? More to the point, why is it important and what can it do for you, the typical Michigan deer hunter?

Scouting is an activity carried out for the purpose of gathering information. Those deer hunters who are consistently successful in bagging a buck do not do it by luck alone. They continually search for information. As a result, long before the first rays of light on opening day, these hunters know where the deer are in their area. They know whether the population is up or down; they know what the deer are feeding on; they know whether the rut has peaked or waned; they know a thousand other bits and pieces of information pertinent to deer and deer hunting.

When these hunters pick a stand, decide upon the course of a still hunt, or plan a drive, they do so based on that information.

One thing is certain. On the average, successful deer hunters know their quarry better than unsuccessful hunters.

This knowledge is not inherent. Good deer hunters are not born, they're developed, and scouting is an integral part of that development. In straightforward terms, scouting will make you a better deer hunter. How much better will depend upon how well you learn the basics of scouting and then how thoroughly you apply them. It takes practice and it is not easy.

In the fall of 1977, I was running a trap line for fox in the area where I planned to deer hunt. Thus, I was in the field every day for several weeks prior to the general gun season. During this time there was one particular buck I watched. Before the deer season arrived I spent so much time studying this one animal that it became an easy matter for me to find him virtually any time I desired. When opening day finally arrived and I chose my stand, I knew that by eight o'clock I would have that animal.

Surprise! Though hunting pressure did not seem heavy, it was heavy enough that even before daylight the buck was alerted and changed his normal routine. I hunted the entire day and never saw a hair. I knew where he'd been bedding for several weeks, since I saw him enter the thicket on numerous occasions. I had always stayed away from it for fear of spooking him, but the next morning I got into the center of it long before daylight. His seven-point rack now hangs in my front room.

One year later I watched an eight-point buck raid an abandoned apple orchard for several mornings prior to the opener. I knew the woodlot across the way had a great many rubs on its saplings, made by that same animal. On opening morning, I strategically placed myself between the orchard and the woodlot. That rack too now rests in my home.

These successful hunts were the direct result of knowing the deer and their routines. Lest I give the wrong impression that scouting entails countless hours of time over a period of many weeks, let me explain. In 1977 and during several other years, I scouted while running a trap line. Last year, I scouted while bird hunting or simply enjoying the fall colors. I love to hunt deer; it's *one* of my favorite pastimes. I have other pursuits too, and I can accomplish more than one thing at a time.

If I had to answer how much time scouting requires, I

guess I'd say it requires whatever you have available, and the more the better. I scout almost year-round, but then that's me. A great deal can be accomplished in far less time, and if done properly, all the time you spend afield will be fruitful.

OK. Scouting is important; it's useful, you say, but how's it done? Just exactly what is it? Let me start by saying that scouting is not the act of deer hunting without a weapon; scouting done in this manner would both needlessly spook the deer and waste precious time. The key thing to remember is that scouting is intended to give you information. Whether or not you see deer in the process is immaterial. Scouting is thus best described as the act of moving through known deer territory and being observant of the signs before you. Scouting is the process that allows a hunter to mentally assemble all the essentials of his hunting environment. The goal of your scouting efforts is an awareness of that environment. (See Chapter 1 to refresh your memory about how the deer are relating to their environment during the fall months.)

Tracks, droppings, rubs, scrapes, the mast crop, and other signs give the observant hunter valuable information. *Nothing about the area scouted should be overlooked.* Crop fields—where they are and what's planted in them—are important. The newspapers, magazines, and other reports may say the deer herd is up. But is it up in your area—in the specific location where you hunt? Are there new roads in your area? Logging operations? Do you know the area well enough to know what's over the next hill before you get there? These are all pieces of the deer hunting puzzle that fall into place by scouting.

A decade ago, a couple things happened to me that I think will highlight the importance of what I've said. On the afternoon of opening day I chose to sit along the side of a hill overlooking a swale where I knew deer frequently bedded down. Directly behind me was a small pine, and beyond that was a fifty-yard strip of heavy brush. This cover then opened into a huge area of open crop fields divided only by occasional fencerows. It was midafternoon and I thought any deer seeking its daytime refuge in the swale would begin wandering out to feed in the crop field toward evening.

Rub with Snowy Background.   This was one of many rubs located while scouting for deer and hunting woodcock several years ago in a dense alder thicket. Due to all the rubs and the several scrapes found in a line leading to the thicket, the author correctly identified this as the bedding area for a nice buck. A beautiful nine-point buck was the end result.

Rub on Pine. While the vast majority of rubs (well over 80 percent) are found on hardwoods or bushes, rubs may be found on conifers as well. In fact, on rare occasion, bucks have been found to rub fenceposts and, in one well-documented instance, a telephone pole!

About 5 o'clock I heard gun shots in the open fields behind me and seconds later the sounds of running deer coming from behind me. I jumped from my seat to the side of the pine, thinking the deer would come straight through the thicket and make for the swale now on my right. I crouched, looking and waiting; the noise stopped and I thought momentarily that the deer were standing and would soon step out into the open.

What I'd forgotten in my haste was the deer run that traversed the cover made a sharp curve to my right. The deer were now standing just thirty yards to my left! Because I had moved I was exposed and, even worse, I was in no position to shoot. Turning ever so slowly, I saw two deer, both does, standing in the open and staring at me. In the dense cover behind them I could make out a third animal but could not tell whether or not it had antlers. All three stood statuelike for what seemed an eternity, then turned and walked straight away.

Now it's certainly possible that the third animal was also a doe, but I'll never know. Taking a stand within thirty yards of a deer run and forgetting which direction it ran is to me inexcusable, and it may well have cost me a buck. If I was more diligent in my scouting, I'd have walked that run before the season, and I probably would not have committed my costly error. (It was this incident that caused me to carry my scouting to the next logical step—mapping—which I'll explain later in this chapter.)

Another incident occurred only one week later. Beginning at dawn I sat watching a thicket that had some old apple trees growing in it. About 10 o'clock, I started to still hunt my way through it. Halfway, three deer moved in front of me. They moved slowly, unalarmed, and I plainly saw that two were does. The third animal avoided the open, and I could not identify its sex.

Watching their progress, I figured they'd follow the fencerow in front of them into an adjacent woodlot; I knew this was a normal avenue of travel for deer in that area. Moving quickly behind cover, I began running with the hope that I would arrive at the woodlot ahead of them. Sure enough, I won the race, and about ten minutes later they moved through. As it turned out, all three were does. But the satisfaction I derived from that ambush was very rewarding. To me, the greatest thrill in hunting is to correctly predict or anticipate the animal's behavior. If you do this consistently, you'll have all the game you ever dreamed of.

In the past couple years, much has been written about both spring and summer scouting. While such activity can be very beneficial, the hunter must relate the information thus gained to the animals in the fall. I've read, for example, that early spring scouting will show you precisely where the deer were and what they were doing the fall before. If you value your hunting time, treat such statements with disdain as they're far too general to be of value. Based upon such analysis, I could show you a hundred places where spring scouting would seem to indicate phenomenal fall usage and where, however, very little occurs. This will be increasingly true as you move north through our state.

Both spring and summer scouting will be more beneficial in some areas of the state than in others. Those areas where early scouting will be of most value are in and immediately around farming regions (regardless of where they occur). Early scouting will also be useful in areas that have clearly delineated habitat ranges, i.e., good habitat surrounded by poor habitat. Areas where early scouting will be of minimal value, and could actually lead you to many false assumptions, are those places where the habitat is uniform over very large regions and deer densities tend to be low or only moderate, i.e., much of our northern Lower Peninsula, as well as much of the U.P.

The reasons for this are simple. Our agricultural areas tend to have fairly high deer densities, and the deer are generally spread uniformly across them—at least over limited regions. These animals frequently have all they require for survival in a small area; they neither move far over time nor do they have major seasonal shifts. Where deer are seen in April or July, they will be seen in October and November. In the U.P., on the other hand, deer are far more likely to undertake major seasonal shifts. They're not spread uni-

Scrape and Oak Tree. This is a typical scrape found in a farmland environment. It was located on the edge of a stubble field along a fencerow that had a limb from a nearby oak tree hanging over it. The buck had not only pawed the ground, but had worked the limb over with his head as well. The process of scouting will disclose many facets of the whitetail's life to you. Be thorough, be patient, and take notes, or create a "hunting habitat map" as described in the text.

TABLE 10.1   Foods most heavily consumed by deer in Michigan's
agricultural areas

clover	goldenrod	winterberry	arrowhead
alfalfa	lespedeza	crabapple	black tupelo
soybean	trefoils	Canada plum	eastern wahoo
corn	potato	black cherry	witch hazel
winter wheat	strawberry	choke cherry	hawthorns
ryegrass	sugar beets	silky dogwood	yellow birch
barley	sunflowers	red osier dogwood	ground juniper
Canada bluegrass	ferns	wild rose	red maple
grasses	bittersweet	wild grape	oaks
cinquefoil	raspberry	mushrooms	poplars
sedges	hackberry	smooth sumac	cottonwood
dandelion	nannyberry	poison ivy	hickory
vetch	red mulberry	viburnums	tulip
sassafras	Russian mulberry	apples	willows
mustard	Downy serviceberry	acorns	paper birch
hawkweed	blueberry	beechnuts	walnut
fleabane	elderberry	lilies	
aster	Juneberry	marsh marigold	

formly across even small areas. Good habitat in spring or summer may well be devoid of value in the fall.

For the hunter with limited available time for fall scouting, spring and summer sorties afield can be beneficial, provided you keep the above differences in mind. Scouting will be most effective when it is closely timed to the time you plan to hunt. Regardless of when or where in Michigan you'll be hunting, I'd recommend no serious scouting be done from January through March and from late May to early July. If you're interested in deer-watching observation, these times can be of value, of course, but don't draw useful hunting insights from your observations. They're simply not there.

If you've done your preseason scouting, you'll be ready to hunt when opening day finally rolls around. Most Michigan hunters are just beginning their scouting activities. The average deer hunter is probably ready to do some really serious deer hunting about the time the season ends. By then he knows the area and he knows the patterns the deer are following; in short, he knows all the things that you knew on opening day—the day you started hunting.

For the successful hunter, scouting never ends. It becomes

TABLE 10.2   Foods most heavily consumed by deer in Michigan's forested regions

pokeweed	mints	winterberry	eastern hemlock
aster	wild grape	wintergreen	oaks
jewelweed	red mulberry	snakeweed	blackgum
poison ivy	pokeberry	goldenrod	white pine
Downy serviceberry	blackeyed susan	bittersweet	jack pine
roundleaf "	marsh marigold	leatherleaf	yellow birch
Juneberry	elderberry	horsetail	white birch
trailing arbutus	ribbonleaf	hepatica	sugar maple
sedges	pondweed	honeysuckle	white cedar
greenbrier	arrowhead	acorns	red cedar
dandelion	water milfoil	beechnuts	poplar
sweet pea	lilies	bush honeysuckle	black spruce
wild strawberry	marsh cinquefoil	willow	basswood
tick trefoil	grasses	silky dogwood	beech
ferns	choke cherry	red osier dogwood	elms
Labrador tea	pin cherry	witch hazel	green ash
blackberry	snowberry	beaked hazel	white ash
spreading dogbane	yellow bellwort	striped maple	black ash
wild rose	mushrooms	mountain maple	Amer. Mtn. ash
wild back currant	staghorn sumac	red maple	fir
arboreal lichens	wild cranberry	American hornbeam	tamarack

Since whitetails are known to consume more than six hundred different food stuffs, these lists are not meant to be all-inclusive nor are they mutually exclusive. The deer throughout our forested regions are unwillingly forced into a feeding pattern of browsing for up to four months a year. Such a diet, especially in areas where both the amount and the kind of browse is limited (low-quality habitat), is generally representative of a negative-balance diet—more energy out than in. Therefore, these regions are not capable of carrying large numbers of animals per square mile.

Our farmland deer are in much better shape, having a far broader choice of energy-rich foods available for a longer period of time each year. Even when these animals are forced into more of a browsing type of subsistence (usually for no more than a month or two), they normally only need to augment their continued grazing and not supplant it entirely.

Another important thing to realize about food lists is they cannot be arranged into a strict order of preference. To a certain extent, as is done here, it is possible to say that some foods are more preferred and of higher quality than others; e.g., white cedar is preferable to spruce, and clover is preferable to red maple. But in large measure what deer consume is also a learned behavior or the result of acquired taste. (Potatoes are one such example. Years ago, little, if any, damage was incurred to the U.P. potato crop. Gradually, as people began feeding potatoes to the local deer herds, damage to the fields increased. Crop damage to potato fields in the central U.P. today is commonplace, as is the feeding of potatoes to deer, especially in the winter months.)

Your scouting goals, as well as your decisions, are many. You should attempt to find an area (preferably several) where you've the best habitat available; a large part of that determination must be based on the availability of foods. Look for plenty of variety as well as ample openings and a good age mix. Once such sites are found, you are then well on your way to a productive season.

a mindset, a way of functioning. No matter what you're doing in the field, the process of scouting—an appropriate aware-ness—should always be ongoing. If practiced and developed, this awareness becomes natural; your scouting proceeds automatically whenever you enter the woods. It becomes effortless, something done almost unconsciously, and all the while it makes you a better deer hunter. (See *Table 10.1* for a list of the foods most heavily utilized by deer in Michigan's agricultural areas, and *Table 10.2* for a similar list common to our forested regions.)

Habitat Maps: Taking the Art of Scouting One Step Further

If there is one thing I've learned about deer hunting over the years, it's this: successful deer hunters are those who minimize errors. There are, of course, many causes for deer hunting errors, but the most insidious are those resulting from the hunter's lack of knowledge about his environment. The deer know their environment thoroughly. Every action they make is based on that knowledge. For example, once danger is detected they instinctively know the escape routes. In normal travel they know the best way to get from here to there, and so on. How, then, can the hunter compete? How can he minimize his errors? The answer is to map out his deer hunting area *in detail*.

Years ago I began searching for better ways to memorize—to learn—the areas in which I hunt. I'm a great believer in the benefits of preseason scouting, and was devoting all my spare time to this activity; yet there remained voids in my know-ledge. Since increasing my time afield was out of the question, I had to come up with another way to help fill in the holes.

Fiddling around home one evening, I decided to see just how well I knew my hunting area. I started with generali-ties. What crops are growing in which fields? Easy! How large are those fields and how do they lie in relation to all the others? Easy! Where are the fencerows and where are the passages? Easy! Where does the creek run? Easy! Where are the hardwoods that produce mast? Easy!

As I started to develop greater detail, to my surprise I began having problems. In a vague, foggy sort of way I knew where the deer runs were, but when I tried drawing them onto the map I couldn't. Does the run cross the creek there, or is it farther down? I was amazed at just how imprecise my knowledge was when I forced myself to put it onto paper! As a matter of fact, I soon realized that my knowledge—of an area I'd have sworn I knew very well—was so incomplete that I could not make an accurate hunting habitat map.

Over the next two weeks I revised my map. I'd sketch in a run, for example, and then go out and walk it. I found I was soon concentrating on particulars overlooked before. Everything—crossing points, thickets, openings—seemed more obvious than it had before. Spatial relationships between various features became much more obvious to me. As a result of this simple exercise, I was truly learning the area. By spending three to five hours a day, within two weeks I knew the particulars much more thoroughly than I'd ever known them before.

Since I've started making maps, my deer hunting has improved and my time afield is much more enjoyable. I feel more comfortable and confident in my ability to predict the deer's actions and movements. Now when I begin my scouting activities each year, I start a new map from scratch. I first draw in the gross particulars: fields, woodlots, swamps, creeks, lakes, and so forth. I then begin on the more detailed aspects, and the specifics for that particular year: which crops are in which fields, the location of the mast, if any exists, the course of the runways, and so on. All the while I cross-check with actual field inspections to be sure of accuracy.

Since making such maps, I've been tinkering with various entries to the map. Seven or eight years ago, I began adding buck sign, along with the date it was found. Since I scout just about every day from the first of October on, I soon have a very detailed account of all buck activity in the area. Rubs and scrapes are not randomly made, and soon patterns begin to emerge on my maps. Unless I kept track of them in a visual manner, I'd probably never notice or fully comprehend these patterns.

The first year I recorded buck sign, for example, I found most of the activity began on the night of October 16. Before there was nothing, but on this night the bucks went berserk! On the seventeenth there was buck sign, in the form of rubs, everywhere I went. Over the next four or five days the sign began to create a definite pattern, and although there was some sign everywhere, it was mostly concentrated in two core areas. One of these areas was a small section of perhaps thirty acres, inside a dense woodlot roughly a quarter-mile square. The other was an area roughly five hundred yards long by fifty yards wide, inside an alder thicket a half-mile long by one thousand feet wide.

On November 4, I found my first scrape of the year; it was inside the core area in the alders. By the seventh I found three more active scrapes, all within a straight line drawn from this thicket. Opening morning, I took a stand on the edge of this area as I'd mapped it. I got to my stand well before daylight, since I figured the buck was using this spot as his bedding area. I did not want him to arrive home before I got there. About eight o'clock, following a run that cut just south of the line of scrapes, came my buck. I'm convinced that if I had just been scouting, without a written record of my findings prior to the season, I'd have never diagnosed this situation so easily. When you attempt to memorize everything there is simply a lot of detail that is going to be lost. When you record it on a map, it is right there in front of you, be it one week or one month later, and patterns, sometimes very subtle, begin to emerge.

Since maps of any area as detailed as what you'll want and need do not exist, and since the entire purpose of the map is its use as a self-teaching tool, I believe it essential to make a new map each year. With as much care as possible, I sketch every detail of the entire area, no matter how small or seemingly insignificant.

My experiences of three or four years ago were even more illustrative. As usual I'd begun my serious scouting around

October 1. From then until October 28 I found nothing in terms of buck sign, and was beginning to become concerned. I saw a lot of deer sign—some of the tracks were huge—but there was no buck sign. On October 28, I found several rubs. The next day I found several more. In the days following I found a great many more, and a definite pattern began to emerge on my map. Three areas were being worked thoroughly by the bucks.

I almost decided on November 11 where I would hunt and wrote in my journal for that day "have made up my mind to hunt the cedars west of the creek, north of the corn, unless something new shows up before the fifteenth." (I keep a written journal, recording weather, hours spent afield, unusual events, sightings, and so forth, in addition to my maps.) Then on November 13 something else showed up. An area west of the other three began showing buck sign for the first time, while the other areas languished. A scrape appeared in this new area while scrapes in the other areas went untouched. Rubs appeared in the new area while no new ones appeared in the others. I doubt that someone not out each day and not recording his findings—along with corresponding dates— daily on a map would have noticed the meaning of this change, but looking at my map it really hit me: the deer had changed locations. Obviously, the does had shifted their feeding areas, and because of the rut the bucks had followed.

I decided on a new stand within this latest area of activity, and on opening morning I collected the biggest buck I've taken in Michigan to date. A big eight-point, with a hog-dressed weight of 202 pounds, came gliding out of the fog between two pockets of cover within thirty yards of my stand.

This all leads to what I believe is the most powerful use of mapmaking: trophy hunting. Based on my experiences with such maps over the last ten years, I'm convinced that any hunter will benefit from them; the map's advantages are absolutely essential for the hunter seeking better than average bucks. Any hunter can, "just by chance," bag a super whitetail on occasion, but the hunter who wants to eliminate, or at least minimize, his reliance on Lady Luck needs the additional insight provided by such a hunting habitat map. No one can memorize so much information. Putting the information on a map reduced errors and oversights.

You can make a habitat hunting map as complex as you desire. Tailor it to your needs and your time constraints. The hunter who has limited preseason time may want to make such a map only to help himself learn his hunting area more thoroughly. To do this, start with a large sheet of blank white paper. I prefer a sheet nine square feet for each square mile I draw. A sheet this large allows the recording of all particulars, no matter how detailed you get, and keeps the map from becoming too cluttered.

Using a lead pencil, draw your hunting area in as much detail as you can from memory. I'm sure you'll be amazed at how easily you'll become confused and unsure. Is that thicket north or south of the fencerow? Are those poplars thick right up to the alders, or is there a slight opening between them? Regardless of how confident you feel, once you've finished that stage of the operation, check your map by actual field observations. Again, I think you'll be amazed at how you pick up details that before would have gone unnoticed.

For the hunter possessing more time, the hunting habitat map is a more powerful tool. Begin your operation the same way I've described above. Then, once the physical layout is complete, record your scouting data as it's found. In order to conserve space and aid in reading, I use the following symbols for recording all sign:

O = rub   ❑ = hunting stand
O̲ = breeding rub   _●_ = major runway
X = scrape   - - - = minor runway

For clarity, the accompanying map is an extremely simplified version of the actual map used in 1979. As with this map, I do all my maps in color for easier reading. Evergreens are green, hardwoods black, thickets, swales and cattail marshes blue, and all buck sign is red.

Obviously, recording data on the map is not itself an end. Once the data are there you must then be able to interpret their meaning; otherwise, the exercise is for naught (unless

Illustration 10.1 **Habitat map**

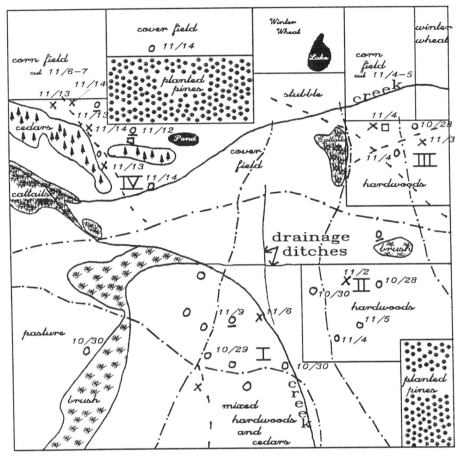

This map conveys the sense of the author's hunting habitat maps, but for our purposes here it is much simplified. The author's actual maps are nine square feet for each square mile of area. Such a large format allows the incorporation of all manner of detail without cluttering the map. Experiment with your own map designs to satisfy your particular needs. One thing you might want to do, for example, is to code for different size rubs and scrapes. The author has never attempted this, preferring to do this in his journal, but certainly this could easily be incorporated into the map's information.

you are simply making a map to better learn the area). This interpretive process is best explained by analyzing the accompanying map (see *Illustration 10.1*).

The bucks began creating sign on October 28. As you can see from the map, all the sign they created initially fell into basically three areas labeled I, II, III. Sometime between

October 31 and November 11, I'd almost made up my mind to hunt area III. I based this decision not on the number of rubs and scrapes I found in the area, but rather on the size of the sign, the forcefulness with which it was made, and the dates—far more important parameters, as I'll explain. In 1978, I'd taken a large eight-point buck from area I, and in the fall of '79 the rubs I found there were all made on small saplings and trees. This indicated to me that a buck had taken over the area vacated by the eight-point I'd taken the fall before, but he was a young, small buck—not the animal I had in mind.

Area II showed better rubs but they again indicated a smaller buck, as did the scrapes within that area. As a general rule, the larger the buck the larger and more vicious his rubs; he'll generally make them a little earlier than his smaller brethren. Also, bigger bucks will normally make bigger scrapes, which will also be made somewhat earlier.

From the map, you can see both the first rubs and the first scrapes were in area III. Also, both rubs and scrapes were larger. Some of the poplars rubbed in this area were six to eight inches in diameter. A buck that tackles trees that large is worth getting excited about! Because of all this data, I planned to hunt where the "❑" is in area III. Notice that there are two "❑" figures within the area. The precise location of my hunt would have been dependent on the wind and overall weather conditions on any given day. Since the deer were feeding in the winter wheat and stubble fields north of area III, I had an excellent idea which way my buck would be traveling both in the mornings and in the evenings. Also, again depending upon the weather, either of the two selected sites would have been perfect should the buck have wandered within the cover during midday, as deer often do. Because you can never be sure of the weather, you should always select at least two or more sites for stands before opening day. This eliminates the need for hasty last-minute decisions.

Critical to any strategy, but often ignored in the literature, is the issue of stand selection. This one aspect of your hunt can very well determine a successful season and therefore must be chosen with great care. (See Chapter 12 for a detailed discussion.) If you know the direction the deer will likely enter the area (as was the case here), the ideal stand is then going to be downwind from that direction. It should also be located so that if deer approach from a slightly different angle or come in early, before daylight, you'll still have a good chance of seeing them later on.

To properly locate a stand there are several things you must keep in mind. As a general rule, bucks who are undisturbed, especially larger bucks, will tend to follow a minor or seldom used runway to get into cover. They'll do this far more frequently than use a major runway. Once in cover they'll frequently amble off the run entirely and slowly pick their way through cover to their beds.

Furthermore, at some point during midday, they'll get up off their beds to stretch and feed, *within cover*, for an hour or two. They will then lie back down until just before dusk. When they leave cover in the evening, they are less likely than does to follow a runway at all. They'll begin their movements to the edge of cover very slowly, picking their way and feeding cautiously.

In heavily hunted areas, bucks will more often travel runways even in midday; when pushed from their daytime sanctuaries, runways offer the quickest mode of escape.

In addition to wind direction you must also consider other aspects of weather. If the wind is blowing heavily, deer are less likely to move because their senses are not as reliable. You'll therefore want to be closer to really dense cover where the deer are most likely to bed. On extremely cold but clear days, you should look for them to move into bedding areas with good southern exposures where they can pick up all the warmth possible from the sun. (See Chapter 11 for a detailed discussion.)

On snowy or rainy days you should again look for deer in the most protected cover. However, to stay warm they will want to wander more than usual unless it's really blustery as well. All of these factors must be weighed carefully before a stand site is settled upon. Once the decision of where to stand is made, the hunter should stay put, especially in lightly hunted areas.

Note the area of the map marked IV. The cornfield north and west of this area had been cut on November 6–7 and the deer had shifted their location in order to feed on the spilled grain. Throughout most of the year a big, dominant buck is not going to forsake his normal bailiwick—core range—just because other deer make such a change; during the rut they often will, and in this case he did. This is an example of the increased vulnerability of bucks during the rut. Note that all sign making by bucks ceased outside of area IV after November 9, and yet sign making within this area was intense. This indicated that all the bucks were within this area, including the real dominant buck.

Another rule of thumb is that big bucks like thick cover to bed. This is their edge—their added protection—and this buck was no exception to the rule. A line of scrapes appeared over the nights of November 12, 13 and 14 that led directly to the densest stand of cedars in the entire area. My stand, again indicated by the "❏" on the right in area IV, was positioned so that I'd intercept him at the edge of his sanctuary. Because of my map—its data, the accompanying dates, and my interpretation of this information—that buck's head now adorns my front room wall.

I fully believe that a hunter who puts the time into creating a hunting habitat map, as I've described, will find it of immeasurable assistance. It is not a replacement for scouting, hard work, knowledge of deer habits, and good deer hunting skills, but it is a very powerful adjunct to all the other assets a hunter brings to his sport. It is one more piece to solving the deer hunting puzzle.

11

The Effects
of Weather

Snow, rain, strong winds, extreme cold or heat, clear skies and sunshine, as well as other dominant weather patterns, have profound influence upon the activity levels and behavior of deer. In order to be successful afield we must alter our hunting behavior with these weather patterns. Here are some of the basics you should know.

In our Upper Peninsula, late November often brings some of the meanest storms of the entire year. Just yesterday, wind gusts of up to seventy miles per hour forced the closure of the "Big Mac" bridge for twelve hours and had driven every deer in the region into hiding. Such conditions rarely bode well for hunting (especially for the line hunter), but today was different—much, much different.

As I drove down the two-track long before dawn, with less than a half inch of snow on the ground, yesterday's winds had died entirely. Visibility was bad, as my headlights reflected more light from the steadily falling snow back into my eyes than onto the trail ahead.

Donning my heavy parka and packs, I slung my day pack over my shoulder and headed toward the cedars a mile distant. Despite the late-breaking daylight, I now had no problem seeing; even in the cedars, the freshly fallen snow had greatly increased visibility. Several days earlier, I had located three cedars growing in a tight clump. Just enough room existed within them to provide a natural blind; it was there that I took up my vigil.

As time passed, I adjusted to the stillness and, with the exception of the softly padding the snow, it was a silent world: no woodpecker's tap-tap-tap greeted this morn, no raucous crows swooped and screamed, no wind stirred the tree tops. I waited silently.

Shortly after eight, I watched a deer drift through distant trees, too concealed for me to identify its sex, and too protected to get off a shot. Time passed, the snow fell, and the silence continued unbroken. By nine o'clock I noticed that the snow completely covered the gun cradled in my arms. Involuntarily I shivered. The snow and the silence seemed, somehow, to make it colder than it really was.

At 9:30, and without prior warning, I heard brush cracking and the sound of a large animal running among the twisted windfalls behind me. The big buck broke into the cedars just as I turned in that direction. He ran several yards and stopped, head held high and very alert. As the cross hairs settled on his chest I squeezed off my shot. He bolted through the trees, I shot twice more and, as suddenly as it had been broken, the silence returned.

Not wanting to track him immediately, I was nonetheless fearful that, with the fast-falling snow, I must or I'd lose him. Reloading, I quickly headed to where he was when I first shot. There, spilled across six inches of newly fallen snow, were several spots of bright arterial blood. Knowing then I'd gotten my hoped-for lung shot, I took off on his track at once. He'd turned after only thirty yards, and leaving the cedars he had headed into an open field beyond. Fifty yards past where he was shot I almost stepped on him, as the falling snow had begun to cover him up. The .30/06 had done its job cleanly; he was dead.

Hanging my orange parka in a nearby tree, I headed toward the truck to gather my camera equipment. On the way,

Doe in Snow. Cold, snowy, moonless nights are followed by heightened daytime activity, especially when the sun comes through. Look to small openings within cover or along the edges where food is prevalent.

I cut six sets of deer tracks and, in the excitement, didn't think much of it at the time. Arriving at the truck, I poured a cup of coffee from my thermos and fiddled with my gear. Warmed by the coffee, I headed back. At once, it dawned on me that my own tracks were now obliterated, and yet I continued to cut fresh deer tracks.

A quirk? Unusual that so many deer happened to be moving on such a day? I can only point to other days, under similar conditions, during which I've either scored a deer, or at least witnessed their increased activity, to counter such a guess. I believe, based on numerous incidents spanning at least twenty years, one of the very best times to be afield for deer is during or immediately following a major snowstorm.

For some reason, whitetails react to the first few big snowfalls of the year as children on a playground. It seems to exhilarate them; they romp, they run, and they cover a lot of territory in a short span of time. As a hunter, I want to be in the woods and fields when they do this. Under these circumstances, I have all the odds stacked heavily in my favor. Since it's the deer who are increasing their activity, in random ways, all I need do is pick an area that routinely supports a lot of deer traffic, and wait. If I'm patient, they then will come to me.

I first noticed this phenomenon many years ago while hunting a thicket adjacent to some agricultural lands in

Does in Snow Covered Pines. These animals were caught in the early morning working along the edge of thermal cover following a bitterly cold night—such movement is typical.

southern Michigan. It had been snowing since late the night before; by dawn we had well over an inch and it was still coming down heavily. By late morning, with five inches on the ground, the only deer I saw, a buck, broke through the brush in front of me. While dragging him the half mile to my jeep a few minutes later, I was amazed at the number of tracks I kept cutting.

Up to that point in the season I had hunted for five or six days and had only seen a handful of deer. Yet coming out that morning, despite the falling snow, I cut fresh tracks everywhere. The reason I stress this point is because many hunters fervently believe that deer lie low during major snowfalls and hence they (the hunters) must also. Perhaps later in the year that's true, but *early winter* snowstorms have just the opposite effect. For the hunter who's nestled next to a campfire, it's a wasted day!

Rain is another major weather pattern that dramatically affects deer behavior. Precisely what that will be is going to depend on several other related factors, including concurrent winds, duration of rainfall, intensity of rainfall, fog, whether it's an isolated rain or a rain in a continuing pattern of wet weather, and the associated temperature. (There may well be other factors, but these are the major ones.)

There's probably nothing that can completely ruin a hunter's day more thoroughly than rain with very high winds. We're not talking about light breezes here, or occasional gusts, but rather unrelenting, tree-bending gales. Such weather makes deer very fearful. Their senses are totally befuddled under these conditions. They can no longer rely on their noses, their ears, or their eyes; all orientation to their world has been quite effectively blocked.

From every direction there is noise and movement. If there's a sudden influx of alarming odor, it's there one instant and gone the next. For the deer it arrives much too suddenly to identify, let alone to pinpoint. Without meaningful exception, this forces deer to lie low. Storms of such magnitude never last long, and the deer will simply ride them out locked up in very dense cover. For the hunter who works alone, such days are better spent doing other things.

Given the right circumstances (proper cover and fellow hunters), however, all is not lost on such days. Years ago, quite by accident, I learned a valuable lesson about hunting in such weather. If you hunt as a member of a party, you may someday be able to use this to your advantage.

It was the kind of day that nobody in his right mind would have been out in, except for one thing: three of us had left home about three in the morning, had driven some two hundred miles, and weren't inclined to just sit around. So, despite the weather, we hunted. The area was cultivated, with scattered pockets of dense lowlands intermixed. Our initial idea was to take up stands in those smaller pockets, hoping for hunters in the surrounding larger thickets to push deer our way.

Shortly after daybreak, when it became obvious we were alone, we changed our minds, deciding that our only realistic hope of scoring was to execute some drives. Despite (actually because of) the driving rain and the wind gusts that threatened to blow us away, we did push deer. In fact, in our third swale that morning one of my companions nailed a fine eight-point as the buck attempted to escape along with a couple does. We saw plenty of other deer that day as well, including other bucks, but somehow never managed to hook up. Nonetheless, it was one of those days that I have never thought worthy, but by driving the deer from small, well-defined cover, I was proved wrong.

In a rainfall that's been ongoing for some time, the deer eventually get to a point where they'll ignore it and get on with their routines. Food must be obtained, and if a dark, threatening, or rainy night precedes a daylong rain, I want to be in the field, rain or not, that evening. In fact, I want to be nestled over a known feeding area by midafternoon. The only exceptions I'd make would be really torrential rainfall, rapidly falling temperatures (in which case I'd be there earlier), and high winds. Even then, small openings in dense protective cover could be a good bet.

For the hunter working alone in rain, still hunting through dense bedding areas during midday periods is a good tactic. The deer under such circumstances are hungry much of the time, and while they may not venture into the open, they will frequently feed for short periods of time within the cover. An excellent approach is actually a combination of still and stand hunting, working thoroughly every area capable of sheltering deer, and remembering that these areas need not be large. In heavily hunted zones, be alert to out-of-the-way plots of cover or any cover that is overlooked by other hunters.

For group hunters, these rainy days are custom-made for driving. Groups large enough to completely cover the area available should block all exits and drive as usual. Small parties, even just two hunters, should post blockers on major runways within the cover being driven. Drive silently and slowly, and the deer will likely try slipping around you rather than exit the area.

A successful approach under such circumstances is for two or three hunting partners to drive smaller pockets of cover by actually alternating their roles. The drive starts, for example, where by prior planning and agreement one of the two hunters begins his drive while the other assumes a stand. This alternation of drivers continues until the drive is completed, or until someone connects. There must be no yelling or talking between the hunters. Everyone knows his functions and responsibilities before the drive begins; he must then carry them out precisely.

The hunter who is moving should do so slowly (but faster than one would if still hunting) and quietly, and he should do so with no regard to wind direction. Research has shown that whitetails seldom forsake their home territories unless hunter densities are extremely high (more than twenty hunters per square mile), otherwise they choose simply to slip around the hunters or to lie low and let them pass by. This is precisely why the above technique works so well.

On occasion you'll have a storm that starts out slowly, with fairly light rains, for example, persists for a day or so, and then intensifies. The hours immediately preceding such changes are an excellent time to be afield. Deer are very alert to an impending change, and will begin feeding heavily just prior to its arrival. The hunter should post up either overlooking feeding areas or on runways leading to heavy cover at such times. Do so regardless of the time of day.

Following such a storm, concentrate your efforts on known feeding grounds, and again do so regardless of the time of day. Deer that have been forced to lie low, even if only for ten or twelve hours, are hungry. They'll feed voraciously as soon as there's a break in the weather, and you should capitalize upon this type of activity. In areas with intense hunting pressure, you should hunt the edges of cover as well as those areas within cover having plenty of browse. In less-pressured zones, look to more open spots. Following prolonged periods of inactivity, deer seem to actually enjoy getting out of thick cover, providing they feel they can do so safely.

Periods of moderate temperatures with slow-to-steady rains are uncomfortable for the hunter but productive nonetheless. Four or five years ago I was again hunting southern Michigan's farm country. It was Thanksgiving Day, about forty-five degrees, and it had been raining steadily since daybreak. Up to that point it had been a very wet, rainy deer season. This served to greatly reduce normal hunting pressures in the area; any deer movement was quite natural, since no one was pushing them. About eleven o'clock a little spike came picking his way through the hardwoods. To me, he looked about as miserable as I felt. We looked at each other for a long, lingering moment; I bid him a good day, and he slowly walked away.

By dawn the next morning the rains slowed, but drizzle persisted. Almost twenty-four hours to the minute after I let the spike go, the buck of my dreams suddenly materialized before me. From a hunter's point of view the story has a sad ending, as my execution left something to be desired, but the point is to see the bucks you seek. An excellent time to do so is in a slow steady rain, especially one that has persisted for several days.

For the hunter who chooses to stand under such conditions, the dark, generally colder nights mean little feeding activity for the deer. Daylight then finds them more active than usual and for longer periods of time as well. Also, the diminished hunter activity assures more predictability. Stands should be selected overlooking known feeding areas and along well-used runways.

For the still hunter, such days of moderate temperatures with slow to steady rains are tailor-made. Though the elements may conspire to make you uncomfortable, they also allow you tremendous freedom. Areas frequently off-limits to the still hunter can now be hunted much more effectively with the combined effect of dripping water to muffle any noise you might make, as well as the lessened likelihood of making noise. In addition, winds are generally more predictable on such days, allowing you to be more certain of where your scent is drifting, and how best to approach cover.

Rainy weather accompanied by nearly freezing temperatures is quite a different matter. Not only is such weather extremely uncomfortable for you, it is miserable for the deer as well. If you hunt such days as a solo hunter, you should get yourself nestled into thick cover and stay put. The deer will feed completely within cover, and in frequent but short periods of time. Two or more hunters working together can again execute simple drives designed to slowly move the deer within the cover.

Fog, of course, is another element often associated with rain. It also provides excellent deer hunting opportunities. Late November, many years ago, I was on a stand in a clump of partridge berry bushes in our Thumb region. It had been wet and dreary for days on end. Late in the season, with temperatures hovering in the forties, I was the only one left hunting this farm.

My stand overlooked a mosaic of broken cover in a sixty-acre parcel, sandwiched between crop fields to the east and a pasture to the west. The slight, intermittent breeze wafted the fog forming over the low-lying cattails in front of me in undulating waves. At times I couldn't see the cedars only twenty yards to my right. Most of the time I couldn't see the cattails fifty yards ahead or the poplars fifty yards to my left. Except for the incessant dripping of the woods, everything was silent. Even the deer (all does) I saw drifted past in a surreal, almost ghostly manner.

At precisely one o'clock, a light gust cleared a path between me and another clump of bushes to the left. There, jutting above the cover, was a wide, heavily beamed rack. Slowly I raised my slug gun and slipped the safety. As the buck's shoulder cleared the thicket, I touched the trigger and claimed my prize. Admiring my trophy moments later, I smiled when I thought of how many times that day I'd consciously reminded myself to continue the hunt despite my numb feet and cold fingers!

Fog lends an air of confidence to deer. Perhaps its accompanying chill also permeates their coats; I don't know, but I do know they move a lot on foggy days. Enveloped in its cloak, they'll brazenly move far out into open feeding areas during midday periods. When fog is widespread, I therefore hunt over feeding areas. Still hunting is highly effective at such times and allows you to work several different areas. When fog is more patchy, I'll actually get right down in it. I especially like to overlook runways weaving their way through lowland, fog-forming areas during these times.

Cold—bone-chilling, teeth-chattering cold—has a way of quickly sapping a deer hunter's enthusiasm, as well as prompting the deer to do their disappearing act. It's as if they said "beam us up, Scotty," and they disappear. But they always materialize again in the thermal cover, and it's here they stay. Several years ago, I was hunting in northern Wisconsin's forested region. For days I had been looking over a goodly number of deer in the uplands while temperatures ranged in the thirties and forties. Overnight, the weather changed. Temperatures plummeted, the mercury disappeared, and along with it the deer.

An inch of new snow preceded the falling temperatures and the next morning, with moderate winds and below-zero temperatures, not a track could be found where I'd seen deer just the evening before. For two days I suffered cold hands and feet, exaggerated by my inability to find deer. In an attempt designed more to keep warm than to locate deer, I headed down off the hillsides. Here, in the hemlocks and the swamps below, were the deer. A maze of tracks and well-trod trails awaited me; tagging a buck became a simple question of biding my time.

In November 1985, my late friend Joe Frankum tied up

with business obligations, missed the first week of the season. When he finally arrived in the U.P., the temperatures hovered in the low teens and below. For the eight hunters in his camp that week, it was an ominous beginning; with six bucks on the meat pole by week's end, their spirits, if not the temperatures, had warmed considerably! They had beaten

Trail in Snow. Trails and runways with activity stand out in the snow. This trail has seen heavy use since the recent snow.

the odds, and beaten them soundly, by heading to thick cover. Lowlands and sheltered areas out of the winds are your ticket to success in cold weather. Cedars, hemlocks and immature, densely planted pines are where you'll find the deer under these circumstances.

In areas where dense cover does not exist, look to thickets of any kind and particularly those in low-lying areas. The deer under these conditions are always going to head for insulating cover. Cattails, tag alder thickets, even tangles of broom grass are often enough to cut the wind and hence appreciably raise the ambient temperatures. The critical question is: "Where, given this particular environment, can I find cover giving the most protection from the wind and cold?" Answer that, and you will have successfully located the deer every time.

Your best hunting strategy under such conditions is to take a stand and wait out the deer. Most feeding is going to take place during the warmer daylight hours. By using such knowledge, a friend of mine finally tagged an old buck that had previously been giving us the slip for a couple years.

We knew this old boy was holing up routinely in a particular thicket, yet despite Jim's persistence after being on stand every morning long before daylight, the buck beat him to cover every day for more than a week. Finally the weather turned bitterly cold with a stinging northerly wind. The next morning Jim slipped into a blind south of the thicket and he tagged the buck sneaking home late.

I'm certain the deer was feeding later than normal that morning as a direct result of the lower temperatures. Deer under such conditions won't normally begin feeding until later, and therefore can often be caught later than usual in the open. In heavily hunted regions, this feeding will occur within the cover itself. In more remote, less-pressured sections, look to openings near the cover, and to areas protected from the winds.

The same approach is required to succeed under unusually hot, arid conditions. You should look for cover offering plenty of shade, and to areas that are low, especially those adjacent to water. Early morning periods are the best time to waylay deer under these conditions. You should be posted early overlooking feeding areas, or on runways leading from feeding areas to cover. Water sources during midday periods and again just prior to dark are also good bets.

The effects of clear skies and bright sunlight are dependent on the weather of adjacent days. Days with clear skies that either precede or follow foul weather are particularly productive, as the deer attempt to satiate their hunger. On clear-breaking mornings, which follow a day or more of inclement weather, position yourself, whether standing or still hunting, to overlook known feeding areas; hunt these until later in the day—much later than you normally would. In heavily pressured areas, hunt bedding sites with southerly exposures and be alert to heightened daytime feeding in these spots.

Under such circumstances, the deer try to make up for lost time, and they'll feed much longer than normal. This is especially true when rainy-then-clear weather coincides with the end of the rutting period. Big bucks—those most heavily taxed by the rigors of breeding—will often feed twice as long, or longer than normal at such times, and they will very often do so even during daylight periods. It is for this reason we find so many of the very best bucks taken each season (especially in our Upper Peninsula) during the last few days each year.

Orchards, mast-bearing hardwoods, and crop fields in less-pressured areas will often have feeding activity by bucks even during midday. In more heavily hunted regions, feeding binges are much more likely to occur within cover, but make no mistake about it: those bucks are feeding somewhere even during daylight hours, and it's your job to discover where.

Sunlight and mild temperatures always affect deer, and generally it makes them more accessible. Many years ago I had the opportunity to watch a big buck that lived near my home. For weeks prior to the season I saw him here and there, as the summer's bounty fattened his body and adorned his headgear. As fall progressed, he gradually became more and more reclusive, and his living space dwindled. He finally took up residence in a dense tangle bordered by planted pines on the east, cornfields on the north and west, and a cover field and thickset fencerow on the south.

As so often occurs, deer season brought us the fall's worst

weather; even when it didn't rain, it was sullen and overcast for days at a time. Each morning I patiently waited and watched my buck's thicket, with every hope that I'd catch him sneaking in late or exiting early. I never did.

At midseason, a cold front moved in quickly and temperatures dropped precipitously. The next morning the winds were out of the east and the skies crystal clear as I took up a stand on the very edge of the thicket, just west of the fencerow to the south. Very early I saw two does feed slowly from the fencerow out into the cover field and then slowly work away from me. Later a lone doe stole into the thicket itself; then, for a long time, nothing moved. By midday, I was enjoying the sun's warmth and my eyes were growing heavy when I caught movement in the fencerow just south of the thicket. Immediately alerted, I couldn't identify what I'd seen. A squirrel? The random flitting of a songbird? I couldn't tell.

An hour passed and nothing stirred, when all at once there he was, standing broadside right where I saw the earlier movement. The lure of the first sunlight in days, as he attempted to garner all its warmth, was his undoing. Just a few short yards from the complete sanctuary in the thicket, he bedded in the fencerow. Such behavior is not uncommon.

Planning your hunting strategy with the weather depends on your ability to predict it. For this very reason I always catch the latest weather forecasts. The particulars aren't nearly as important as the trends. A few degrees one way or the other is insignificant, a shower or isolated thunderstorm means little or nothing, but major changes should be noted and capitalized upon. The deer, as most animals, seem to have a built-in ability to foresee weather changes, and they react to them long before they're obvious to you and me.

In camp, or while traveling to and from camp by car, I always try to pick up the latest in weather news. To be sure, an awful lot of information and insight must guide us in our hunting efforts, but weather is one of the key criteria that few hunters seem to understand and many simply overlook. When employed properly, it's the one factor that just might determine the outcome of your whole season!

12

How to Select
a Stand

I've every reason to believe that my deer hunting career began in a fairly typical fashion. My father hunted deer for years, but due to an arthritic condition, which cold weather greatly aggravated, he had to stop hunting when I was about ten. He then entrusted my hunting education to my brother-in-law and my brother-in-law's dad. My brother-in-law's dad was a man in his fifties with a good deal of deer hunting experience, and in my fourteenth year—the first year it was legal for me to hunt deer—we began planning my initiation.

No expense was spared. My father bought me a new rifle topped with a 2.5X scope of good quality, a new heavy woolen hunting outfit, insulated underwear, and the finest boots available. In addition, I received his old army compass and an in-depth explanation to its use, plus a beautiful new hunting knife, drag rope, gloves, hat, and sundry other paraphernalia. I had everything a deer hunting novice could ever ask for. Numerous trips were also made to a local gun club where I became familiar with my weapon. To my mentors' way of viewing, nothing had been overlooked.

At least every couple weeks during the summer and early

fall, my brother-in-law and I would review in detail when the season opened, when we'd "go north," where we'd hunt, how long we'd stay, and so on. The evening before our departure, the three of us, my brother-in-law, his dad, and I, went grocery shopping. As a result of all this advance preparation, plus the deer hunting savvy that had been directed my way over many months, I was confident that inside of five minutes in the woods I'd have my deer—no, even more confident than that—I'd have my buck! There was no way I could fail.

Opening morning, long before daylight, we pulled the car into a fire trail and parked. I was instructed, "John, you go down there, find a stand and stay put! Whatever you do, *don't get lost*! We'll meet back at the car at noon. Good luck!" As I wandered through the darkness, heading for "a stand," doubt began creeping into my mind. When I reached the edge of a hillside, I decided—still under cover of darkness—that this was the spot and I took "a stand." When daylight finally came I wasn't sure; the place didn't look quite right, so I moved. A short time later I moved again—then again, and again.

I'm not sure how many times I moved that morning, but I am sure I spent more time moving than standing. My five-minute journey to success turned into a three-year trip! The problem was that no one bothered to tell me what was involved in selecting "a stand." Whether you begin hunting in Michigan's north country, as I did, or the farmlands of our southern counties, the problem of selecting a stand is universal.

It has been my experience that this process of selecting a stand is usually glossed over and thought to be either so obvious, or so extremely elementary, that it is not worthy of intelligent discussion. Generally some cursory mention is made about wind direction and about picking a site along a runway, but beyond that you're left hanging. Not wanting to appear totally ignorant, most novices, and even some experienced nimrods for that matter, simply go stumbling off in the dark.

After twenty-five years of deer hunting, I've concluded that *stand selection is the most difficult and important single event of the deer hunter's entire season*. If it's done correctly, you're practically guaranteed your deer; if done in haste (as is usually the case) or with a lack of knowledge, you're probably doomed to a fruitless season even before first light.

To begin, correctly done, *a stand must be selected before opening day and you should always have more than one in mind.* To begin deer hunting as I did, on that day many years ago, not knowing where you're going to stand beforehand, is foolhardy.

In addition, you must decide what you're after—and what your expectations are—before choosing a stand. Do you want a very high probability of success, and are you therefore willing to take just about any deer that happens by, or are you after a trophy, and therefore willing to chance a lower probability of success (a higher probability of failure)? This is a critical issue that must be addressed *before* choosing your stand.

A good friend and an excellent deer hunter has for the past eleven years taken a deer—a buck—every year from the same stand. His stand is on heavily hunted state land in our northern Lower Peninsula, and he's never been forced to hunt beyond the third day of the season! He's performed this feat although the success ratio for buck hunters in Michigan is roughly 1:6 on an annual basis. Of these eleven bucks, seven have been spike horns, two three-points, and two were small four-points. He has never even seen a larger rack, although he tells me about many days when he's seen forty or more deer. It's unusual for him to ever see less than fifteen to twenty deer a day. His hunting satisfaction derives from seeing as many deer as possible, and putting his tag on one of them. To do less is a disappointment for him. Obviously his stand location fulfills his needs beautifully.

In contrast to his record, I've taken but seven Michigan bucks during those same eleven years. I've never taken two deer from the same stand and, in fact, seldom hunt the same stand twice. However, four of my seven deer have been eight-points, one a nine-point, one a four-point, and one a three-point. Very often during our season in Michigan, I'll go two or three days in a row without even seeing a deer, and I consider a great day to be one in which I sight four or five deer! Without question, *where you choose a stand is going to determine both the quantity and the quality of the deer you see.*

Author with Buck. The author waylaid this four-point by covering an escape trail in the late season between heavily hunted feeding areas and escape cover farther in.

When choosing a stand there are many characteristics of white-tailed deer to be considered (a thorough review of Chapter 1 is in order here). Very briefly, mature white-tailed bucks are loners, or at least they shy away from congregations of other deer. Conversely, the rest of the deer herd is gregarious in nature and generally sticks pretty close together. In addition, for much of their travel, most deer—

does and smaller bucks—rely on runways when not actively feeding. Older, mature bucks usually shun runways except when pressured, or when moving through marshy areas or around watercourses.

Whitetails also follow certain patterns when moving to and from feeding areas. Does and smaller bucks will usually feed until well after daylight and then pick a run to follow into their bedding area. If these are the deer you seek, your stand for a morning hunt should take this behavior pattern into account and should overlook a run leading to a bedding area. Both bedding and feeding areas must be located prior to the opening of the season.

I personally do most of my scouting to gather such information in the middle of the day and seldom ever look for the deer themselves. Deer sign is much more telling than actual observation, and deer sign is far easier to detect in good light. To determine where deer are feeding, the hunter should look for tracks leading into crop fields, hardwoods containing mast, and thickets in which the foliage is within reach.

Ideally, this scouting should be done within a week or two of opening day. It does little good to know where the deer were feeding on the first of October when the season doesn't open until mid-November. For equally obvious reasons *all scouting should therefore be timely in nature.*

Depending upon cover density, a stand should be anywhere from twenty to forty yards away from the run you're watching, never closer. Frequently you'll find around a bedding area one or more heavily used runways leading to its edge. As the runs enter the bedding area itself, they'll splinter into smaller runs until they just disappear. The area, for a morning hunt designed to show you the highest number of deer—does and smaller bucks—is where a major run enters a general bedding area.

For an afternoon hunt you should select a different stand, since deer behave differently. In the morning deer feed as long as possible and then rather quickly get into cover; in the evening they begin feeding at a more leisurely pace. They'll slowly leave their beds, one at a time, and begin feeding immediately, upon whatever is available. They'll drift toward their

Bucks Browsing. Where you hunt—the type of habitat—will determine both the quality and the quantity of the game you see. Generally speaking, the more deer you see, the less likely you will see a truly big buck.

main goal, be it a crop field, mast, or whatever, but this leisurely movement may take two or three hours. In selecting an afternoon stand, you should realize that deer will seldom be on runways; rather, they'll be ambling through cover in a random manner, moving gradually toward their main feeding site. Because of this pattern, an afternoon stand should be located between the bedding and feeding area, but closer to the beds than the morning hunt. It should be kept in mind that the runway is not nearly as important as it was earlier in the day.

A mature white-tailed buck, in contrast with the above, is unlikely to remain feeding in the open until daybreak. He may feed in the same general area with the rest of the herd, but long before daylight he'll abandon this area and drift into thicker cover. Once in cover he'll continue to feed as he slowly moves into his bedding area. A hunter, wanting to waylay this guy, will not do so by watching runways, especially runways carrying other deer. Mature bucks seldom rely on runways (there are a couple of specific exceptions that I'll get to later) and they rarely bed with other deer. To begin your quest for a large buck, first find his bedding area and home range. Rely on tracks, cleaning rubs and direct observation to gather this information. *If you're truly committed to tagging a bigger than average white-tailed buck be prepared to spend weeks nailing down his movements.*

Pinpointing a big buck's behavior and movement is not that difficult but requires a good deal of time. The specific areas of the buck's home range that should interest you include: where he's bedding at that time, where he's feeding, and the buffer zone between the two. This search is greatly simplified by remembering the buck's biological needs at that time. In the fall months, big bucks, whether the rut is in full swing or not, will not stray too far from the rest of the herd. Wherever they're feeding, he'll feed. Wherever they're bedding, he'll bed nearby—within a mile.

This is why buck rubs will give you a lot of useful information. Bucks rub their antlers wherever they happen to be when the mood strikes. Wherever the bulk of the bigger rubs in the area are found is the area or areas utilized most frequently by the biggest bucks. (Again, this is where a "hunting habitat map," discussed in Chapter 10, can be of great value.)

Once all such information is gathered, you should then give thought to stand location. The important thing to keep in mind is that big bucks rarely get caught in the open. You'll want a stand that's located in cover, and you'll want to be there for your morning hunt *before* the buck arrives. This

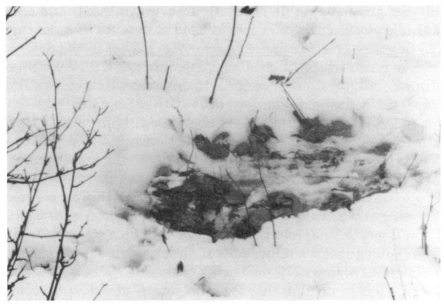

Bedding Area. Two deer bedded here recently. Frequently you'll find one or more heavily used runways leading to the edge of a bedding area. As the runs enter the bedding area itself, they'll splinter into smaller runs until they just disappear.

means that you should be on your stand a good half-hour before legal shooting light to avoid spooking the buck. A big buck is always nervous about being in the open and therefore gets into cover early; once in he's quite content to take his time—seldom does he hurry while in cover. Frequently, he'll feed contentedly late into the morning on the perimeter of his bedding area, especially on mornings following stormy, moonless nights. A stand for a morning hunt should then be along the perimeter of the buck's actual bedding area.

It's true of whitetails in general, but even more so of fully mature bucks: at some point during midday they'll usually stretch and feed for an hour or so. Perhaps big bucks do so more often as the result of stiffness, or the aches and pains of old age. In order to capitalize on this trait, I'll move—very quietly—from the perimeter of a big buck's bedding area directly into the bedding area itself. Keep in mind that a buck's bedding area will cover anywhere from twenty to fifty acres in size. Just exactly where, within this area, he'll bed on any given day will depend on several different factors, including wind direction, temperature, precipitation, and the degree of human intrusion.

Big bucks begin their evening feeding routine much like other deer, only they wander about within the bedding area for a longer period of time. They'll drift about within this cover, nibbling freely on whatever is available. Seldom do they vacate the cover before total darkness. When you're located within the area, you should stay put until nightfall. By hunting in this manner, it must be reiterated, you're not likely to see many deer, but an extremely high percentage of the deer you do see will be bucks, and a high percentage of them will be better than average in size.

There are other factors that a hunter must consider, in addition to "typical" whitetail behavior, when choosing a stand. These factors are the rut, the weather, and the amount of hunting pressure.

Hunters fortunate enough to have an open season during the rut are blessed indeed, but some of the latest research on deer behavior may surprise you. Although sitting on a scrape may very well place venison in your freezer, it probably won't belong to the buck who made the scrape! The biggest, most dominant bucks—those who make the most active scrapes—seldom ever visit them except under the complete cover of darkness. Most of the other bucks within the area, however, will visit them , and frequently they'll do so during daylight hours. Remember, here in Michigan, it's our archers who are most successful hunting scrapes.

If you're interested only in the big bruiser that made the scrapes, then you should locate several scrapes to find the pattern made by their locations and then attempt to find where the buck holes up during the day. Chances are it isn't far away. Remember, a buck wants to be available to the does who will seek him out. Look for him to bed in a nearby thicket; the more dense and impenetrable it is, the better the odds that's where he'll be. Put yourself in the middle of it. Once on stand in the morning, and you must do so well before daylight, you shouldn't move until after dark or you'll only succeed in spooking him. Once spooked, your odds of scoring drop precipitously.

Weather, of course, plays a tremendous role in where you should select your stand on any given day (see Chapter 11). Everything I've said about stand selection so far has assumed fairly decent weather conditions. That all changes, however, when high winds, rain, snow, or extreme heat or cold enters the picture. Deer do not like wind, it befuddles their senses. They cannot hear, smell or see as well on windy days. Their solution is to lay low and remain inactive as much as possible. If you're looking for a day off to do chores, this is the day. If you hunt, do so in thick cover and expect, in all probability, to see deer only very early and very late in the day.

Rain, snow and cold can be uncomfortable to hunt in, but these are frequently very productive days and worthy of the extra effort and discomfort. I remember vividly two snowy days—in different years—hunting in southern Michigan. It's unusual for dear season in southern Michigan to open with snow on the ground, but some ten or twelve years ago the unusual happened. Opening morning found a heavy, wet covering of four inches on the ground. This was the first snow of the year; it had fallen just hours before. Just like children at a playground, the deer were ecstatic. By nine o'clock that morning, I saw more deer than the entire season the year before, and had a nice four-point on the ground.

Some seven or eight years ago, it began snowing after I had reached my stand in the morning, on about the fifth day of the season. By noon we had two or three inches, and I became chilled. Deciding to stretch my cramped muscles and warm up a bit, I wandered slowly to an opening. Immediately I began cutting fresh deer tracks. All morning long sitting in the thicket I saw nothing; now wandering across the open field I discovered why! From the tracks present, it seemed apparent that while I waited in heavy cover, the deer were all enjoying the new-fallen snow by romping in the open. If you can do so, this is probably one of the best times of the entire season for still hunting. I'd recommend covering a variety of habitats—openings, thickets, edges—just to ensure wherever the deer are on that particular day you'll find them. Keep in mind that later snowfalls do not have the same effect, and late season archers and muzzle-loaders should probably head to insulating cover on such days.

Rain, snow, and falling temperatures make the deer cold and uncomfortable as well, and they'll frequently move more than usual on such days. Therefore, unless the weather is extremely bad, I like to stand on the edge of thick cover all day when such conditions exist. If the weather is truly excessive, I'll move into thick cedars, planted pines, or other similarly dense cover, but regardless, I'll hunt the entire day. Such days are often the very best of the entire season. If you encounter a day, excessively cold but bright, look for deer to bed in areas where they are exposed to the sun. They'll attempt to get all the warmth possible from such a day; they'll move more than normal and they'll bed down in the middle of the day when the sun is at its zenith.

Hunting pressure definitely has an effect, usually negatively, on your chances of success, but with some forethought you can use hunting pressure to your advantage (see Chapter 8). The first thing to determine is whether there is a lot of pressure in your area. If you've hunted there previously, you should have a good idea of what to expect. If the area is new to you, then check with local farmers, residents, or the DNR in the area.

If the area is hunted lightly, then keep in mind the factors pointed out. If the area is hunted heavily, you must alter your habits and strategy, especially after opening morning. The early season salvos of gunfire completely change the routines of all whitetails and especially those of the bucks. The effects can be so great as to completely shut off the rut for a time. It will also affect your chances of success.

Generally speaking, hunters in heavily hunted areas should get to their stands earlier and stay later than those in lightly hunted areas. Early in the season, all deer—including big bucks —will depend more heavily than usual upon runways. The reason runways are made in the first place is because they offer the fastest possible route between two points. Therefore, when deer are pressured, they need to exit in a hurry; that's generally how they'll go—using the runway.

Look for deer in heavily hunted areas to resort quickly to

nocturnal habits, especially when hunting in remote areas as compared with farm country. They'll move less frequently, at least in scant cover, during the daylight. This is especially true during periods offering good moonlight when deer can comfortably feed the entire night. Stands should therefore be located in thick cover, far from openings, and the hunter should be on his post early and should stay later than usual. Also be aware that hunters, leaving the woods at lunchtime and returning for the afternoon hunt, unintentionally move a lot of deer. Personally, I never leave the woods all day. Instead I use the movement of other hunters to my benefit.

Be cognizant of where other hunters enter and leave the woods. If there are parking areas, or campgrounds, or special access sites—a dead-end road for example—this information can be used to your maximum advantage. Get there first, and let others entering the woods later drive the deer to you. Look for especially inaccessible pockets of cover in which to take your stand.

Six or seven years ago I took a deer on the fifth day of a trip to Georgia. During my days in the woods, I saw waterfowl taxiing back and forth routinely. So the next morning with scattergun and decoys in hand I was in a swamp south of my deer stand. As the sky brightened, I could make out an island in the middle of the swamp. Wading through chest-deep water I wondered if I'd make it. As I cleared the water's edge onto the island, three deer—two does and a massive buck—broke cover and swam to shore. Chances are great that if I hadn't wandered out there, those deer would have safely spent the entire deer season isolated there. Such pockets of cover, be it an island or simply a thicket in the open, exist in all hunting areas and should be sought. If it's too far, or too difficult, or too small, chances are excellent that it harbors deer! The wise hunter locates a stand in such a pocket.

Try to obtain a working knowledge of how the hunters in your area work the cover even though this takes time and experience. There are some areas within every hunting locality that, for one reason or another, hunters seldom check. As an example, a place I frequently hunt in southern Michigan has a good-size woodlot and a large cedar swamp, separated by a quarter-mile long thicket that nearly everyone hunts. The hunters enter the woodlot from the roadway, hunt its length, sneak along either north or south of the thicket, and then hunt the cedars. Seldom do they ever enter the broken thorn apples north of the thicket, between the woods and the swamp. I can only guess that they believe the cover is too open to be suitable, but in six seasons of hunting there off and on, I've taken two nice eight-points. The deer very quickly learn the areas where hunters do not go, and so should you.

It should be obvious, from what I've said, that a stand selected with the hope of providing you with a full season of deer hunting is inadequate. The knowledgeable hunter should have at least ten or twelve places in mind where, depending on the rut, time of the season, time of the day, hunting pressure and weather, he can hunt. The decision about where to hunt on any given day is best made the morning or afternoon of the actual hunt. Everything I've mentioned should be considered when making that decision; whether it's made correctly or not, it's the most important decision of your entire hunt!

Part IV

A Geographical Guide to Michigan's Whitetails

Preface

Section IV of this book is devoted to the detailed delineation of those regional areas within Michigan in which, I feel, deer hunters could do well, providing they hunt hard and employ good, sound deer hunting practices. This delineation has been accomplished on a county-by-county basis for the entire state. Hopefully, it will help you zero in on those areas to hunt, and also on those areas to avoid. For each region of the state, the counties are listed, to the best of my ability, in descending order of productiveness. For example, in Chapter 13, while Sanilac County may not be more productive than Jackson County, clearly both of these are more productive than Macomb, Monroe, and Wayne counties. This is reflected by the order in which they appear in the text.

It may not be obvious (before I began this field work, it certainly was not obvious to me), but this was an immense undertaking. My desire was to do the best, most thorough analysis of every area of the state as humanly possible. I can only hope I've succeeded—you'll be my judge.

The field work involved took me more than a year and a half to complete. In doing so, I put more than one hundred thousand miles on my research vehicle. When it was finished,

I had more than one hundred hours of tape-recorded information, and copious notes from which I have extracted both the
maps' graphic details, and the county-by-county descriptions.
In addition, I made countless telephone calls, and talked with
scores of people across all of Michigan. But obviously, no matter how detailed, and regardless of how meticulous, some gaps
will remain. I simply could not drive every road, nor tromp
every woodlot, in every county throughout the state.

Genesee County is a case in point. Notice the huge areas
I've shaded as being totally inadequate for even a local
hunter. The sprawling mass of civilization radiating outward
from Flint is such that a local hunter, in say most of Mount
Morris Township, could not find a large enough block of land
where he could gain access to make an extended hunt worth-
while. Let's assume you own, or know someone who owns, a
twenty- or forty-acre parcel in this area. If you've a half day
to hunt, fine—hunt it. But would you consider a three-day
hunt there? A week? The whole season? I think not.

That's why I've shaded that area in as being inadequate.
It's not that there are no deer, nor is it that a few aren't
taken each year, for they certainly are. In this case, it's simply an overwhelming access problem. This land is so cut up
and fragmented, with so many different owners, that very
few locals are going to have access rights to even small
parcels. To gain access to an area large enough to have a
realistic hope of locating a buck, and then being able to
implement a plan, is, in my opinion, nearly impossible.

Another common reason for calling an area inadequate is
simply local ordinances. Many southern Michigan townships
are off limits to all hunting. I should point out that I've made
no attempt to shade in every small area thus unavailable,
i.e., I've not shaded in small villages or subdivisions. I have
attempted to do this as assiduously as possible with larger
areas. There will be exceptions. If you, or someone you know,
owns a six hundred acre farm in Clayton Township (Genesee
County) and you know there's a good herd there (which there
probably is), then by all means hunt it. Keep in mind, however, that I'm referring to an average situation with the
accompanying graphic details.

There's one other common reason for calling an area inadequate to all deer hunting, and that's an overwhelming lack of habitat. Areas such as Buena Vista Township in Saginaw County or Peninsula Township in Grand Traverse County, for example, are so intensely cultivated and/or developed that there's no habitat available for deer. Thus, although there will undoubtedly be a stray deer here and there, these areas overall are inadequate. The same is true in some areas of our Upper Peninsula, where the habitat is simply too mature to support sizable numbers of deer.

An additional piece of information found in the text for many of the Lower Peninsula counties: Commercial Forest Act lands. CFA lands are open to hunting (without written permission), but they are not marked in any way. I've noted the acreage enrolled in this program by county where that amount is significant, except in the U.P, where the holdings are so vast that I have not listed them. Maps of CFA lands can be obtained from township, county or U.S. Department of Agriculture offices in each county.

I stick by these maps and by the county descriptions found in the text. I hope and trust they will be of value to you. Michigan has just about anything a serious deer hunter could ever wish for, from the farms of the south to the big woods of the U.P. It's all there—take advantage of it.

Number of antlered bucks harvested per square mile during the 1992 archery, firearm, and muzzle-loading deer seasons

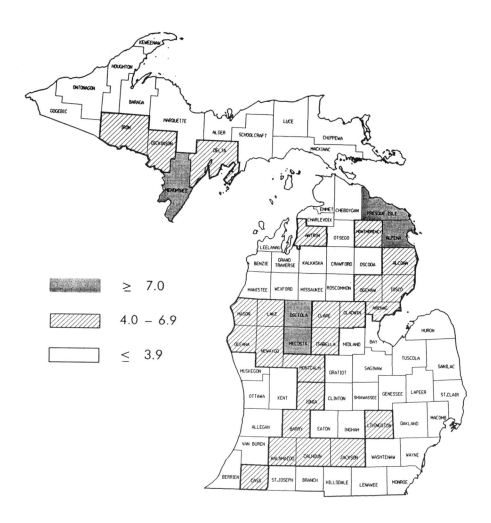

13

Southeastern Michigan

Southeastern Michigan presents us with a mixed lot. Deer densities throughout the area range from a low of two or three per square mile to as high as seventy or more. Areas such as Monroe and Wayne counties can make the deer hunter searching for habitat and hunting space cry, yet areas such as western Jackson and northern Lapeer counties can brighten the deer hunter's darkest day. From the farmland environment of Shiawassee County to the northwoods aura of Tuscola's Deford State Game Area, southeastern Michigan has it all. In recent years fully one-third of Michigan's "trophy" deer have been taken out of these counties, and the future of trophy hunting here looks bright. In fact, there are more counties (fifteen in 1992) in this area that produce a higher percentage (30 percent or more of their legally antlered bucks) of eight-point, or larger, bucks than any other region of the state.

Generally speaking, the habitat and potential deer hunting improves as you move north and west in this region. Based on DNR statistics, and my own research, the areas with the greatest potential for nonlocal hunters are Jackson,

Map 13.1
Southeastern Michigan

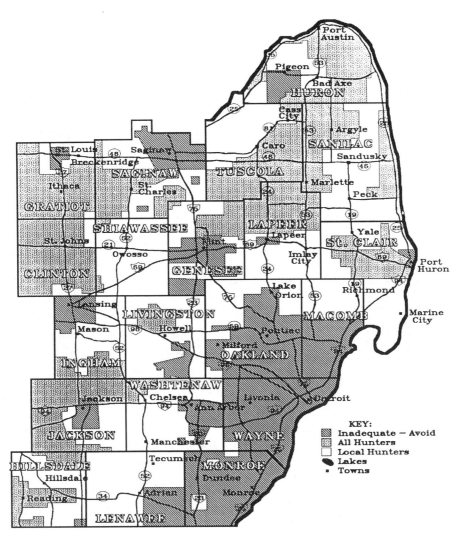

Hillsdale, Tuscola, Sanilac, Clinton, Gratiot and Huron counties. But be forewarned, access to other than state and public access lands can be very difficult to obtain. Nonlocal hunters must begin their search for hunting space in this corner of the state early—far in advance of the actual season—and should be prepared for a lot of rejection. There is opportunity here, but you'll have to work hard to find it. Keep in mind, too, that the closer you are to the major metropolitan centers the more difficult it will be to obtain access—start looking early!

Local hunters will fare best in all of the above-mentioned counties, plus these as well: Lenawee, Washtenaw, Shiawassee and Saginaw. Following is a short description of each county's deer hunting potential in this region, plus an analysis of the best and the worst townships in each.

Sanilac County

On March 13, 1988, I conducted my final field research in Sanilac County for the first edition of this book. I have never in all my years of travel, not only in Michigan but elsewhere as well, seen as many deer in a single day as I did that day. While totaling estimates from my field notes and my tape recordings later that night, I calculated a conservative estimate of 860-plus deer seen in one day!

Most of Sanilac County is privately owned and is therefore, for the local or resident hunter, one of the best deer hunting bets in the entire state. Deer densities are high—although down roughly 20 percent since 1989-90's high—and increase as you move north through the county. Townships of particular interest are Greenleaf, Evergreen, Argyle, Lamotte and Marlette on the west side of the county, and Minden, Wheatland, Forester and Sanilac on the east side. Townships, or more properly parts of townships, I found wanting even for local hunters were sections of Moore Township on the west side, and Delaware Township on the east side. Still, nearly the entire county offers exciting possibilities.

The whole of Sanilac County is agriculturally based. The only exception is in Forester Township, which is currently a resort area with a large number of summer cottages. A lot of original farmland has reverted to cover, and the deer population is quite high. Gaining access for the nonlocal hunter could be a problem, but one well worth the hunter's efforts.

Although there are several small chunks of state land throughout the county, by far the biggest is the Minden City State Game Area. This is an area of roughly four thousand

Deer in Snow-Covered Field. Scenes such as this are commonplace in many areas of southeastern Michigan, where some of the highest deer densities in Michigan are recorded.

acres. It is essentially flat, low-lying land, in the north-central portion of the county, and heavily covered with soft hardwoods, mostly poplar and birch, plus a lot of brush. The state is doing an excellent job in selectively cutting different stands, and plenty of browse is available.

Speaking with several local landowners surrounding this state land, I found that their lands are all posted because they themselves hunt. Courteous requests (preseason) for the second half of the general deer season would probably get positive results. Preseason scouting, at least in terms of setting up access, would be critical for the nonlocal hunter. Elsewhere, there are more than 1,900 acres of hunter access lands in the county.

The remainder of the county offers its best cover along the numerous waterways: particularly the Cass River and its many tributaries in the northwest, Ossintosh Creek in the north, Elk Creek in the southwest, and all of the creeks flowing into Lake Huron on the east. Knee-high rubber boots, perhaps even hip boots, are the order of the day in these areas.

Jackson County

Jackson County offers exciting whitetail possibilities for local and nonlocal hunters alike. The areas with the best overall habitat are the townships in the extreme north, as well as those in the extreme south. Specifically these are Waterloo, Henrietta, Rives, and the eastern half of Tompkins in the north, and Pulaski, Hanover and Liberty in the south. The area immediately adjacent to the Sharonville State Game Area is also very good for local hunters.

Springport, Parma, Sandstone, and the western half of Tompkins townships are only marginal for nonlocals. The reason is that the percentage of cultivated lands increases quite dramatically in these townships. I believe gaining access to the land in these areas would be extremely difficult for the nonlocal. The habitat that exists in these areas is excellent if access privileges are obtained. These townships are top-flight for local hunters.

Much of the area that lies east and south of Jackson is only available to local hunters. There are some areas in this vicinity that have excellent cover, but the surrounding human population is so high that I doubt anyone hunting with a gun could do so safely. This is particularly true in areas around the region's lakes. This includes parts of Summit, Spring Arbor, Leoni and Grass Lake townships, as well as most of Columbia Township.

Jackson County as a whole is a moderately contoured county, with very little flat land anywhere. The gentle hills form many valuable pockets of cover. An excellent mix of cover and habitat types results. Hardwood woodlots are common throughout, but there are also thickets, swales, cattail marshes, some abandoned farmlands, a good many brushy fencerows and some abandoned orchards.

With the exception of the area from the city of Jackson south and east, Jackson County is a sparsely populated rural area. Within the county roughly 2,100 acres of state lands are open to hunting, but only 250 acres of farmlands are enrolled in the hunter access program. (There are no CFA lands.) The county is heavily hunted, especially the state-owned and state-leased lands—personally, I'd avoid most of these areas.

Huron County

The two days I spent researching Huron County for this section were a couple of the first really nice days we had in March 1988. If you remember the winter, you'll then know why the deer were excited about spring—and excited they were! I was unable to count them precisely, but I know I saw at least three hundred deer in two days of scouting there.

For the hunter without access problems, there's tremendous hunting potential here, but due to the absence of state lands, access is generally limited. For the most part, local and nonlocal hunters alike can forget about hunting Brookfield, Winsor and Oliver townships. These areas are intensely cultivated and totally lacking in cover. The land is very flat, and unless the hunter knows about a specific deer in a specific location, he can cross these townships off his list.

There are three widely separated areas, however, that will appeal to both local and nonlocal hunters. These areas are all on private lands, but I believe, with early preseason requests and ample preseason scouting, these areas would offer excellent sport. The first is the land just north of Sanilac County, particularly in Grant, Sheridan and Bingham townships. That area off Bach Road, between Trumble and M-53 and a mile north up to McAlpin Road, seems especially appealing to me. It's a mix of hardwoods, cedars, and lowland brush; the cover is dense and runs for four or five miles, essentially unbroken. I get a good feeling every time I'm in the area! The gentle rolling countryside around Mud Lake seems to be calling me as well; I think this is tremendous deer country!

The area adjacent to M-25 from Port Hope all the way to Caseville Township warrants close scrutiny, especially for local hunters. Hunting areas are scattered here—there is no single mass of territory—but for the local hunter with access permission, there's phenomenal potential here.

That area next to Wildfowl Bay (some of which is state land) is simply incredible! Wildfowl Bay itself is off-limits, being closed to all hunting until at least the year 2010; however, there's plenty of habitat adjacent to it. This is flat countryside with lots of brush and marsh area, as well as some hardwoods. Much of the private land is posted, but again, ask. The potential is there, it's up to you to make the most of it.

With the exception of townships mentioned earlier, all of Huron County can offer the local hunters excellent sport. The deer population is high, and cover, though spotty, serves to concentrate the deer once the crops are in.

For out-of-towners, areas I'd particularly concentrate on are Paris, Sigel, Bloomfield, Huron, Port Austin, Dwight, Hume and Lincoln townships. Huron County has roughly two thousand acres enrolled in the hunter access program. These, of course, warrant checking out, especially by early season archers.

Tuscola County

In terms of good-looking habitat, Tuscola is the best of the Thumb areas. With more than 25,000 acres of state lands, as well as more than 2,200 acres of state-leased private lands, there is ample hunter access as well.

Speaking in broad terms, the area south and east of Highway 81 is the best in the county, but this comprises more than half of the county! The southwest corner contains the highest hills and the least level ground in all of the Thumb. In the east, there are many marginal, abandoned farmlands, particularly around the Deford State Game Area. The habitat more closely resembles northern Michigan habitat than it does the rest of the Thumb.

In areas such as Elkland, Arbela, Tuscola and Millington townships, there are a lot of mature mast-bearing hardwoods, but ample browse is present as well. In other areas, such as Wells, Novesta, Kingston and Juniata townships, there's little mast but an immense amount of both crop fields and browse. The woodlots in these townships are mostly

Buck with Squatting Doe. Some areas of the northern Thumb region register the greatest antler development in yearling bucks of anyplace in Michigan.

five- to twenty-year-old stands of poplar, birch and a mix of evergreens; they provide excellent cover and browse.

One of the nice things about the state lands is that they're not big blocks, but rather consist of a series of fragmented chunks, all closely spaced. The Deford area, for example, covers something like thirty-seven sections of land and yet is only 9,600 acres. This provides a large number of access points and helps to spread out hunting pressure. These state areas, thanks to our DNR, are actively managed for small and nongame species, mostly upland birds. This is exactly the same kind of management that best suits the whitetails' needs, and hence deer densities are high, although down probably 20 percent from their peak numbers of four or five years ago.

Tuscola County is an agriculturally based area, but the farmland in the east and south sections is marginal at best. Much of it today is not actively farmed, and there's little grazing of cattle. The rest of the county, particularly Wisner, Gilford, Fairgrove, Denmark, Columbia, Akron and Elmwood townships, is heavily farmed. This is high-quality farmland and hence the fields are very large, there's scant cover, hardly any fencerows, and the woodlots tend to be more mature than those in the rest of the county. There are deer in these areas, but they're not really plentiful, and all the land is private. Except for the local hunter, I certainly couldn't recommend hunting it.

The nonlocal hunter should hunt in and around the state lands. Since the water table in these areas is very high, rubber boots are highly recommended. Hip boots will take the hard-working hunter into many areas in this part of the county avoided by other hunters.

Hillsdale County

Despite conducting my research in Hillsdale County on a sunny and mild day in June, I saw deer throughout the day; not a great many, eight or nine probably, but they were out and moving nonetheless. Hillsdale is an excellent area for locals, and much of it should be good for nonlocals.

The entire county is agriculturally based; corn, wheat, oats and barley are the dominant crops. There are considerable numbers of livestock—mostly cattle, but also hogs and horses.

Hillsdale is a very contoured area, providing a good deal of pocket cover. The only exceptions to this are Wright and Ransom townships in the extreme southeast corner of the county. These two townships thus offer the poorest deer hunting potential for the locals and offer nothing at all for nonlocals.

Good stands of mature mast-bearing hardwoods are found throughout the county as well as younger woodlots in most areas. There's also excellent pocket cover provided by all the nooks and crannies produced by the roll of the land. Everything is there in terms of cover, except evergreens. There are good thickets, swales, brushy fencerows, abandoned orchards and vacated farmlands.

Typical of the rest of the county is the area around Milne in the north-central part of the county. With pockets of intensely cultivated lands containing absolutely no whitetail cover, there also are thick patches of cover that border these areas, providing deer with needed food and shelter, in both summer and winter.

The townships I'd recommend for nonlocal hunters are Somerset, much of Moscow, the western half of Pittsford, as well as Jefferson, Cambria, Reading, the western half of Camden, and the southern part of Woodbridge. The biggest problem a nonlocal hunter will encounter in this area is gaining access to the land. Many of these landowners are extremely protective of "their deer herd," and gaining access is questionable.

More than 2,150 acres of Hillsdale's farmlands are enrolled in the hunter access program, as well as over 2,374 acres of state lands within the Lost Nation State Game Area. Your best shot at access to private lands will be a very early start!

Saginaw County

For the local hunters in Saginaw County, deer season must be a much anticipated event, for I'm convinced that throughout much of the county a serious deer hunter's efforts will be greatly rewarded. The county is agriculturally based, so much so that some areas lack adequate cover and hence cannot be considered as huntable, even by the locals. Blumfield, Buena Vista, Saginaw and Kochville townships fall within this category.

Elsewhere, the county shows the dichotomy of both a northern Michigan type of habitat in places and that of southern Michigan in others. It has, for the most part, the crop fields of the south, and, in places, the open hardwoods of the south. But much of the cover, as around the Gratiot–Saginaw State Game Area, has the mixed woodlots and bracken fern so common in the north. The county is flat everywhere, much of its soil is very rich, and its water table is very high.

There is precious little state land for deer hunting, and few farms are enrolled in the access program. The state land, which does exist, is of two types. The Gratiot–Saginaw State Game Area is typical of most state lands in southern Michigan. It's a dynamite area, consisting of more than 3,600 acres of land spread out over several square miles. The state land itself is mostly mixed woodlot, with a good mast supply, sandy soil, and a high water table. The land in between is mostly marginal farmland (in other words, excellent whitetail habitat) providing the deer with both food and cover. Gratiot-Saginaw is a good bet, as are the surrounding private lands, if the nonlocal wants to invest the time in seeking necessary landowner permission.

The other public land is the Shiawassee River State Game Area and the Shiawassee National Wildlife Refuge. These adjoining blocks of land, located in the corner of the county, cover roughly nineteen thousand acres. Both areas are managed primarily as waterfowl areas, although both contain sizable deer herds. To control crop damage, and to help ease the burden on surrounding farmers, deer are maintained at appropriate levels through hunting.

All deer hunting is by special drawing or on a preregistered permit basis. There are, usually, both archery and gun seasons, although they change from year to year. The best advice is to check well in advance of when you wish to hunt (I'd check no later than mid-September to avoid missing application deadlines).

Townships of little or no interest to anyone are parts of Frankenmuth, as well as Blumfield, Buena Vista, Saginaw, Kochville, and parts of Tittabawassee. Townships of interest to nonlocals are the western part of Jonesfield, Lakefield,

Fremont, Swan Creek, Brant, Chapin, Brady, Marion, Maple Grove, Taymouth, and parts of Albee.

Livingston County

Livingston County is an unusual area; there is absolutely beautiful cover for deer throughout almost the entire county, and yet I cannot suggest much at all for the nonlocal hunter. Even locals have problems in certain areas, principally between Pinckney and Brighton. This is truly a dichotomous area. There is beautiful cover; the land is heavily contoured, with a lot of mature mast-bearing hardwoods, interspersed crop fields of corn, wheat and barley, nice brushy draws and thick swales. Then thrown right in the midst of this will be a subdivision or cluster of fifty to one hundred homes! The problem, then, is that though good habitat is available, supporting a goodly number of deer, there are severe access problems. I really doubt that even most locals are able to gain access.

Throughout the rest of the county, the land characteristics remain about the same—it's fine habitat, and the human population is much less. Livingston County is an agriculturally based county, with high numbers of livestock. It's heavily contoured, with plenty of mast, woodlots, brush, heavy cover fields, and, especially up in Tyrone and Deerfield townships, a lot of little marshes.

There are only two hundred acres of farmland enrolled in the hunter access program and no CFA lands in the county. There are roughly five thousand acres of state lands available to hunters, but as is the case with all the state lands near our major metropolitan centers, they are so heavily hunted that personally, I'd avoid them. Hunter densities on most of these lands range as high as one hunter per every ten acres on opening day!

Although I really can't recommend much of the county to nonlocals, I want to make it clear that the deer and the cover are both available. If a nonlocal is willing to put a lot of time and effort into gathering access, he could do well. I am particularly impressed with the area along the M-59 corridor, and also that area along Owosso Road from Fowlerville north. Compared with the rest of the county, the population is far less in Howell, Osceola and Deerfield townships, and I believe that even nonlocals could do well in these areas.

Clinton County

Clinton County, for the past thirty years, has been an area in transition. Thirty years ago thousands of sheep were pastured here; today few remain. The soil is poor, the drainage is bad, and cultivation on much of this land is unprofitable. As a result, successional brush and second growth has since sprung up, especially along the hundreds of miles of ditches and creeks. The result is a much improved whitetail habitat and a flourishing whitetail herd. In an effort to maintain control of crop damage, the DNR has been attempting to hold this herd at roughly ten to twelve deer per square mile; I don't think they can do it!

. With the exception of Dallas and Bengal townships, which offer only marginal hunting because they're very open with little cover and large crop fields, the county offers local hunters excellent deer hunting opportunities. I particularly like the following townships for local hunters: Bath, Dewitt, Watertown, the eastern half of Olive, Victor, Ovid, Duplain and Lebanon. These townships have lots of cover and a mixed habitat. The contoured land offers plenty of pockets, lots of brush, mixed woodlots and good browse. Mixed in are rather smallish crop fields of twenty to forty acres, and brushy fencerows.

For nonlocals there are only 500 acres of farmlands enrolled in the hunter access program, and no CFA lands, but there are more than 9,500 acres of state lands. Additionally, a lot of the private acreage is available, if you make early arrangements. This is particularly true the farther you move away from the greater Lansing area.

Gratiot County

Like Clinton County to the south, Gratiot, in the recent past, was home to large numbers of sheep. As the bottom fell out of this market, the numbers of animals grazing here sharply dwindled. Habitat has improved as a result, and deer numbers have increased.

From a hunter's point of view, some parts of the county are still uninspiring; Bethany township, as well as parts of Wheeler, Emerson, Arcada and Pine River townships fall into this category. This area, due to its intense cultivation, is of only marginal value even for the local hunters.

There are, however, a lot of bright spots in Gratiot County. The biggest and brightest is the Gratiot–Saginaw State Game Area. This area contrasts sharply with the remainder of the county, for it closely resembles a more northern type of habitat than anything else in the county. The soil here is sandy, and the flora is typically northern: poplar, birch, alder and other soft hardwoods, as well as lots of bracken fern, thickets, swales and plenty of brush. There are plenty of deer as well, and the surrounding landowners should have phenomenal hunting. Hunting pressure on state lands, especially during the gun season, is intense.

The area in and immediately adjacent to the Maple River State Game Area is also of interest, although less so. Also of interest is the region around Beaver and Mud creeks in the extreme northwest corner of the county. These three areas are all highly recommended, even for nonlocal hunters.

The areas having the most promise for local hunters are those along the Pine River flood plain on the west, the North Branch of the Bad River on the east, and North Shade, New Haven, Sumner and Seville townships on the west side of the county.

It's recommended that nonlocals, seeking access here, begin early and attempt to build a good relationship with the landowner. Perhaps begin by seeking permission for either the archery or small-game seasons. Access rights for the latter part of the regular gun season will be a lot easier to obtain than permission for the opener.

Ingham County

Ingham County is an agricultural county, but has many problems that beset the deer hunter; it is heavily cultivated, has a high human population, and the habitat is much too mature to be appropriate for whitetails. Exemplifying this is the area in Wheatfield Township adjacent to the corner of Williamston and Dennis roads. This area has such extensive cultivation that there's simply inadequate cover. Any existing cover is in the form of mature mast-bearing hardwoods. They're too mature, thus assuring that when winter comes, there's little whitetail food and totally inadequate cover.

I'd rate Delhi, Alaiedon, Wheatfield, Leroy, Vevay, Ingham and White Oak townships as offering only marginal opportunities, even for local hunters. Locke Township, in the extreme northeast corner of the county, is excellent for local hunters and could even be considered as marginal for nonlocals, although gaining access is going to be exceedingly difficult.

Stockbridge, Bunkerhill, much of Leslie, and Onondaga townships offer nonlocals a good opportunity. They are, of course, excellent for locals. There are also 4,100 acres of land in the Dansville State Game Area that are good for nonlocals but very heavily hunted. Fewer than nine hundred acres in Ingham County are enrolled in the hunter access program, and much of this is on poor whitetail habitat areas. Aurelius Township is very good for locals.

Finally, there's the entire northwest corner of the county encompassing the Lansing, East Lansing, Okemos, and Holt metropolis. This area, despite some habitat (and undoubtedly a few deer) is totally off limits to all. There are so many people in this region that all hunting, except perhaps archery, would, in my opinion, be unsafe.

Why, if much of Ingham County is unsuitable for the serious whitetailer, does the county continue to produce fairly good numbers of trophy bucks? Ingham is a perfect place for the occasional buck to grow into a real wallhanger. There are undoubtedly areas within the county that seldom see a hunter; with so few deer, most hunters will search elsewhere. Those few are given the chance to mature into the trophy-age classes. The same is true in sections of many other southeastern Michigan counties as well.

Lenawee County

Lenawee County is monotonous and uninspiring from a deer hunter's perspective. It's a heavily cultivated, agriculturally based county, especially the south and east sides. A line drawn from the southwest corner through Adrian up to the northeast corner nicely separates the county. With rare exceptions, anything east and south of the line is of only marginal value to the serious deer hunter, due to the dramatic decrease in deer numbers. That area which lies north and west of the line ranges from marginal to very good.

Woodstock, Cambridge and Rollin townships have the most potential—although only for local hunters. There's little state land offering the deer hunter anything of significance, and although there are six hundred acres in the county enrolled in the hunter access program, almost all of this is located in the poorer areas. Much of the better private land is also heavily posted.

Medina, Dover, Madison, Raisin and Macon townships are only marginal at best, while Rome, Adrian and Franklin are fair for the local hunter. The problem in these areas is a lack of adequate habitat. The entire county contains very mature stands of mast-bearing hardwoods, in forty- to eighty-acre woodlots. The townships in the south and the east literally have no other cover to offer. Cover throughout the northwest corner varies from marginally adequate to very good. For nonlandowners, access is going to be very difficult to obtain anywhere in the county.

The Lake Hudson Recreation Area contains 2,600 of the 3,100 acres of state lands found in the county. If managed properly, this area holds substantial promise for the future, but presently the cover is sparse throughout much of the area. It's going to take another ten to fifteen years before this area attains its optimum potential in terms of habitat.

Oakland County

Oakland County may well represent the worst case of urban sprawl in any county in Michigan. With the possible exception of some very limited opportunity in Lyon Township in the extreme southwest corner, the entire southern half of the county is off limits to all. There's simply too much congestion to safely hunt within most of this area, and there are local ordinances prohibiting it in the others.

The northern half of the county, though still congested, does offer some limited opportunity in townships such as Springfield, Oakland, Highland and Rose. The best areas overall, though still only fair, are in the northern tier of townships: Holly, Groveland, Brandon, Oxford and Addison. There are roughly nine thousand acres of state lands in this area. So there is some chance for nonlocals, although realistically they are slim.

Washtenaw County

Overall, this is a very good-looking county for local hunters. With the exception of Augusta Township in the extreme southeast corner, and some leveling out in the northern portion of Lima Township, as well as Scio Township, the county is heavily contoured. The hills and dales, thus created, lend themselves to a lot of pocket cover, that is, small dense areas providing perfect whitetail habitat.

The county has excellent stands of mast-bearing hardwoods, and most of the county has a good mix of thickets, overgrown fields and swales mixed in as well. The only exceptions are a few scattered areas along the southern boundary areas, such as southwestern Augusta Township and a few scattered areas along Willow Road in Saline and Bridgewater townships. The whole southern tier of townships is just marginal even for local hunters. There are few deer and little habitat. This area is more intensely cultivated than the rest of the county, and all the pocket cover has been cleared.

The remainder of the county, with the obvious exception of those areas immediately adjacent to Ann Arbor and Ypsilanti, has excellent possibilities for local hunters.

I won't recommend any of the county as being good for nonlocals. However, in some areas of Webster, Dexter, Sylvan and

Sharon townships there is so much good cover that a nonlocal who diligently gains access rights should do all right. The state land—Pinckney and Waterloo recreation areas—are very heavily hunted, with as many as one hunter per ten acres on opening day of our gun season. Personally, I wouldn't hunt here and I won't recommend it, although deer are taken in these areas. Very little land in Washtenaw County is enrolled in the hunter access program or in CFA lands.

St. Clair County

Spread out near the northeast corner of St. Clair County is the Port Huron State Game Area. There are roughly five thousand acres of land here, contained in a dozen different chunks. This land is generally quite flat, except right near the Black River; much of it is covered with fifty-year-old hardwoods. There's generally a good mast crop in the area.

Although no southern Michigan lands are managed by the state specifically for deer and deer hunting, these lands are actively managed for hunting, and the results favor deer as well as other targeted game and nongame species. There are strip plantings of corn, sorghum, and barley, as well as dense rows of olive and multiflora rose. As on many other state lands in southern Michigan, there is also some share-cropping done between the state and local farmers. In share-cropping, the farmer farms the state's land, harvests three-fourths of his crop and leaves one-fourth of it untouched for the benefit of wildlife.

The state lands offer nonlocals an excellent opportunity, but your scouting efforts must be preseason for the best results. Be forewarned that hunting pressure is intense. This is particularly true the first couple days of the gun season, on weekends and over Thanksgiving. Bowhunters may well have the best opportunity on state lands in this area.

I've been impressed with many of the private lands surrounding these state lands, particularly with those south of it. The Kimball, Wales and Smiths Creek areas have a large percentage of abandoned farmlands. This countryside has a lot of twenty-year growths of hardwoods and plenty of brushy fields. These areas offer the hunter excellent opportunities, and the deer herd is up. Keep in mind it's private land and permission is mandatory. For the nimrod on opening morning, permission is going to be a real problem, but a lot of this land is available if the hunter is courteous enough to call well in advance of the season, and if he makes a good appearance. There are five thousand acres of hunter access lands in the county.

Both throughout the state land, and the rest of St. Clair County as a whole, water can be a problem. The Black River flows through the very heart of the state game area, and it simply prevents movement. The hunter desiring to go from one side to the other must search out a bridge; it is not possible to wade across at any point. Most of the other waterways do offer crossing points, but the hunter would be well advised to wear knee-high rubber boots or even hip boots.

A great deal of St. Clair County offers excellent hunting for local hunters. I particularly like the northern and southern townships. For nonlocals, I like Emmett, St. Clair, Kimball and Wale townships.

Lapeer County

With only a couple very minor exceptions, Lapeer County offers solid deer hunting opportunities for local hunters. Deer numbers increase dramatically as you move north through the county. In terms of nonlocal hunters, the southern portion of the county is so chopped up (ten- to twenty-acre parcels) that, for the most part, access is almost impossible.

The northern portion of the county is a different story altogether. There are over 7,000 acres in the Lapeer State Game Area, as well as 2,850 acres of farmlands enrolled in the access program, mostly in the northern tier of townships, giving the nonlocal ample land access. The deer population, while not as high as in some of the other Thumb counties, is nonetheless substantial.

Lapeer County is a rural county with a considerable amount of agriculture. Hardwoods are widespread throughout, as well as crop fields, swales, thickets, and some abandoned farmlands. The southern tier of townships, along the west of the county, consists of some of the hilliest, most contoured lands in the Thumb. This area offers the hunter some really scenic and exciting hunting opportunities, and at the same time gives the deer plenty of cover.

Townships of particular interest to the nonlocal hunter are Rich, Burlington, Marathon, Deerfield, North Branch, Burnside, Mayfield, Arcadia and Goodland. Again, provided he's going to put the work required into scouting, the local hunter could successfully hunt anywhere in the county.

Shiawassee County

This is an agriculturally based county containing, overall, a good mix of crop fields and cover. The southern half of the county has a lot of contour to it. Its gently rolling ground forms little pockets of cover and a wide variety of habitat types. There are plenty of brush, cover fields, mast-bearing hardwoods, brushy draws and swales all interspersed with moderate-to-small crop fields. This entire area offers the local hunter excellent opportunity.

The northern half of Shiawassee County is flat. Its crop fields are considerably larger, and the amount of cover is far less, although generally adequate. That area in the northern townships of Rush, Owosso, New Haven, Caledonia, Hazelton and Venice will still offer local hunters sufficient areas in which to hunt, but it's the poorest area of the county. Most of the cover consists of hardwood woodlots. There are no cedars, and very few evergreens anywhere in the entire county.

With the possible exception of the Rose Lake Wildlife Experimental Station and some of the lands immediately adjacent to it, I cannot honestly recommend anything in Shiawassee County to the nonlocal hunter. Rose Lake allows deer hunting but, due to the various experiments that they conduct there, this situation should be checked year to year. At any rate, the amount of acreage is small, roughly eight hundred acres, and is heavily hunted. The area of Rose Lake and its adjacent lands looks more like northern Michigan than the rest of the county. There is very little land in Shiawassee enrolled in the hunter access program, and that is scattered throughout the county.

Genesee County

As I mentioned in the introduction to this section, much of Genesee County is consumed by the city of Flint and its burgeoning population. What's left of the county is a hodgepodge of blocky cover and open agricultural lands.

There are deer in Genesee County to be sure, and local hunters in those townships, along the county's northern tier, should be able to do quite well. I like Montrose, Vienna and Forest townships for the local hunter, and I would also include Forest and Thetford townships for nonlocals since some 1,500 acres of this land are in the hunter access program.

Some of this land is contoured with good stands of hardwoods and plenty of thick patches of cover. The soil is sandy and the water table is high, offering a good amount of marsh, bog and cattail cover as well. Every year a couple of real wallhangers are taken out of Genesee County, but it requires a lot of preseason scouting and a healthy dose of luck—or both.

For the remainder of the county, I have doubts how effective even a local hunter can be. Areas like Fenton Township or Argentine Township probably see deer die of old age simply because they're able to slip around protected by the smaller chunks of private lands.

Macomb County

Macomb County, along with Oakland County (and others), is one of those areas that is a puzzle to our DNR biologists. There's good habitat, capable of carrying many more deer than are currently present, and although some of the population data indicates the herd is growing, it is not increasing at anywhere near the rate of surrounding areas.

It appears to me that deer in this area are highly stressed, perhaps by heightened and intolerable levels of human intrusion, by free-roving dogs, and by poachers. They are stressed to the point that infertility and stillborn fawns are too often the norm. While I was scouting the area, I was absolutely amazed at the number of dog tracks—everywhere. The DNR also feels strongly that many more deer are taken illegally by poachers in areas such as Macomb County than taken by hunters.

The very best area of the county is the extreme northwest corner, with Bruce, Armada and the western half of Washington townships being the local hunter's best bets. Richmond, eastern Washington, Ray and Lenox townships are all marginal at best. These areas are marginal, not due to a lack of habitat, but rather a lack of deer. Because of this, it's conceivable these areas could improve somewhat in the future.

Monroe County

While a few deer are taken each year in Monroe, the county as a whole offers very little to the average local hunter. The county is intensely cultivated and rural in its population distribution, with the extreme southern townships serving as high-density outskirts of Toledo and Monroe. The land is flat and the habitat, in whitetail terms, ranges from nil to bare minimum.

The few harvested deer are in the extreme northwestern townships. Of interest to me was the location of three separate areas in which there was much improved habitat: the eastern half of Summerfield Township, the central to western portion of London Township, and the north-central to northeastern portion of Exeter Township. These three separate areas have adequate habitat, and could hold more deer in the future. At this time, however, they are only marginal.

Wayne County

While there are some deer in Wayne County and a few are taken each year, particularly in Sumpter Township, I cannot in good faith recommend any of the county as offering the serious deer hunter any realistic possibilities.

14

Southwestern Michigan

The state lands of southwestern Michigan (as is true of our state lands throughout all of southern Michigan) are heavily hunted, as are scattered areas of private holdings as well in Montcalm, Kent, Eaton, Allegan, Barry, Ionia and Calhoun counties. Nonetheless, this region offers excellent hunting with tremendous trophy-hunting potential in most areas. It's of interest to note that the top six producing counties (Montcalm, Barry, Eaton, Calhoun, Ionia and Kent) account for almost 65 percent of the bucks taken here.

While the herd structure will vary slightly in specific areas (fewer legally antlered animals in the most heavily hunted areas, with slightly more in less-hunted regions) generally speaking, southwestern Michigan's prehunt composition runs 15–45–40. That is, fifteen bucks, forty-five does and forty fawns for each hundred animals. This is a better buck-to-doe ratio than anywhere else in the Lower Peninsula and the DNR is working diligently to keep it that way. The thrust throughout this region is to maintain the herds at roughly their present numbers, with some minor adjustments required by specific circumstances.

Map 14.1
Southwestern Michigan

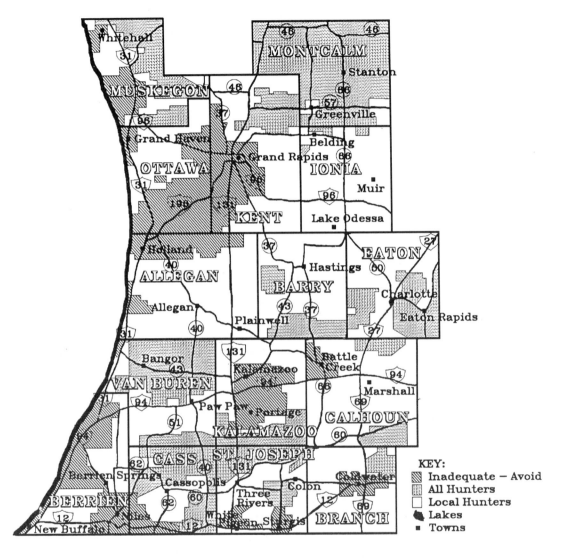

Many specialty crops are grown in this area—asparagus, celery, blueberries, orchards, and ornamental trees and shrubs—which makes the control of crop damage a particularly vexing problem, but one that remains tolerable at current levels. In the southeast and the southwest the herd has exploded within the past twenty to twenty-five years. Deer densities currently run from a low of five to eight animals per square mile in places like western Berrien County to as high as sixty per square mile in areas like western Calhoun County. While still requiring preseason effort, access is usually more easily attained throughout the southwest than it is in the more densely populated and developed southeast.

Following is a brief description of the counties in the southwestern region and the most promising areas in each.

Montcalm County

This county, with a solid agricultural base, is largely rural in nature, especially in the north. In fact, the extreme northwest corner of the county has a pronounced northern Michigan flavor. Cultivated lands are about 50 percent, but in areas such as the extreme southeast corner, cultivation climbs to about 80 percent. Throughout, there is a good mix of brushy fencerows and scattered woodlots. The woodlots are generally hardwoods in the south, but they gradually change to softer woods as you move north. In the extreme west-central area some pines are thrown in.

Habitat throughout the county runs hot and cold. Some areas have a lot of brush and much heavier woodlots that are larger and more interconnected than elsewhere. For nonlocal hunters, as well as locals who do not care for driving deer, I'd try these areas, especially after the first few days of the season. Traditionally, the other areas are heavily driven.

Most of the county is suitable for nonlocal hunters, but your best choices will be Crystal, Evergreen, Pierson, Richland, Home, Winfield, Fair Plain, Eureka and Reynolds townships. There are fewer than 1,400 acres of hunter access lands, and fewer than 200 acres of CFA land, widely spread throughout the county.

For local hunters, most of the county is excellent. Nonetheless, I particularly like Crystal, Evergreen, Bushnell, Bloomer, Fair Plain, Eureka, Ferris, Maple Valley, Pierson, Pine, Richland, Home, Cato, Winfield and Reynolds townships.

Barry County

Resident hunters in the southern sections of Barry County must look forward to the deer seasons with great expectations, and well they should. Deer populations are very good and the habitat is exciting. This land has a lot of contour and is covered by a solid mix of habitat: plenty of hardwoods, lots of brushy draws, heavyset fencerows, cattail and other swales, and plenty of thick waterways.

As you move north, especially along the sides of the county, the quality of the habitat diminishes, as do the number of deer. Despite this, the north-central area between Freeport and M-37 remains very good. Agriculture markedly intensifies and deer numbers plummet in places like Coats Grove, where as much as 95 percent of the land is tilled. The habitat in the northern tier of townships consists of mature oak-dominated woodlots. There's no brush, and no winter cover; improvement is found only within a few miles of the northern county boundary. Archers do well in this area, especially in years of a heavy mast crop, with deer densities

Author with Fallen Buck. Trophy hunting potential is excellent throughout most areas of southwestern Michigan—particularly in those areas with the fewest hunters, and the most limited access.

between twenty and twenty-five per square mile.

For local hunters, I particularly like Assyria, Johnstown, Barry, Maple Grove, Baltimore, Hope and Rutland townships. For nonlocals, I like southern Assyria, Johnstown and Barry townships. There are 4,700 acres of hunter access lands and 300 acres of CFA lands widely spread throughout the county. There remains good-to-excellent cover and good numbers of deer up into Baltimore and Hope townships, but many of the better lands here are heavily posted—the nonlocal hunter would have to work hard to gain access. Deer numbers in Rutland Township, although the cover is good, slip to about twenty animals per square mile while those areas to the south average roughly thirty.

Eaton County

Why do so many of us love this animal—the whitetail? Doing the research necessary for the first edition of this book, there were many times I became very discouraged. I found myself locked in my truck, miles from home, for endless days with no distractions except the land—it was very tedious and lonely. The day (Easter Sunday of 1988) I finished Eaton County began with that frame of mind. I headed north out of Battle Creek on I-69 at daybreak. When I entered Eaton County, I exited at Olivet and turned west, heading toward Bellevue. I hadn't gone a mile when a group of five deer crossed the road just yards in front of me, flags all aflyin'. That seemingly insignificant event changed my mindset. The rest of the day was pure pleasure—such is the power of the whitetail over me. I hope they affect you in the same way!

Eaton County offers the local resident good hunting potential. It's an agriculturally based area, with fairly low human populations. There are areas, such as Walton, Carmel, Chester and Roxand townships, where the amount of land under cultivation is so high that cover is scant, but such areas are spotty and not extensive. The rest of the county is a very solid mix of woodlots, thick fencerows, brushy fields and thickets. The local resident should have little problem finding good deer hunting. I particularly like Bellevue, Kalamo, Vermontville, Benton, Windsor, Eaton, Eaton Rapids, Hamlin and Brookfield townships.

This is a tough county for the nonlocal, since a moderately high percentage of the very best lands is posted, and the cover is spotty—especially true in the northern half of the county. Your best bet is to get out well in advance of the season and make prior arrangements. There are only 1,700 acres of hunter access lands as well. Bowhunters will have much better success in gaining access than will gun hunters. For the nonlocal, I think the following townships and isolated areas have the most promise: Bellevue, Kalamo, Hamlin and Eaton townships. I'd also try some of the river drainages such as Thornapple and Little Thornapple, both in the northwest.

Calhoun County

Calhoun, overall, offers the local hunter excellent opportunity. The land varies from sharply contoured in the extreme northwest, to gently rolling flats in the county's center. Calhoun, in general, is an agriculturally based area, but it's more rural than cultivated in the northwest. The extreme northwest corner is really exciting for the local resident. Its sharp hills are topped with hardwoods and its hollows have a mixture of tamaracks, cattails, water, and dense thickets. Nonlocals be forewarned—this area is congested and heavily posted—you will not be welcomed here with open arms.

The area east of here is perfect for the nonlocal. A solid mix of crop fields, cover fields, plenty of brush and thickets, heavy fencerows, and beautiful hardwood woodlots. Areas like this assure plenty of whitetails in southern Michigan for years to come. The habitat in the southeast corner of the county is similar except it has less contour.

For the local hunter, a great deal of the county has a lot to offer, but I particularly like Sheridan, Convis, Lee, Clarence, Homer, Clarendon, and Athens townships, as well as the northern portion of Bedford, and the area in Leroy Township near East Leroy.

For the nonlocal I like Lee and Clarendon townships, as well as the western section of Homer and the eastern portion of Convis townships. There are only 1,400 acres of hunter access lands in the county.

Ionia County

A clear reciprocal relationship exists between the numbers of deer and the amount of agriculture. In the south, 80 percent to 95 percent of the land is under tillage. As you move north the percentage decreases and the number of deer increases. The habitat has good cover, being mostly hardwoods in the form of scattered woodlots, brushy fencerows and thickly covered flood plains. The hunting from I-96 south is only marginal at best, however, due to intense cultivation.

Between highways 96 and 21, both running east-west, there is a general improvement in the habitat; there's simply more of it and hence more deer as a result. The best area lies between and just south of Ionia and Lyons. From Highway 21 north, there is a marked increase in deer numbers and a decrease in the percentage of lands under cultivation. Scattered, isolated hardwood woodlots generally hold more brush than those farther south. This is an excellent area for the local hunter. In particular I like North Plains, Keene, Ionia, Ronald and Orleans townships.

Overall there is not much for nonlocal hunters, since many of the best parcels in this area are heavily posted. There are, however, a few scattered pockets that do hold promise and 2,600 acres in the hunter access program. I especially like western Keene Township, the area surrounding the Flat River State Game Area, and northern Ronald Township.

Kent County

Kent County, in large measure, is dominated by its high human population as well as by intense agriculture, with both orchards and grain crops. The greater Grand Rapids area is

Doe in Orchard. Mild winters and energy-rich crops mean that southern Michigan's deer herd is controlled more by political considerations—how many traffic/deer accidents are tolerated, how much crop damage can our farmers absorb, how many deer we want to see—than by the habitat's carrying capacity.

heavily developed with both industrial and residential areas. Along with this development is an intense orchard industry. This all leads to a lack of hunting opportunity throughout much of the southwest quadrant. The remainder of the county is spotty, both in terms of its habitat and deer population.

The northern and southern tiers of townships are particularly spotty. Hunters working these areas will have to be highly selective, especially in the later seasons once crops are in. I'd pay particular attention to the various watercourses here, hunting the brushy corridors that they form. Stick close to the heaviest brush in other areas as well. Deer numbers will run roughly twenty-five to thirty per square mile, but only in those areas with the best habitat.

There is a marked improvement in the quality of the cover beginning just north of Rockford and spreading to the south and east. Nonlocal hunters will fare best in Grattan, Solon, Spencer, Tyrone, Algora, Courtland and Oakfield townships. There are almost 5,600 acres in the access program, and roughly 500 acres of CFA lands in the county, with the bulk of them being in these townships. For local hunters I like the following: Courtland, Plainfield, Oakfield, Grattan, Cannon and Vergennes townships.

Allegan County

Allegan County does not offer the serious whitetailer much to get excited about. Intensely cultivated almost throughout, the major problem is a complete lack of cover. This problem is so pervasive that even within those isolated locations where there is some cover, deer numbers remain low.

There's no hunting to speak of in the extreme north, as more than 95 percent of these lands is under tillage. Just south of this area is a subtle decrease in cultivated lands, but the hunting is at best for locals only. This paucity of cover continues south, especially on the east side of the county. The only areas that show any promise are the southern halves of Lee and Cheshire townships. Despite a marked decrease in the percentage of cultivated lands, deer numbers in the southern portion of the county are still low.

That area surrounding the Allegan State Game Area is somewhat more promising than the rest of the county, but deer numbers remain low. Although there's little here to excite the nonlocal hunter, there are 1,600 acres of hunter access lands, and 650 acres of CFA lands in Allegan County. Bear in mind, however, that the area is heavily hunted.

Autumn Buck. Rut-crazed and unafraid (note the swollen neck), the mature autumn buck is master of his domain.

Branch County

An intensely cultivated area, Branch also has a great deal of livestock. The amount of land under cultivation ranges from roughly 60 percent to 70 percent in the northeast to as much as 90 percent in the central portion. The quality of hunting is obviously affected. Overall, the county is slightly to moderately contoured and, with the exception of the M-12 corridor between Quincy and Coldwater, the entire county is agriculturally based.

Existing cover consists of small blocks of mostly hardwoods and swales of various mixes. A lot of brush, overgrown fencerows and thickets contribute to plentiful browse in the extreme northeast corner. This is also true in the northwest corner of the county, only not as great. The remainder of the county shows a clear lack of adequate habitat except over small areas. Deer numbers reflect this also. My advice to nonlocal hunters is to concentrate on the low-lying areas immediately adjacent to the various rivers, creeks and drainages. Try making landowner contacts well in advance of the season. There are over seven thousand acres of hunter access lands here.

Local hunters do all right throughout most of the county with the exception of the area from Matteson along Highway 86 east to Coldwater and then to Quincy on Highway 12. This area is simply too populated and devoid of cover. Areas with the most promise for local hunters include Bronson, Bethel, Ovid, Butler, Girard, Union, Sherwood, Gilead and Noble townships.

Most discouraging, from a deer hunter's perspective, is that despite the intense cultivation that now exists in Branch County, there is still even more land being cleared and cultivated. This does not bode well for the future. Another hindrance to the herd here is an alleged severe poaching problem. Several locals indicated that a serious problem exists, and the DNR seems to agree.

Kalamazoo County

A mixed bag! Better in the south, problematic in the north, particularly the northeast quadrant. The southern third of the county is heavily cultivated, running at about 50 percent to 60 percent in most areas with some as high as 90 percent. Between the cultivated fields is an excellent mix of both mast-bearing hardwood lots as well as scruffy, softer hardwoods. There's also a significant amount of brush in this area, as well as a lot of swales, heavy fencerows and brushy, weed-choked watercourses. If I lived here, I'd figure out ways to employ both hip boots and canoe to hunt these waterways, but keep in mind you'll need permission of the adjacent landowners. Nonlocals could do this also but it would require a lot of intense preseason work.

A huge area extends outward from Kalamazoo that, while hunted, has to be considered very weak. It's heavily populated, with lots of subdivisions and other developments around the many small lakes. Within this area lies the Gourdneck State Game Area. This place would get my vote for being the most unusual state game area anywhere in Michigan. Not once did I see a game area sign (vandals keep ripping them down!). Even with signs, trying to figure out what was public and what was private would be a nightmare; such is the chopped-up nature of the area. On top of that, much of it lies within the marked city limits of Portage—filled with homes. Perhaps local archers, intimately familiar with the area, could do all right here, but I certainly couldn't recommend it to anyone else.

The northernmost tier of townships is a strange lot as well. Your best bet is the northwest corner. This land is mostly dominated by oak, with some brush, and intermixed with numerous openings. It is heavily contoured, lending itself to lots of cover. The problem, however, is too many people. The northeast quadrant is even worse with several major landowners in the area having heavily posted lands. This is the home of the Kellogg Bird Sanctuary, for example, as well as MSU's Biological Station, an Audubon Sanctuary, and others. There are undoubtedly a few locals who have sufficient access rights to be successful but they must be a minority.

Muskegon County

A rural, essentially nonagricultural county with a sparse human population except for the Muskegon Heights–Muskegon–Whitehall complex on the extreme west side. There's a moderate amount of farming done in the south just west of Ravenna, and a lesser amount done in the extreme northwest and extreme northeast. If I were a local hunter, I'd concentrate on these areas.

Muskegon County more closely approximates northern than southern Michigan. There's some bracken fern with an awful lot of oak and scattered pockets of pines. The big problem, especially in the northern half of the county, is lack of browse. I'd concentrate on the brushy spots, lowland areas, and whatever tangles of cover I could locate in this area. For example, along River Road the high bank falls away to the river. If I hunted this area, the opposite side of the river would be mine. Hip boots, waders, or canoe—whatever it took—I'd get to the lowlands on the opposite side. I would avoid those large, flat expanses of oaks and I'd concentrate on the thickest cover I could find. In so doing, you'll avoid at least 90 percent of the other hunters and you'll then have them pushing deer to you.

For local hunters, I especially like Ravenna, Fruitport, Sullivan, Dalton and Holton townships. For nonlocals, the only one I really like is Dalton Township. The other areas require a lot of creative hunting to have them pay off for you.

Ottawa County

Conducting the research for this section was an eye-opening experience. I've lived, traveled, hunted and fished all of my adult life in Michigan. I thought I knew our state well and I had some preconceived notions about what I'd find in any particular county at the onset. Many counties surprised me, but none more than Kent and Ottawa counties.

For some reason I thought that these two areas had excellent deer hunting opportunities, but for the most part I was wrong, especially in regard to Ottawa County. Due to the extreme lack of cover (heavy cultivation) throughout much of Ottawa County, there is little hunting, even for the local nimrods. Deer populations are generally low. I'd strongly recommend that nonlocals avoid these areas—both Kent and Ottawa counties—as there are simply too many good areas nearby.

For the local hunter, Chester Township is probably your best bet, with Crockery Township next and then the northern half of Polkton.

Cass County

Cass is a continuation of the same habitat as that present in St. Joseph County to the east. The land ranges from slightly to very hilly. The most rugged expanse is around the Crane Pond State Game Area; you'd better have good lungs and legs if you plan to hunt here.

Overall there's marginally less intense cultivation in Cass County than St. Joseph County. Some places the habitat actually falters badly due to the amount of tillage (as high as 90 percent). The central and the southwest portions of the county are the most affected. In the southwest, there's a human population problem as well, as Niles sprawls eastward just north of the Indiana border.

Taken as a whole, the best habitat runs along the eastern quarter of the county. For nonlocal hunters, I especially like Marcellus, Newberg and Porter townships, although Volinia, Wayne and the northern half of Penn are good also. All of the county's 1,400 acres of access lands are located within these townships. For local hunters, I like those townships already mentioned plus Lagrange, Pokagon and Calvin. The other townships in the county will prove to be inadequate or very spotty, with a lot of preseason work required for them to produce.

Berrien County

Although Berrien's deer herd has increased quite dramatically in the past five years, the numbers were so low initially that even now they're still very low. Overall, the county has little to offer its deer hunters. Either due to intense development and settlement, as along the Lake Michigan shoreline, or due to the intense planting of orchards and vineyards throughout the central portion, there's little habitat available to support deer.

The best areas are found in the extreme south, just above the state line, and on the extreme east side, north of Berrien Springs. The better townships are Galien, Three Oaks, New Buffalo, Berrien and Pipestone. I really can't recommend the area at all for nonlocals, but if you're in a pinch for a place to go, try New Buffalo or Pipestone. These two areas will offer you your best bet.

Van Buren County

Van Buren County is the capital of our wine industry and as such the southern portion of the county—that area south of I-94—is a solid mix of vineyards, orchards and grain fields, all nicely interspersed with hardwood woodlots, brushy draws and thicket fencerows. Throughout this area the better habitat is spotty, however, and some areas have plenty of cover; these are the places to concentrate your hunting. Very little of this land is posted, but deer numbers are quite low throughout.

From I-94 north, you enter a different world—the world of the blueberry bog. There's a dramatic increase in the amount of brush and thicker cover, with a lot of reclaimed or marginal farmland. There's a tremendous decrease in the amount of land under cultivation. Deer numbers are moderately higher throughout this region. Nonlocal hunters will fare best in Geneva, Columbia, Bloomingdale, Pine Grove, and northern Bangor townships in the south. Somewhat less than half of the county's 1,500 acres of hunter access lands, and 900 acres of CFA lands, are located in these townships.

Local hunters will do well in all those areas plus Almena, Waverly, Arlington, South Haven and Covert townships in the north, and Keeler and Hamilton townships in the south.

St. Joseph County

St. Joseph County is an intensely farmed county with grains and hogs the major products. It's highly cultivated throughout, but particularly so in the southern, flatter sections of the county. Those areas most highly contoured offer the deer hunter the greater promise. These areas are invariably covered with plenty of mast-bearing hardwoods and they have plenty of brush, swales, thickets and heavy fencerows as well.

Across the northern tier of townships there is somewhat less farming than elsewhere; the deer populations are good and there's a very solid mix to the habitat. For the nonlocal hunter I particularly like Flowerfield and Leonidas townships, although Park and Mendon townships are good bets as well. The east-central portion of the county around Perrin is a nice area, with again, a lot of cover and contour.

An excellent hunting approach in this area would be to sit or still hunt early and late and to conduct small, two- or three-man drives throughout the rest of the day. This would be especially productive after the first couple days of the season.

Local hunters have most of the county in which to hunt with good prospects for success, but I particularly like Fawn River, Colon, Fabius, Flowerfield, Leonidas, Mendon and Park townships.

15

Northeastern Michigan

Our northeastern Lower Peninsula counties have the distinction of supporting many of Michigan's most heavily hunted lands. These are the traditional counties that Michigan hunters hunt when they "head north." Clare, Gladwin, Alcona, Ogemaw, Roscommon, Oscoda, Montmorency and Midland counties shoulder the bulk of this deer hunting burden. Although hunting pressure has been reduced throughout the region in the past few years, these nine counties still bear more than 65 percent of the deer hunting pressure that is exerted throughout the seventeen counties comprising the northeastern Lower. Deer hunter densities on opening day of the gun season on some state lands in these counties are as high as fifty hunters per square mile. Throughout the area, hunter densities on public lands average twenty to thirty per square mile. The public lands of Clare, Gladwin and Roscommon counties are the most heavily hunted of the lot. Normally 80 percent to 85 percent of the buck kill in these counties is composed of year-and-a-half-old animals. But because of a very significant fawn crop loss in 1992, in '93 only 50 percent of these animals were yearlings. Spike horns

Map 15.1
Northeastern Michigan

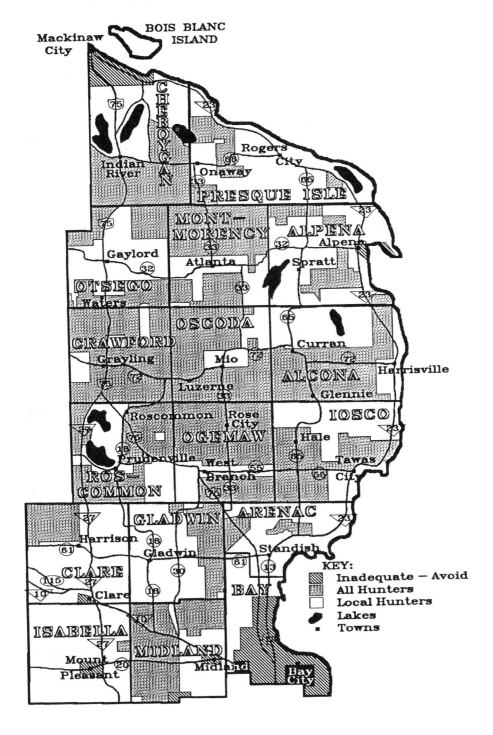

or small four-points comprise the bulk of the kill. Trophy-hunting potential, overall, is very poor (see Chapter 3). Nonetheless, hunters here hold their own as hunter success rates run from a low of 10 percent in Crawford County to a high of 25 percent in Alpena County (statewide average in Michigan is roughly 17 percent).

It is in the northeastern Lower that the lion's share of Michigan's deer hunting clubs are located. The counties of Alpena, Oscoda, Montmorency, Presque Isle and Cheboygan epitomize Michigan's "Club Country." An increasing trend in Michigan is the leasing of private hunting lands. While its introduction in the northeastern Lower counties is fairly recent, it has been a common practice in the southeastern United States for many years. Whether we like it or not, the leasing of prime hunting land is clearly the direction of the future. Clare, Gladwin, Arenac and Isabella counties probably head the list of Michigan counties for acreage under lease rights at this time, but this is something that will spread throughout all of the Lower Peninsula in the next few years. Leased lands currently run the gamut from a low of a dollar or two per acre each year to as much as ten dollars per acre, for really prime hunting lands. Currently, the average cost is somewhere in the vicinity of three dollars per acre.

Following is a brief description of the northeastern counties and their better hunting areas.

Clare County

An excellent area on the whole, Clare County is one of the most heavily hunted counties in all of Michigan. Deer numbers range from good to excellent and they are high throughout the entire county. Two separate and distinctive areas divided by M-61 characterize the habitat in the county. South of M-61 is an intensely cultivated area where most of the residents live year-round. Close to 90 percent of the farmlands and livestock in the country are found in this area. North of M-61 is mostly rural with a few scattered pockets of agriculture, most of it located in the extreme

Deer in Winter. Currently there's sufficient thermal cover in the northeastern Lower to carry the bulk of our herds, but what about in the future? The prospect is not good when we look twenty to thirty years down the road. Now is the time to act, so we don't have to react to a future crisis.

northwest corner of the county in Winterfield Township.

Nonlocal hunters can simply forget about any other than the public lands in Clare County; access is out of the question on private lands throughout. There are only 560 acres of CFA lands in the county but these warrant investigation. For the local hunters though, the southern half of the county is an outstanding area, especially Garfield, Freeman, Hatton and Arthur townships. Deer numbers are excellent in these areas, running from twenty-five to thirty-five per square mile. In the northern half of the county, I particularly like Winterfield, Frost, Franklin and Hamilton townships. Deer numbers are also excellent here and the habitat is generally beautiful. The dominant tree species here is the poplar, but most often associated with the agricultural lands in the middle of the county. There is also a good number of mast-bearing hardwoods. With very few native pines, there is planted pine, especially in the northern sections. Cedars can be found in scattered pockets but are not numerous. There's lots of brush, both naturally occurring (in the lower elevation areas), and that which is commonly found on abandoned farmland.

Gladwin County

Nonlocal hunters flood the state lands in Gladwin County (as high as fifty hunters per square mile), as they find it virtually impossible to gain access on private lands. Deer numbers are excellent—thirty to forty per square mile—in the southern half of the county, but fall markedly (fifteen to twenty) in the northern half.

In the south, the habitat is predominantly mixed poplar, tag alder and willow. There's a small percentage of scrub oak thrown in as well. The northern half of the county shows some pure stands of mast-bearing hardwoods, principally surrounding the farmlands. There's no cedar and very few pines in the south with more pines and some cedar found in the north, particularly in the northwest. The habitat is far superior in the southern half of the county; in the north, it is too mature and sparse in most areas, due largely to widespread cultivation.

Livestock, intense cultivation, and the degree of development make most of Butman, the eastern half of Sherman, and most of northern Gladwin townships the least attractive areas of the county. Deer numbers and habitat improve markedly, however, in the southern half of Gladwin Township.

Hunters should fare best in Beaverton, Bentley, Grout, Tobacco, Billings and Grim townships, as well as in the southern half of Gladwin Township.

Alpena County

The county is predominately covered by forests, with a good mixture of northern hardwoods (which are too mature in many places), softer hardwoods and conifers. There's ample thermal cover, but as is the case throughout practically all of northern Michigan, it is too mature to be optimum. There is an adequate number of openings here as well. Small-scale haying operations are found throughout much of the county. Two areas with more intense agriculture can be found around the M-32 and M-65 intersection and in the south-central townships of Ossineke and western Sanborn. Most of what is grown here are high-energy grains.

Good numbers of deer exist throughout, but the highest concentrations are found in the western half of the county. Local hunters throughout Wellington, Green, Long Rapids, Maple Ridge, Ossineke, and western Sanborn townships will have the best hunting.

There are plenty of deer for the nonlocal hunter on the extensive state lands (roughly 8 percent of the county), especially those on the west side, but there's also some opportunity for access to private areas if you work hard at it. Such efforts would be well worth your while as state lands are very heavily hunted. Stay away from the southwest quadrant in particular as there are numerous hunt clubs throughout this region. Access, of course, is out of the question. Be advised, as well, that the state lands are not found in contiguous blocks; you must be aware of the boundary lines in most areas or you'll quickly find yourself in trespassing difficulties.

Presque Isle County

The most exciting townships in Presque Isle County are Ocqueoc, Moltke, Case, Bismarck, Belknap, Metz, Posen and Krakow. That's the good news. The bad news is that unless you're a local landowner, or hunt on one of the many private clubs within this area, you're out of luck.

The areas I mentioned are very good, with excellent habitat over much of the area and good deer numbers, although down considerably (as much as 40 percent) from their peak of 1989–90. The cover throughout more than half of this region occurs in small chunks, interspersed with crop fields and pastures. The rest lies in larger masses of unbroken woods, swales, thickets and marshes—this is particularly true in Bismarck Township. Throughout the entire area there's plenty of mix to the cover with scattered stands of mast-bearing hardwoods, poplar and birch, plenty of pines and cedars, and lots of brush, especially willows. There are numerous clear cuts and plenty of areas within the various club properties where heavy selective thinning is being intelligently practiced. This produces a lot of browse and excellent cover.

Since nonlocals are going to be confined essentially to the state lands, be advised that they're very fragmented. Early in the season, hunt the periphery of the state lands bordering the areas I mentioned. As the season advances, then hunt farther into the dense areas and the interior of the state lands.

Some of the habitat, particularly in the western half of the county, is much too mature in places. In some areas it's downright monotonous, such as the jack-pine stands in the extreme southwest, but overall it's quite good. Deer numbers are spotty, but again they're quite high overall.

Alcona County

Cover runs both good and bad throughout this area. Alcona County is primarily forested around the edges and hardwood stands dominate. The very best habitat is found on the actively managed deer hunting club properties in the northwest corner. This is where the highest number of deer are found as well, with some areas running as high as forty animals per square mile. The best cover is found in the various corners of the county—the northwest, northeast, southeast and southwest. Throughout most of the private land, the dominant trees are hardwoods and they're badly in need of logging. Deer numbers generally reflect this need.

The Huron National Forest area in the southwest is a bit too mature overall, but it's not too bad. There's a good mixture of tree species here and somewhere between 7 percent and 10 percent have recently been logged. There's a pretty good age mix to the cover throughout this area as well. Deer numbers run between thirty and forty-five per square mile.

Agriculture is found in scattered pockets throughout the private lands. The southwest quadrant has some cattle and sheep operations, but the only place there's any intense agriculture is in the southeast. As a result, the area north of Mikado and south of M-72 is so devoid of significant habitat, it's only of marginal value even to local hunters once the crops are in. Many other areas of private lands are heavily posted. This is particularly true in the area south and east of Hubbard Lake (it is interesting that this is chiefly private hunting land, and it is some of the most poorly managed land in the entire county), and the area south and west of Mikado. In a lot of other areas, hunters scouting early and politely asking permission will be able to gain access onto some of the private lands.

Wherever you hunt, avoid the solid stands of hardwoods and concentrate on the mixed timber, the younger growth stuff, and the flood plains along the many watercourses.

Ogemaw County

A rural, heavily forested county in most areas, there's some agricultural activity and livestock with two core areas: along the M-55 corridor east of West Branch over to the Iosco County line, and the area south of Rose City and north of Campbell's corners.

Roughly one-third of the county lies within state and

national forests. The Au Sable State Forest southeast of West Branch, the Au Sable State Forest in Klacking Township north of West Branch, the Huron National Forest around Goodar Township, and the Au Sable State Forest southeast of Rose City are the best bets. The Au Sable State Forest lands in the extreme northwest may offer better hunting in the future—if they're more heavily timbered—but that's a few years down the road at best.

For the nonlocal hunter, gaining access onto private lands may be difficult, but this is where the best hunting will be found. A high percentage of these lands is posted, so begin your search early, and concentrate your efforts on the agricultural areas. The extreme southwest corner is the weakest area of the county, and there's no hope for improvement without massive timbering (which is unlikely). This area, which is composed of essentially unbroken mast-bearing hardwoods, offers no cover whatsoever, and while there is good hunting the first day or two of the regular season, it quickly fades.

Habitat, in general, improves as you move north through the county. You'll soon see an increase in pulp trees and the only cedars to be found anywhere in the county. Deer numbers are higher—forty to fifty per square mile—although deer numbers are also excellent in the southeast corner (running thirty to forty per square mile).

For local hunters, good-to-excellent hunting can be had, with minor exceptions, throughout the county with Horton, Mills, Richland, Hill, Goodar and Rose townships offering the best bets. Goodar Township contains 360 of the county's 460 acres of CFA lands.

Roscommon County

The northeast quadrant shows a real strong mix of habitats, with good numbers of openings, cuttings, and mixed forests. There are poplars, cedars, planted pines, naturally occurring pines, swales, and thickets here. Good-to-excellent deer numbers—running thirty to thirty-five per square mile—are found throughout this area of the county.

The southeast corner is hilly and primarily covered with hardwoods and, despite an appreciable amount of logging and young growth timber, there's a dramatic decrease in deer numbers. The deer are heavily stressed throughout this corner of the county by the unusually heavy use of ORVs on a year-around basis. Deer numbers run roughly fifteen to twenty per square mile in this area. There are few cedars or yarding areas here and the hardwoods are all too mature. Several hunt clubs are found in this corner of the county and, generally speaking, their lands are better managed than the public lands.

If you're going to hunt the southeast corner of the county, stay near the lakes and watercourses. Since a lack of wintering areas severely limits the number of deer here, the waterways will offer you your best shot.

The habitat in Roscommon County suffers from a litany of problems typically faced by whitetail habitat statewide: roadways and fire trails are too numerous; monogamy of timber stands (stands containing identical species) is too common; absence of adequate wintering areas is also common in the north; timbering activity needs to be increased by threefold to fivefold; at least ten to fifteen times the current number of forest openings are needed. Before we see any significant increase in our northernmost deer herds, these problems need to be addressed and, realistically, this is not likely to happen soon.

The northwest area of Roscommon County, around the big lakes, is generally very poor habitat; this area is very highly developed. Amid the congestion, however, are pockets here and there of good cover where local hunters, especially, should do well. I like best those areas in the northwest that lie near the heavier pine cover.

The best habitat overall in Roscommon County is found in the northeast quadrant where deer numbers are good. However, the hunting pressure is heavy.

Oscoda County

A county that is truly open for all to enjoy! With roughly three-quarters of the land mass in the public domain, Oscoda County offers little advantage to the local deer hunting fraternity. Even the Feds have done a pretty good job here (it may well have been to help the Kirtland's Warbler rather than any concern about the whitetail, but let's not quibble).

The Feds demonstrate their undying devotion to the pine tree throughout much of the southern half of the county; with the exception of the southwest corner of the county, these stands have an excellent age mix, as well as being host to other plant life. There's a considerable amount of mixed timber stands in the county, particularly in the extreme northwest and the extreme southeast. In fact, essentially the only place the habitat diminishes is on the private sector lands, chiefly in Clinton and Comins townships in the northeast. Deer numbers are good to excellent throughout the area (forty to fifty per square mile) but they fall off in those two townships, since the area is dominated by hardwoods that are much too mature to be adequate.

In 1980, a controlled burn that was originally set to improve Kirtland's Warbler habitat got out of control. Before it was over, more than six thousand acres were blackened. This area is excellent now and should continue to improve over the next five to ten years.

In October, archers should check the edges of the mast-bearing hardwoods, particularly in the area northeast of Luzerne. I especially like the area around and just north of Luzerne as well as the northwest tier of the county.

Iosco County

Although both the Huron National Forest and the Au Sable State Forest occupy considerable chunks of Iosco County, in most cases mediocre hunting opportunity awaits the nonlocal hunter. The forested area in the northern half of the county is unbroken and composed entirely of pines, both planted white pine and natural occurring jack-pine. It is all too mature, has virtually no browse whatsoever, and is inadequate as wintering habitat. Deer numbers run from ten to, perhaps, twenty per square mile, but are uniformly low in most areas. Exceptions to the poor habitat can be found in the extreme northwest corner where there are some brush and hardwoods, but the area is privately owned and heavily posted. Another is in the northeast corner, where, north of the Foote basin, there lies a sparsely forested region of scrub oaks offering little browse and no winter habitat. Slightly to the east there is a good-looking, although small, area of dense tag alder bottoms, cedars, younger planted pines and young poplars, intermixed with agricultural lands. The problem is that it's all privately owned, heavily posted, and the former Wurtsmith Air Force Base lies right in the middle of it.

By far the best habitat in the county is found in the southern half, particularly on the southwest side. The area for several miles around Whittemore is absolutely beautiful. Depending on where you are, anywhere from 30 percent to 50 percent of this land is under tillage, with the remainder being a very solid mix of cedars, planted pines, poplar, birch, and some mast-bearing hardwoods as well as alder/willow bottoms. Wintering areas range from sufficient to ample and there's plenty of browse. Even the western half of the Au Sable State Forest is excellent. The problem for the nonlocal hunter is that the vast majority of the really good habitat is privately owned and heavily posted. There are several large hunt clubs in the county as well as some large private ranches, all of which are posted, of course.

Locals will fare best in Burleigh, Sherman, Reno, Grant and Plainfield townships, all in the west-southwest, as well as in Wilber Township, in the east-central area. Deer numbers run as high as thirty-five to forty per square mile in these areas. Nonlocals will do well in these areas if they can gain access, but that's highly questionable. Overall, your best bets will be select areas within the Au Sable State Forest, as well as in the Huron National Forest, closest to and north of East Tawas.

If you're going to hunt in the northern portion of the county, hunt the heaviest cover you can find—that with

some mix to it—and pay particular attention to the creek
bed areas, some of which are adequate.

Montmorency County

It is hard to imagine a more exciting area than Montmorency
County! A near perfect blend of forest lands, parklike openings
and farm fields are all nicely spaced and provide plenty of valuable edge. It is a credit to both the DNR and the various hunt
clubs, particularly in the southern portion of the county, that
this area is wisely managed for multiple use. The area is aesthetically pleasing, efficiently and productively timbered, and
has good to excellent whitetail numbers throughout. The only
place that can be considered weak is the area west of Atlanta
to the county line, where many miles of essentially unbroken
but mature hardwoods need to be selectively thinned.

For the local hunter, I particularly like Rust, Loud, Albert,
Hillman, Avery, Vienna, Briley and Montmorency townships.
Local hunters should probably avoid the state lands, especially during the general gun season, and hunt instead along
their perimeters.

Nonlocal hunters can do well on the various parcels of
state land, but be forewarned that, especially in the southern half of the county, there's no access on the private lands
and the state land is not found in contiguous blocks. You
must be aware of the state boundaries or you'll find yourself
in trespassing difficulties. I especially like the state land
four to six miles east of Lewiston as well as all of
Montmorency Township. The private land in the north is
more family-owned than in the south, and access, although
not assured, may be available if you're courteous and ask
permission prior to the actual season.

Arenac County

A flat, heavily forested county, Arenac has an immense
amount of diversity, as much as I've seen anywhere in the

state. Through most of Turner, Whitney and Sims townships, the agriculture is so intense that very little habitat remains. Some of what does remain has been rendered totally worthless to whitetails by the grazing of cattle within the woodlots. Despite this, the highest deer densities in the county are to be found just west of this area in western Turner, eastern Mason and most of Au Gres townships.

Agriculture throughout all but the western side of the county is found in isolated pockets. This creates ideal conditions for the local hunters. The open, cultivated lands should be ignored. Hunt the periphery of these areas and the thickset, brushy patches in between, particularly once the crops are in. Early season archers will do well posting up right on the edges. In the later seasons, drives would be ideal in these areas.

The state land on the west side of the county is exceptional, as it is heavily covered with a solid mixture of habitats. Cedars and true hardwoods are scarce, but there are some pines in the brushy bottomlands where the deer can winter. Birch and poplar of a good age mix are plentiful, the result of numerous small clear cuts made over many years. There's a substantial number of swales and thickets, as well as a lot of alder, willow, cattails and swamp grasses in this area. The private lands surrounding the state lands here have essentially the same composition.

Throughout the entire county, the private lands are very heavily posted and access for the nonlocal is nearly impossible. The west side of the county holds thirty to thirty-five-plus deer per square mile, and this entire area should provide good-to-excellent hunting. State lands are uniformly heavily hunted. The east side of the county ranges from poor to excellent—local hunters should hand pick their spots, however, as the deer distribution can vary greatly in this area.

Midland County

Midland County is an area dominated by poplar woodlots, and dotted with pockets of agriculture, particularly in the southern half. Cedars are conspicuous by their absence, and with the exception of Lee Township, there are very few pines. The deer winter throughout the county in the denser thickets, found in the bottomland areas. Running north-south through the center of the county is a band of mast-bearing hardwoods; elsewhere there are few to be found. Deer numbers run as high as thirty to forty per square mile, particularly in the north and in the west.

The city of Midland, along with the Dow Corporation and the resultant sprawl of development, usurp a large area in the east-central portion of the county; otherwise, local hunters have free reign over most areas. With very minor exceptions, the land is flat, and in the northeast corner of the county there's a considerable number of wet marshes and swamps. The habitat runs hot and cold throughout the county, but seldom is it poor, except around the city of Midland itself and the extreme southern section.

The extreme south and the southeast corner are, in places, so intensely cultivated that precious little habitat remains. There are areas in southwest Jasper Township, southeastern Porter Township and the southern tier of Mount Haley Township where there's simply no whitetail habitat whatsoever.

Access for nonlocals on any private lands is almost impossible to attain. The state forest lands run from good to excellent, but they're very heavily hunted, with hunter densities running as high as forty to forty-five hunters per square mile. Deer numbers are good on these lands, though, particularly early in the fall. Early season archers especially fare well here.

Local nimrods will fare best on the lands immediately adjacent to the state lands, as well as in the northern halves of Warren and Jasper townships. Edenville, Hope, Mills, Greendale, Lee and Geneva townships all offer the local hunting population excellent opportunities as well. I particularly like the area surrounding the Porter Oil Field in the southwest corner of the county; it's excellent! Due to intense cultivation, much of Porter, Mount Haley and Ingersoll townships is marginal at best. Deer probably number fewer than ten per square mile throughout this area, especially when the crops are in.

Successful hunting strategies would include sitting by hunters on, or immediately adjacent to, the state lands. For those who are physically capable of getting into the interior regions of the state properties, the latter part of the general gun season may be most promising here. For local hunters, drives in the latter part of the season should pay off, especially in the brushier, low-lying areas. The county has only 600 acres of CFA lands and these are widely scattered.

Isabella County

Both habitat and deer numbers are spotty throughout the county. Most of the cultivated lands and most of the mast-bearing hardwoods are found in a swatch, running north-south through the center of the county. Within this area the habitat ranges from adequate in the south, to totally inadequate throughout the entire central area; it slightly improves again to the north. Deer numbers are uniformly down throughout, but are highest in the western half of the county and lowest in the southeast.

The area radiating outward, northwest of Mt. Pleasant, is intensely farmed, with as much as 80 percent to 85 percent of the land under cultivation; there's a lot of livestock as well and the only true cover is fully mature mast-bearing hardwoods. There's no browse here whatsoever, no brush, and no winter habitat. Deer numbers are predictably low, and human populations and development are relatively high. Even locals will find it difficult to connect here.

The western portion of the county offers by far the best habitat and highest deer densities. For the most part, this area is a good mix of agricultural lands with mixed forest and plenty of brush, as well as marshes and heavy fencerows. If a nonlocal hunter desires to hunt here, he absolutely must make contacts and arrangements weeks ahead of time. The very best areas are in Rolland, southern Broomfield, Sherman, Coldwater and Gilmore townships, and for nonlocals the best hope of entry is to be found in these townships as well.

Doe in Autumn. There are plenty of deer in the northeast, especially in the more southerly counties. Unfortunately, buck-to-doe ratios are badly skewed, running as lopsided as 1 to 40 or even 1 to 50 in places like Gladwin and Clare counties; trophy-hunting potential is extremely poor.

The above townships, as well as Vernon in the north and Denver Township in the east, are the local nimrod's best bet.

Otsego County

Not a particularly exciting area, Otsego is dominated by hardwoods, which generally are too mature. Quality habitat in terms of summer range is lacking and winter range is in even worse shape.

There are no cedars, and hence suitable winter range areas are lacking in all but a few sections of the county. Such cover is only to be found in the extreme northern tier of the county, as well as in places along the extreme eastern side and in the southeast corner. Late season muzzle-loaders and archers would be advised to check here.

Deer numbers are low through the county's central section, but pick up considerably in the eastern portion and along the southern tier of townships. Quality of cover is so poor and deer numbers so low that many areas, particularly the areas on either side of Gaylord, are only of marginal value even for the local hunter. Local hunters will find Charlton and Dover townships good to excellent, as well as the northern half of Elmira Township.

The best bet for nonlocals is the state land in the extreme northeast where the habitat improves considerably and the deer have responded, numbering between thirty and forty per square mile in select areas. Stick to the more remote and dense cover here, especially after the general gun season begins. Nonlocals would be well advised to steer clear of almost all privately owned lands. Access is almost impossible, and remember, too, that northern Otsego County is elk country.

Cheboygan County

A rural area with a smattering of farms spread throughout, the most intense area being along the central-eastern region. The habitat is quite mixed throughout the entire county. There's a sizable amount of pines, planted pines and cedars, as well as plenty of brush, mostly tag alders, but there are some willows and sumac also. Overall, the dominant tree is the poplar and there's plenty of birch, too. Surrounding the farm fields and around the lakes area there's plenty of mast-bearing hardwoods that are, invariably, much too mature. The contour varies from nearly flat in the northwest and southeastern corners, to heavily contoured in other areas.

Beyond a doubt, the greater deer numbers—fifteen to eighteen per square mile—and best hunting potential is in the southern portion of the county, particularly in Mentor, Wilmot, Nunda, Ellis, Walker and Forest townships. Moving north of highway M-68, the habitat becomes increasingly mature and spotty. There's little here at all for the nonlocal hunter, although the locals should do well in Aloha, Koehler, Grant and Waverly townships. Benton Township, in the northeast corner of the county, is a problem. If a nonlocal puts a lot of time into scouting he could do well here, but it will take work.

I'd seriously suggest a lot of scouting anywhere you intend to hunt in Cheboygan County, but in the northern half of the county it is imperative. Deer numbers are extremely spotty there, with the better areas carrying up to eight to twelve animals per square mile. Hunt the periphery of the farming areas and immediately adjacent to the numerous clear cuts and brushy thickets, while avoiding the mature coverts. Deer numbers are probably highest in the south-central region, to lowest in the northwest corner.

Crawford County

Unbroken stands of pine stretching for miles characterize the whitetail habitat in Crawford County as a disaster area. They are too mature to provide any food value or cover, and from what I can see, there is no effort whatsoever to provide understory or herbaceous matter either. As might be expected, the situation is far worse in the southeast quadrant, in the area of the Huron National Forest, and even the state has gotten into the act on its lands here.

In areas where other forest types exist, as in Maple Forest, Frederic and Beaver Creek townships, they're far too mature, offering minimal browse and virtually no cover. It's testimony to the amazing adaptability of whitetails that so many deer are found here (six to fifteen per square mile); it's not the result of any meaningful management efforts. As a matter of fact, the large parcel of land in the north-central area that forms the artillery range for the National Guard has no white-tail management at all and yet this area supports as many (or more) whitetails as any other area in the county!

The only saving grace is the multiple cutting sites that, while poorly managed and inevitably replanted in pine, provide at least some food stuffs for a few years prior to their complete deterioration.

In general, the west side of the county is stronger and has more to offer than the eastern half. Maple Forest, Frederic, Beaver Creek, and the area south and west of Lovells, are your best bets. With minor exceptions, access is readily available throughout the entire county. The forest fire that occurred in May 1990 involved some five thousand acres of land four or five miles east of Grayling and should have no noticeable impact on hunting.

Bay County

Bay County may well be the most intensively cultivated area in all of Michigan. From the east-west running Cottage Grove Road, lying in the center of the county, south to the county line, at least 80 percent and in most cases 90 percent of the land is under cultivation. The land is perfectly flat, and the only habitat is in the form of small widely scattered woodlots containing hardwoods. These are true mast-bearing hardwoods and maples. There is no brush, no fencerows for cover, and no browse.

As you move west in this area, the habitat improves slightly, but it's still very poor. Deer populations are extremely low (three to seven per square mile) and the human population quite high. There is no state land in the county, with small exceptions along the lake Huron shoreline; a few bucks are taken here each year. Any of the habitat south of Pinconning Road is very marginal at best, due to poor ability to satisfy the whitetails' needs. Garfield and Mount Forest townships offer some hunting for those few locals who intently study the herd and have ready access.

The best habitat in the county lies north of Pinconning Road. Its character changes here, as does the soil. The rich soils of the south give way to sand, and the mast-producing broadleafs give way to poplars and birch. There's more brush and browse here, created by younger woodlots. There's also much less cultivated land here as well—perhaps only 20 percent in the north. This area would be adequate for hardworking locals, but deer numbers are still quite low, probably not exceeding ten to fifteen per square mile anywhere. The northern half of Mount Forest Township, much of Pinconning, and all of Gibson Township would fall in this area.

16

Northwestern Michigan

Discussing the northwestern Lower Peninsula is, in many ways, like discussing two separate areas. There are areas south of highway M-55 (the southern third of the northwest) such as Osceola, Lake, Mason, Mecosta, Newaygo and Oceana counties, which have some of the highest buck-kill figures per square mile anywhere in the state. Hunters in the better areas of the northwest can realistically expect to see twenty-five, thirty, or even more deer per day while afield.

Compare these facts and figures with those of the northwestern counties north of highway M-55. Counties such as Emmet, Leelanau and Charlevoix have much reduced deer herds, along with low buck-kill figures, and yet their buck-to-doe ratios and antler development figures are much improved. Naturally, we should question why.

Contrasting soil types and winter severity are the two major factors contributing to this dichotomy. South of highway M-55 we witness a marked increase in the number of conifers and suitable lowland areas, as well as a heightened nutritional diversity to satisfy the whitetails' needs. Winters are noticeably milder—in both temperature and annual snowfall—and

Map 16.1
Northwestern Michigan

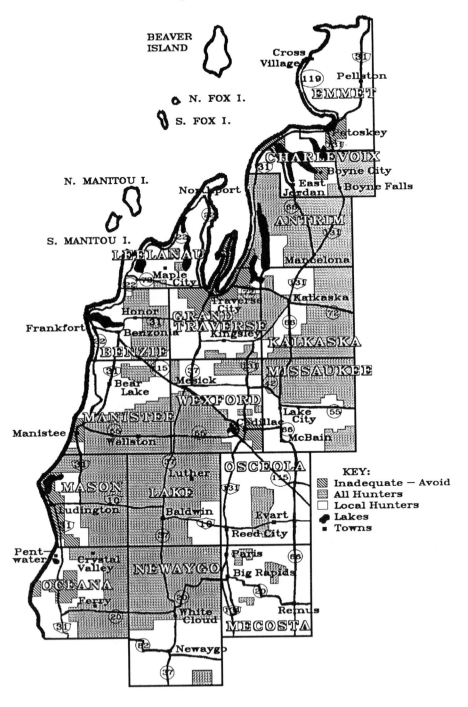

quality food is more readily available. The results are much higher deer densities. From 1980 to 1990, deer numbers in this region increased more than 50 percent and, although they've dwindled somewhat since then, they're now quite stable, and essentially right where the DNR wants to seem them.

North of highway M-55 we have more fertile soils, fewer lowlands, and a dramatic increase in winter severity indexes. The so-called lake effect results in the dumping of more than 120 inches of snow annually in such areas as Traverse City and Boyne City, whereas Grayling to the east and Baldwin to the south receive 90 inches annually, and Bay City to the southeast gets only 45. When winter winds howl and temperatures plummet there are no suitable yarding areas in this region to shelter the deer.

Beautiful and majestic northern hardwoods dominate the northerly northwestern counties. Yarding areas are scarce, since the soil types are wrong. Even in mild winters (such as the winter of 1986–87), the deer herd suffers. Winters such as we had in 1985–86 are devastating. Historically, these counties have supported fewer deer—they do today and they always will—but it's for these very reasons that there are fewer hunters, better buck-to-doe ratios, and more mature bucks.

Following is a short description of each northwestern county and its more productive areas.

Newaygo County

The specter of the National Forest Service rears its ugly head again in Newaygo County. I suppose the mature, unbroken hardwood stands here are more aesthetically pleasing than the pines of southeast Crawford County, but they're no better at fulfilling the needs of our wildlife! The lion's share of the deer are found in the northern half of the county. Pay particular attention to those areas with varied habitat and, if forced to the federal lands, hunt their perimeters.

Moving east-west across the northern half of the county, the situation improves. Highest deer numbers are found in Lilley, Troy and Beaver townships. As you move south, you'll

find increasing agriculture, development and population—
and fewer deer. Deer densities run anywhere from near fifty
deer per square mile in the northern portion of the county to
below twenty per square mile in the southern areas.
Essentially the only cedars in the county are in the extreme
north, particularly the northwest. While the deer this far
south don't always yard up, nonetheless they could benefit
from thermal cover, but none is found.

Local hunters should score anywhere, but Sheridan
Township is especially weak since as much as 85 percent of
this area is under tillage. Locals will fare best in Troy, Lilley,
Home, Beaver, Monroe, Lincoln, Wilcox, Norwich, Goodwell
and Denver townships. Parts of Ensley and Grant townships
in the south should be pretty good as well.

Nonlocals will do best in the northwest quadrant and it's
here (specifically in Troy and Beaver townships) that the
bulk of the 2,300 acres of CFA lands is found. Be mindful of
the private lands, however, as they're heavily posted.

Mecosta County

For the past decade, Mecosta County has consistently racked up
some of the highest buck-kill figures per square mile of any
county in the state. Deer numbers are very good throughout the
county, running from thirty to nearly fifty per square mile.
Overall, deer densities throughout the county are very dependent
on the habitat in the immediate vicinity. The greatest numbers of
deer are found where habitat is the strongest. With the exception
of the public lands—of which there are few—nonlocals should
avoid Mecosta County. Access to private land is next to impossible, for both gun hunters and archers. There are no hunter access
lands and only two hundred acres of CFA lands in the county.

The habitat in Mecosta County is dominated by hardwoods. Grant, Chippewa and Sheridan townships provide
some lowland conifers, and that's about it for the entire
county. The smattering of planted pines is of minimal value.
Habitat is somewhat too mature, but due to the active logging here in the past decade, deer numbers have exploded,

and the habitat is very good.

The best areas are Martiny, Morton, Deerfield, Mecosta, Chippewa and Grant townships, as well as the eastern half of Millbrook and the southern portion of Austin. Hunters will also fare well if they stick to the better habitat along the waterways. Hip boots are beneficial.

Lake County

Private lands throughout the county are a nice mixture of small crop fields (mostly hay), natural openings, mature hardwood woodlots, and thick brushy areas as well as swales. The state lands are primarily forested, but there's a good age mix to the cover. Hardwoods dominate, along with some planted pines and a few naturally occurring conifers. Not surprisingly, the weakest areas are those of the Manistee National Forest. These lands are primarily hardwoods with scattered stands of pine as well. Nowhere are there enough openings on the national lands and there's far too little cutting; the habitat is too mature.

Nonlocal hunters may have some difficulty gaining access to private areas. However, there are slightly more than 1,700 acres of CFA lands so I believe opportunity is here for those who look for it. I'd recommend the following areas: Yates, Webber, Cherry Valley, Sweetwater, Peacock, Newkirk, Pleasant Plains, Lake, Eden and Elk townships. I also like the area east of Wolf Lake that the state timbered not too long ago.

For local hunters, there's a cornucopia of opportunity with deer densities running to forty-plus deer per square mile throughout the center of the county. I particularly like the western half of Chase Township, as well as all of Yates, Pinora, Newkirk, Ellsworth, Eden and Elk townships.

Osceola County

Overall a good and very consistent county, Osceola is quite evenly covered with mixed hardwood woodlots and small scale but plentiful farming operations. There are plenty of swales, brush, and thickets as well. Most of the farming consists of haying operations. Close to 30 percent of the land is composed of openings of one kind or another, and about 70 percent is forested. The habitat is slightly on the mature side of being ideal, but it's not bad. Deer numbers are good throughout. During the past decade, Osceola County has consistently had one of the highest buck-kill figures per square mile of any county in the state. It's consistently near, or even above, 7.0 per square mile!

Marion and Highland townships are more open than the others and, hence, success rates could be somewhat lower here. Any predictions about potential worth of the individual townships prior to the actual season are difficult to make. If you're an archer and there's a mast crop, the area could be very effective. However, if you're hunting the regular gun season or one of the late seasons, and if the crops have already been harvested, hunting will be much more difficult.

Planted pines are scattered throughout the county, but the lowland conifers are mostly concentrated in Lincoln and Cedar townships, as well as along the waterways elsewhere. The entire county is gently contoured and, as a result, there are numerous lowland thickets. Deer numbers are good, averaging thirty-five to nearly fifty per square mile throughout, being somewhat higher in the southeast corner.

Unfortunately for the nonlocal hunter, access to other than public lands is a severe problem. Your best bets will be in eastern Orient, Burdell, Lincoln, Osceola, and the lakes area of Rose Lake townships. The only significant state land, the Chippewa–Pere Marquette State Forest, is very heavily hunted (fifty to sixty hunters per square mile), despite being among the poorer areas of the county. There are also 2,475 acres of CFA lands, all located in the western half of the county. Even though habitat is too mature, deer numbers remain fairly good.

Local hunters can realistically expect to take deer anywhere, but I especially like Orient, Sylvan, Burdell, Lincoln, Osceola, and the lakes area of Rose Lake townships. Avoid the few, widely scattered areas throughout the county that are too mature and too uniform (principally hardwoods), unless they're bearing mast in the earlier seasons.

Missaukee County

A nice blend of forest and croplands combine to form a very good area overall. With a gentle contour to the landscape on the western side, the county starts out strongly in the north and deteriorates as you move south. The southern half, particularly the area south of M-55, is very poor, even for local hunters. The large crop field throughout Richland Township limits the only cover in the area to open and very mature hardwood woodlots. Lake Township is very poor for the same reason, although the northwest corner is much stronger. Deer numbers are low throughout.

There's a marked improvement in the habitat as you move west to east in the southern portion of the county, with decreasing numbers of mature hardwoods, a much improved mixture to the habitat and far less open land. The northern portion of the county also improves west to east, but it starts out much stronger in the west than does the area farther south. Poplar forests prevail in this region, but there's a healthy mixture of both naturally occurring and planted pines, as well as some hardwoods, brush, swales and lowland conifers. When you reach Norwich, West Branch and Enterprise townships on the east side, you'll find plentiful young growth as well as dense stands of willow thickets and numerous swales and swamps. Hunters working some of this region should consider donning hip boots or even consider working a canoe into these places.

For local hunters I particularly like the following areas: southern Bloomfield, Caldwell, Lake, Forest, Pioneer, Reeder, Butterfield, east Clam Union, western Enterprise, Norwich and West Branch townships.

For nonlocals, I like northern Bloomfield, Pioneer, Forest, Holland, eastern Enterprise, Norwich and West Branch townships. The lion's share of the five thousand acres of CFA lands is located in these townships. I also believe that a hard-working, courteous nonlocal could gain access in parts of western Enterprise, Reeder, northern Riverside and western Butterfield townships. The extra work required could be well worth the time spent.

Wexford County

Very heavily forested throughout the southern portion, deer numbers here run roughly twenty per square mile. If it weren't for the farming operations—both old and ongoing— there'd be few deer here at all. Western Cherry Grove, all of Henderson, and much of South Branch townships are covered with unbroken stands of towering hardwoods and fully mature planted pines. Boon and Slagle townships immediately to the north are similar. Parts of Selma are good, due to the increased number of openings around the private lands and logging operations, but much more logging is required in this area for the habitat to improve. Deer numbers run hot and cold here, so hand pick your spots and stick to, or at least near, the private sectors.

Throughout the main body of the county there are a lot of large Christmas three plantations, usually surrounded by towering, open hardwoods. There are fewer than ten deer per square mile in these areas, especially in the later seasons.

Things improve considerably to the north. While the predominant trees in the south are oaks and beeches, poplars prevail in the north and the state has done a good job of management here. The state lands abound with· young growth forests, plenty of openings and lots of brush as well as cedars and naturally occurring pines. Deer numbers are good running upwards of twenty-five to thirty per square mile. Public lands carry roughly the same number of hunters per square mile here during our regular gun season. Nonlocals must be careful not to trespass throughout this area as the private sector lands are heavily posted. Wexford Township is the poorest spot in the northern part of the county, since it's dominated by cultivated fields in the north and large Christmas tree plantations farther south. Consumers Power holds a lot of land in the northeast corner of the county, and this acreage is open to hunting.

For local hunters, I especially like Cherry Grove, South Branch, Selma, Cedar Creek (other than the Fife Lake State Forest area), Liberty, Colfax, Greenwood and Hanover townships. I also like the northwest corner of Haring Township.

For nonlocal hunters, I like all of the state and Consumers Power land in the extreme north, as well as the Fife Lake area south of Manton. In addition, South Branch, Selma, southern Cedar Creek and western Cherry Grove townships also show promise. There are four thousand acres of CFA lands in the county; unfortunately, the great majority of them is found in the poorer townships.

Mason County

Mason County has much to offer both local and nonlocal hunters. While the entire county is dominated by its mast-bearing hardwoods, in most regions there's a very nice mixture of crop lands, planted pines, poplars, cedars, naturally occurring jack-pines and ample brush. This is particularly true on the east and north sides. Deer numbers are strong, running from thirty to thirty-five per square mile in these areas.

The southeast is the strongest area of the county, and while too mature and too heavily forested, a solid mix of forest and cultivated fields provides a lot of excellent habitat. Several active logging operations in recent years now provide dense cover with young poplars. The farming areas of Eden and Custer townships are very nice with good numbers of deer.

North of U.S. 10 on the east side of the county the habitat falters a bit, becoming too monotonous and mature, but it's adequate, and in many areas, like the village of Fountain, it's near-perfect. Hunters working this region should concentrate on the edges of forest openings and carefully pick those spots with variety and younger growth.

As you move west to Lake Michigan into Grant Township, the habitat becomes increasingly mature, but it's still good. For local hunters, I particularly like Logan, Branch, Eden, Custer and Free Soil townships. For nonlocal hunters I like all of the aforementioned areas as well as Sheridan, Meade and Grant townships. In addition to the plentiful federal lands, there are more than 11,700 acres of CFA lands. Almost all of these public lands lie within the strongest areas.

Due to the abundance of people and development, Dow Chemical and Consumers Power lands, and the number of orchards, no one will find good hunting in the area from Ludington State Park south to the county line. Even much of Amber Township is of marginal worth, at best, for local hunters.

Manistee County

If aesthetics had any influence on deer hunting potential, Manistee County might win first prize. Undulating terrain and mature hardwood stands are things of beauty, but by themselves are incapable of providing for the whitetails' basic needs. From the mature oaks and pines of the south and southeast, to the open orchards and hardwoods of the west, the county is very weak in terms of whitetail habitat. There's little here for the deer.

The western townships that border Lake Michigan are the weakest of the lot. Western Cleon Township in the northeast corner of the county, as well as Norman, Dickson, Brown and Stronach townships in the southern tier, are the strongest parts of the county. Deer numbers run as high as thirty per square mile in the better areas, with both hunter and deer densities peaking in the southernmost townships. In addition to the vast federal and state land holdings, there are nearly seven thousand acres of CFA lands. Hence, access is readily available.

Early season archers may find the animals working the oak stands throughout the county if a mast crop exists, but this is less likely as the season progresses. Move closer to the scattered pockets of heavier and younger growth as time goes on. Work the bottoms adjacent to the numerous creeks and rivers as well, where the majority of the wintering areas and dense habitat is found.

For local hunters, I'd especially recommend eastern Pleasanton, southern Brown, southern Norman, select areas (younger, brushier pockets) of both Maple Grove and

Springdale, as well as most of Cleon townships.

Nonlocal hunters might try the state lands around Pleasanton and Springdale townships, as well as western Cleon, southern Brown and southern Norman townships.

Oceana County

Not a whole lot inspires the deer hunter here; Oceana is blanketed around much of its perimeter by forest lands, most of which are far too mature and unbroken. Hardwoods dominate throughout, with 5 percent to 7 percent of the forests consisting of jack-pine. Scant cedar or other lowland conifers are limited to the banks of the watercourses. Considerable agriculture is found in the area and from the looks of it, Oceana County supplies most of the Midwest's asparagus needs. There's also a healthy orchard industry, especially in Golden, Hart, Benona and Shelby townships. In fact, orchards are so prevalent in Hart Township that there's precious little cover left.

Nonlocal hunters will do best in the northern and eastern sides of the county. Deer numbers run from a low of roughly fifteen per square mile on the west and through the middle of the county, to a high of thirty-plus per square mile in the east. I especially like Weare, Colfax and Leavitt townships. The south-central area between Grant and Otto townships and north into Ferry Township is also promising for the nonlocal crowd.

Locals will do best in Weare, Crystal, Colfax, Ferry and Newfield townships. A lot of the remaining sections of the county are of marginal value to even local hunters with very low deer numbers resulting from a badly declining habitat. There are more than 2,800 acres of CFA lands; unfortunately, they are all found in the weakest areas of the county.

Benzie County

While not having tremendous deer densities, Benzie County has excellent deer hunting opportunities for local and nonlocal hunters alike. The habitat undergoes a slight decline in quality as you move east to west through the county, but with the exception of those areas having the highest percentage of cultivated lands and orchards, the entire county has good potential. The weakest areas are Homestead (too much homogeneity and maturity), Joyfield, eastern Benzonia and Almira townships. With the exception of Homestead, all of these areas have rather intense cultivation and in the western townships, quite a few orchards.

The remainder of the county is largely forested, almost completely dominated by northern hardwoods. Find those areas with the youngest and most diverse growth. The townships on the eastern border of the county match this criteria nicely, and they're all quite good. Deer numbers run as high as twenty-five or thirty per square mile in the better areas. For local hunters, I like Inland, Colfax, Almira, Platte, Weldon, Blaine, western Gilmore and northern Crystal Lake townships. Nonlocals will do well in Colfax, Inland, Platte and Weldon townships. In addition to vast state land holdings, there are over 3,200 acres of CFA holdings in Benzie County.

Kalkaska County

Kalkaska County is one of the few examples of poor state land management of whitetail habitat in the Lower Peninsula. With the exception of the state lands in Oliver and Bear Lake townships, state lands here are invariably too mature and too homogeneous throughout. In the Rapid River Township area, the situation is so bad that unless you're a local resident and already have a bead drawn on a buck you've been watching, I wouldn't recommend that anyone hunt here.

There are many very mature mast-bearing hardwoods spread widely throughout the county. Many of these hardwood stands are found lining the higher ridges; Clearwater, Blue Lake, Boardman and Orange townships have a lot of them. Deer populations, with the exception of the east-central region of the county (fifteen to twenty deer per square mile throughout this area), are not high anywhere, but they're generally better on the east and north sides.

For local hunters, I recommend Clearwater, Boardman, Springfield, Oliver, Bear Lake and select areas of Blue Lake (avoid the areas without variation) townships.

Nonlocal hunters should try southern Kalkaska, northern Boardman, southern Springfield, Oliver and Bear Lake townships. There are vast state land holdings in Kalkaska County as well as 3,200 acres of CFA lands.

Grand Traverse County

The entire western region of Grand Traverse County has very little to offer in terms of deer hunting potential. The major tree throughout this area (and throughout most of the county as well) is the oak, and the major type of cover is the hardwood woodlot. The entire region is far too mature overall, with intense cultivation of typical farm crops in Blair, Mayfield, and most of Grant townships. There are few deer, under ten per square mile, throughout the western townships, but the best areas are found in southern Long Lake and western Green Lake townships. The extreme north is weaker yet, and essentially is inadequate for all hunters. Acme and Peninsula townships are heavily planted in cherry orchards. The habitat there is very mature, and Peninsula Township is punctuated with houses and small subdivisions its entire length. Much of eastern Long Lake, Garfield and western East Bay townships lies within the populated and developing areas that surround Traverse City; hunting is impractical or illegal here.

The habitat improves markedly on the state lands of Blair Township, and includes the area east and somewhat north of there. The best areas are found a few miles northwest of Kingsley, the area around the lakes of southern East Bay Township, and the state lands in the extreme northwest corner of Whitewater Township. The state lands in Whitewater are not very exciting, but some of the private lands immediately surrounding them are.

For local hunters, I'd recommend the following: eastern Blair, southern East Bay, Whitewater, Union and Fife Lake

Hunter with Buck. Some of Michigan's nicest bucks come each fall from our northwestern counties. John Lengyel of Flint took this monster from Leelanau County's South Fox Island. In general, the greatest number of deer are taken in the southernmost of these counties, but the bulk of the trophy animals come from the more northerly counties. (Photo by Donald Brown)

townships. For nonlocals, I'd try eastern East Bay, Union, and the state lands in western Whitewater townships. There are 3,400 acres of CFA lands in Grand Traverse County. Unfortunately, most of these are found in the poor regions.

Demographic studies of the Grand Traverse County area all point to the further development of the Traverse City region and its continued outward sprawl. Increasing population will inevitably hurt deer hunting potential, which is not that great now, and will undoubtedly deteriorate further in the future.

Leelanau County

Although Leelanau County as a whole is nothing to get terribly excited about, the bulk of the best habitat and a lion's share of its deer are found on the eastern side of the county. As a rule, in Bingham, Suttons Bay, eastern Centerville and Leland townships, the best cover and greater number of deer are to be found nearer the water. These spots hold most of the cedars, heavier brush and the younger growth.

The area with the most potential is a north-south corridor from Cedar over to Maple City in the south, then north to Good Harbor Bay and east to the village of Lake Leelanau. I especially like the Victoria swamp area within this corridor. There's heavy growth, brush, wintering areas, poplars, hardwoods, adequate young growth, and ample openings around its periphery to provide for the deer's needs. Deer numbers here run about fifteen animals per square mile, and each year some very nice bucks are taken from this general area.

Most of Cleveland, Kasson and Empire townships in the extreme southwest are very poor, the vast majority of their area being covered with unbroken stands of very mature hardwoods. There's little here for the casual nonlocal hunter (the serious trophy hunter with plenty of scouting time could do well), as much better options are available. For the local hunters, I like the following areas the best: Elmwood, Solon, western Centerville and eastern Cleveland townships.

Antrim County

Antrim County is actually like two separate areas: the hilly, open farm and orchard regions of the west and the more rural, forested areas of the east. Both areas possess their own attractiveness.

The entire county is heavily contoured and much of it has good areas of isolated pocket cover. The only area presenting tremendous problems for the deer hunter is the southwest corner, in the Elk Rapids–Elk Lake–Torch Lake region. This corner of the county is simply too congested and open to offer much to anyone, particularly nonlocals.

The farmlands of Banks Township in the northwest corner, while open, are not that congested and offer good hunting potential, although deer numbers are not great. Access for nonlocals will take work, but it's worth investigating.

The remainder of the county can be hunted, but the region I like best is formed by Star, Warner, Jordan, Chestonia and Kearney townships. A large section of the Gaylord State Forest falls within these townships, and the entire area is heavily forested. It's still contoured and there's a solid mix of soft hardwoods—with a healthy age mix—as well as cedars, planted pines, thickets and brushy fields.

Charlevoix County

A solid area with plenty of potential, Charlevoix is not what it could be if its state lands were more aggressively managed for deer. The entire eastern area of the county, including Melrose, Boyne Valley, Hudson and Chandler townships, is dominated by extremely mature, and essentially unbroken, hardwoods. Virtually no timbering is being done here—certainly nowhere near enough—and there are too few openings, especially on the state lands. Nonetheless, there's good potential here for local and nonlocal hunters alike. Melrose and Chandler townships both offer fine sport to the hunter who is selective in his efforts. Concentrate on or near the few areas that have been cut over, and the lower elevations

Deer in Winter. Neither habitat nor climate in the northwest lends itself to great numbers of deer. There's not nearly enough thermal cover and the winter's temperatures and average snowfall are brutal.

where there's a good mixture to the cover. Avoid the higher ground and areas with the most maturity.

The western portion of the county has considerable agriculture (mostly traditional crops and cattle, but some orchards as well) and the best cover is to be found around these agricultural plots. Deer numbers run only about five to eight deer per square mile, but the buck-to-doe ratio is very good (1:3 to 1:4), and hunting pressure is low. Some very nice bucks are taken out of this area every year. Again concentrate on the younger growth areas, and those containing the most cedars, poplars and brush. These areas are abundant throughout. Avoid the mature and barren hardwoods, most of which are found near crop fields.

For local hunters, I especially like Norwood, Marion, South Arm, Eveline (but be selective here, stick to lower ground and the most varied habitat), Wilson, Hayes, Melrose, Hudson and Chandler townships.

Nonlocals will find Melrose and Chandler townships the most promising, but again selectivity is essential. I also like southern Wilson Township, and if a nonlocal hunter were to work hard at it, access to some of the better private areas could be obtained.

Emmet County

From the deer hunter's perspective, Emmet County leaves a lot to be desired. Bliss, Readmond, Friendship, Pleasantview, West Traverse, Resort, Little Traverse and Littlefield townships are all essentially carbon copies of one another and of little worth except to the dedicated trophy hunter. Each is dominated by mature hardwood woodlots and extensive hardwood forests, particularly along the higher ridges. Cultivated fields vary in these townships from roughly 20 percent to 40 percent of the total area and throughout there's a smattering of planted pines and occasionally some lowland thickets. There's little brush and essentially no wintering yards in these townships.

The areas with the most promise are Wawatam and Carp Lake townships in the extreme north, as well as most of McKinley and the central section of Center townships a little farther south.

For local hunters, I'd recommend concentrating on the following areas: Wawatam, Carp Lake, McKinley, eastern Maple River, northeastern Littlefield, southern Bear Creek and very select areas of Springvale townships (the dense, heavier lowlands).

Deer populations throughout the county are so low that I honestly cannot recommend anything here as suitable for nonlocal hunters—too many better options available. However, if you are to hunt here, I'd recommend Eastern Carp Lake and the younger growth sections of Wawatam townships.

17

The Upper
Peninsula

The Upper Peninsula runs the gamut in terms of deer hunting potential. Wildlife District II, comprising Menominee, Dickinson and Iron counties, offers some of the very finest deer hunting to be found anywhere in the world. Other areas, such as Keweenaw, northern Houghton and extreme northern Ontonagon, are extremely poor, and very likely will never improve.

In general, it would be advisable for nonlocal hunters to concentrate on the southern half of the U.P. Trophy hunters or those searching for a "quality" deer hunting experience should investigate Gogebic, Ontonagon, Marquette, northern Schoolcraft or northern Luce counties. Buck-to-doe ratios in these regions run in the neighborhood of 1:4 or even 1:3— higher than anywhere else in the entire state—and eighteen-month-old bucks account for only 25 percent of the buck harvest from these areas as compared with more than 70 percent statewide. Hunter densities run perhaps one to two per square mile, while buck hunter success runs 25 percent or more.

Local hunters who scout diligently during the preseason

Map 17.1
Upper Peninsula

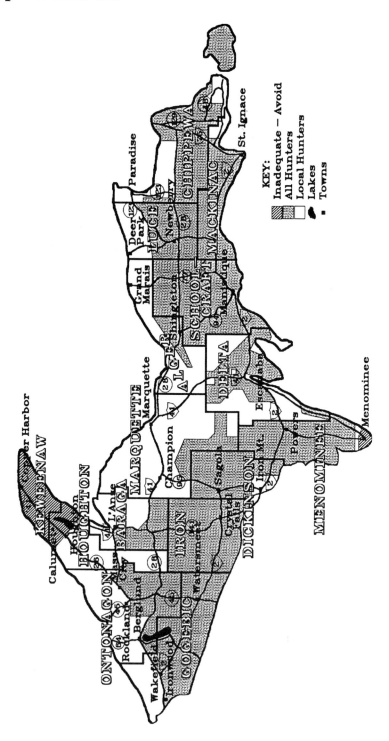

can expect to do reasonably well anywhere throughout the Upper, but even for these hunters, hunting the extreme northern regions will reduce their chances of success.

Following is a short description of each U.P. county and its better areas.

Menominee County

Menominee County bills itself as "The U.P. Dairy Capital" and indeed it is. As much as 30 percent of the land mass in the southern half of the county is under cultivation. Most crops are grains—corn and wheat—used as cattle feed; there are few specialty crops. Locals who plant a garden are practically forced into putting up a deer-proof fence or they simply waste their time. Deer numbers are probably higher here—fifty to seventy per square mile—than in any other place in the entire state.

The southern half of the county is basically flat. In between the croplands are dense stands of cedars, planted pines, poplars and alder thickets. Nowhere in this entire region is there a single woodlot that's too mature. Food and shelter for deer abound. And have they responded!

The northern portion of the county changes radically. Only about 2 percent of this area is cultivated, and unbroken forest dominates. Population and development decreases dramatically. The habitat, however, remains strong and productive. While essentially unbroken, the forest has plenty of edge. Ongoing timbering has created a nice mix in the age distribution of the timber, and pulp production has been very high for years.

In the extreme northwest there are some hardwoods and cedars well past their prime for whitetail habitat, but a lot of cutting is occurring here too. The northern half of the county is sprinkled with mast-bearing hardwoods and has a gently rolling contour. Deer numbers run from twenty to thirty per square mile.

Much of the county is privately owned and access, especially in the southern half, will take some preseason work.

There's a section of the Menominee State Forest in the southeast that has excellent access, high deer densities and a good covering of poplars, birch and cedars. While deer numbers have slipped considerably since their peak in 1988–89, deer hunting potential in Menominee County remains excellent. Hunters are likely to be successful anywhere in the county.

Dickinson County

Dickinson is dominated by its Copper Country State Forest, which covers roughly three-quarters of its land. Only about 1 percent of the land mass is under cultivation and potatoes are the main crop.

The extreme southwest corner is mostly a mix of poplars, birch, mast-bearing hardwoods and cedars, all of which are too mature to provide optimum habitat. This is only a small area in and around Iron Mountain and Norway. It is also the only area of the county that's dominated by large hills.

The remainder of the county is composed of a beautiful mix of cedars, pine, poplar and birch, as well as plentiful alders, willows, and numerous swales. The land rolls continuously with low, gently sloping hills. To manage a forested habitat specifically for deer, you should harvest roughly 2.5 percent to 3.5 percent of the forest per year. By doing so, you'd harvest essentially the entire area once every thirty to forty years. In so doing, you'd always provide essential browse and cover. Dickinson County closely approaches this ideal and is assuredly one of the finest deering hunting counties in the entire state. Deer densities run from fifteen to twenty in the northwest to thirty in sections of the east. If we can regenerate wintering areas in this region, there's every reason to believe deer numbers could return to their levels of the late 1980s, but that's a big "if."

During the 1980s, a tremendous contrast existed between those counties farther west, and Menominee County to the south and Dickinson. Although the situation is now changing because of an increase in logging in those western counties, formerly they were dominated by their unbroken forests. They had little edge, far too much maturity, and inadequate browse to support large numbers of deer. Southern Menominee, on the other hand, was and still is broken by large areas of cultivation, and provides excellent whitetail habitat by its variation. Dickenson County, for the past twenty years, has provided optimum habitat by its broken forest edges. Very little of this edge is provided by the agricultural operations. The majority is formed by the logging operations. Much of this logging is in the form of clear cuts, some in the form of thinning. The overall result is ideal habitat. Hunters can realistically expect to score most anywhere in the county.

Marquette County

Marquette County ranges from extremely rugged terrain in the north to very nearly flat in the south. It ranges from inadequate habitat through much of the north (although this is beginning to change as logging operations have picked up considerably in the past five years), to excellent in parts of the south. Deer densities are better in the southern portion of the county. Overall, densities run from three or four deer per square mile in the north to as high as thirty in parts of the south.

The north shows very rugged terrain—some of the higher peaks carry the title of "mountain." In reality these are high and rock-studded hills. There are a great many rocky outcroppings in the northern half of the county. The forest is unbroken and consists of a solid mix of oak, maple, beech, softer hardwoods, and brush, as well as some pines and cedars in most areas. This habitat is too mature but, as mentioned, logging operations have increased greatly the past few years and the openings thus created, as well as the resurgent growth already present, are proving beneficial—deer numbers are increasing. Still, in many areas of the north there's little browse and the forest canopy towers to sixty feet or more. There's also a large private tract of land in the extreme northwest called the "Huron Mountain Club." Deer numbers in the surrounding area are relatively high but access is extremely limited; nonlocals should probably avoid this area.

In the southwest part of the county a definite decrease in the maturity of the forest occurs, as well as a very active forestry operation. Limited agriculture is also found in this area, principally along the extreme southwest side of the county, consisting of haying operations; there's little if any actual cultivation. Few true hardwoods thrive in this area causing an increase in both poplar and birch. There are markedly more deer, running about fifteen to twenty per square mile in all but the extreme southern tier of townships, where the numbers increase to twenty, or even thirty per square mile. Thanks to the limited agriculture plus timbering, there's a lot of useful edge and plenty of browse. The result is a much improved habitat.

The southeast portion of the county is rather a blending of good and poor habitats. Around the city of Palmer in the northwest corner of this area, and then both south and east of there, a noted increase in mast-bearing hardwoods and habitat age is found. The canopy is too high and there's a lessened amount of browse. A huge area of very mature planted pines is around the Sawyer Air Force Base. Browse is scarce in this region, which also lacks suitable winter habitat. Consequently, there are few deer. The southern half of this area is then the best of the lot—it is excellent!

There's a nice blend of cedars, pines and soft hardwoods. There's also plenty of brush, and some mast-bearing hardwoods. Around the village of Watson there's also some active farming, with potatoes being the primary crop. A good percentage of timber is being cut in the area from Forsyth Township in the center of the county, south to the corner of the county, and then east to Ewing Township. The result is very good habitat; there's an excellent mix of food and cover and the deer population right now is high. This area also includes much of the deer yard that I specifically referred to in Chapter 2. The herd in this area has declined in the past five years and, although it may well stabilize now, it will not increase until new conifer growth (not planted pine) occurs. Hopefully, this can be accomplished; we'll just have to wait and see. Access on the private lands in this area is difficult to obtain as well; nonlocals wishing to hunt here should get an early start.

Iron County

Coming into Iron County, heading south along U.S. 141, the first thing you notice is a significant increase in cedars. As you then move south through the county, pines and cedars continue to increase. Once you get away from the highway itself, you realize that this is truly deer country. From east to west the composition of the habitat also changes, with many more true hardwoods being found on the western side of the county.

With a couple minor exceptions, Iron County is heavily forested throughout. There are many poplar and birch, as well as cedars and pines across much of the area. In the southwest and the northwest, there are large stands of true hardwoods—oaks and maples. Sadly, Iron county is also a good example of whitetail habitat on the verge of going bad. Much more of it needs to be timbered if it's to remain productive.

The northeast corner, from Amasa east and north, is a whitetail haven. There's a solid mix to the cover. There are some very large cedar swamps, a good stand of mast-bearing hardwoods, plenty of both young and old poplar and birch, and many alder thickets. A lot of edge is thus formed, and the deer have responded favorably; the herd numbers twenty to twenty-five deer per square mile throughout this corner.

While the rest of the county still offers good-to-excellent hunting, its habitat is generally declining; it's too mature to provide optimum whitetail habitat. The area north of Winslow Lake in the north-central portion of the county is a case in point. That area is heavily forested with fifty- to sixty-year-old hardwoods. The forest floor is completely open and the canopy soars to eighty feet. There's precious little browse and while some deer will survive forever in such habitat, it will never hold good populations.

Overall, the hunter's best bets are the southwest and the

Cut Logs. The state of the U.P.'s deer herds is dependent upon our logging industry. Whether or not we will have viable herds in the future will be determined by how wisely we balance our needs for forestry products with the whitetail's requirements.

entire eastern half of the county. Deer numbers are highest in the southwest, ranging as high as thirty-five per square mile.

Delta County

The habitat in Delta County improves as you move north to south, especially in the eastern half of the county. It also improves as you move east to west. The eastern half of the county is essentially unbroken forest that becomes more mature the farther north you go. The extreme northeast is composed of very mature hardwoods as well as fully mature planted pines. The area south of U.S. 2 in the east and around the town of Garden down to Fayette State Park has some small-scale agriculture. This creates a lot of edge. There's a lot of cedar, mixed woodlots and young poplars, as well as some dense brush in this area. The Garden Peninsula has excellent habitat, but be forewarned there are severe access problems. Deer numbers run about twenty to twenty-five per square mile in the Garden area to nearly twenty per square mile in the extreme northeast of Delta County. Deer numbers have more than doubled in the northeast corner of Delta County in the past five years.

The southwest portion of the county is an extension of the Menominee County habitat to the west. Like Menominee, this area of Delta County is exceptionally populated and developed for a U.P. county, and again, severe access problems will confront the nonlocal hunter in this region. As much as 30 percent of the land is under cultivation, being mostly hay, corn and potatoes. The area farther north has a good mix of cover, but is mostly forested, with lots of cedars (all too mature), brush and young growth in spots. You'll want to concentrate on the areas of younger growth—be selective. Consider hunting within a quarter of a mile or less of the creek beds and river flood plains in this area. There's lush, dense growth with good cover and plenty of food in these areas. Nonlocals will fare better here by sticking to the state and federal lands.

Archers in the early season can concentrate on the more open areas, those with plenty of young poplars, and near the agricultural edges. Gun hunters should look a little farther into the cover, especially in areas with moderate to heavy hunting pressure. Late season muzzle-loaders and second-season archers should head to the cedars or at least closer to their edges. With the exception of the northeast corner, several large yards are widely spaced throughout the county. Late season hunters should always migrate closer to them, particularly if there are deep early snows.

Avoid the heavily planted pine areas as well as the hardwoods that are too open underneath. Your best bets overall will be those areas south of and along the front of U.S. 2, Garden Township, Nahma Township, the private lands north of Rapid River, and the entire central portion of the county.

Chippewa County

Chippewa's best habitat and, not surprisingly, its greatest number of deer are found in the extreme southwest corner.

The habitat is an excellent mix. There are far more poplars and birch than anything else, but there are good stands of cedars, pines, plenty of tag alder and willow thickets, some clear cuts and a few scattered pockets of true hardwoods. Overall, the habitat is too mature, but acceptable. The land is gently contoured. Deer numbers have nearly doubled in Chippewa County in the past five years, and now range from a low of perhaps five to ten per square mile in the north to a high of twenty-five per square mile in the south. The best areas in the entire county are Hulbert, Trout Lake, Rudyard and Kinross townships.

As you move north and east from here, the habitat declines. In the north existing habitat is far too mature; there's no cedar, and no yarding areas. Deer numbers suffer. In many areas the habitat consists of pure stands of pine—jack, white and red. In others, it consists of pure stands of true hardwoods. Nowhere is there adequate browse or cover. The entire area is essentially forested. These areas offer good trophy hunting opportunities, particularly in the early season; late season archers and muzzle-loaders should stick to areas south of Highway 28 for best results.

The eastern side has a very large area of intense agriculture, mostly haying with plenty of livestock. As much as 80 percent of the land in the northern half of the county is under cultivation. The habitat that does exist is far too mature, with no yarding areas and very few cedars or pine whatsoever. Deer numbers range from ten to perhaps twenty per square mile. Access is available, provided you're courteous and make arrangements early.

Gogebic County

Gogebic County, for the past five years or so, epitomizes the changes occurring throughout the western U.P. Logging has increased dramatically and this is good news for the deer. Numbers have more than doubled during this time so that many areas today are carrying from twenty to twenty-five deer per square mile that traditionally carried fewer than ten. The entire eastern side of Gogebic, from the Wisconsin border to Ontonagon County, is good. The cover is unbroken and the habitat is amazingly consistent. There's a very solid mix of hardwoods, both mast-producing and softer hardwoods. There are plenty of thickets, swales, and marshes produced by the gentle contour of the land. There are hemlock and pine as well, unfortunately in poor shape and getting worse. Trophy hunting potential is excellent. Gogebic, Ontonagon, and perhaps southern Houghton counties may well represent today the most improved deer hunting opportunities in all of Michigan.

The southern region of the county is absolutely covered with lakes and is known as the "Land-O-Lakes" region. The only place I believe the habitat needs improvement is west of Lake Gogebic. This is a very expansive area of mature hardwoods, but there are still deer here, running about fifteen to twenty per square mile.

The north and east sides of the county falter in comparison with the east. The habitat is mostly hardwoods and they're well beyond their prime in terms of providing whitetail habitat. Their thick canopy leaves the forest floor devoid of browse. Yet within this area I did locate some pockets of fair to good cover. The area around Bessemer and somewhat north is an example. Erwin Township is as remote and wild as you can imagine, and the habitat is quite good. There's lots of marsh, brush, and a solid mass of cover. Deer numbers have improved dramatically and now run around twenty to twenty-five per square mile. Trophy hunting potential is excellent.

Mackinac County

Mackinac County runs both hot and cold. The best areas are those in the central to southern portion of the county. That surrounding Allenville is good, and typical of some of the small-scale farming operations found throughout the area. Agriculture, always in the form of haying operations, is intense over small areas followed by unbroken forest. There are plenty of cedars (but they're in poor shape) and pines, providing winter habitat in some places and yet they're totally lacking elsewhere. In large sections, such as the extreme east side of the county, the habitat is far too mature to be considered as more than just adequate. Deer numbers run ten to fifteen per square mile.

Moran, Brevort and St. Ignace townships are the best of the lot, while Hudson, eastern Garfield and western Newton are all good choices. Northern Portage, surrounding the Black Creek flooding, is excellent as well. Deer numbers are highest in the west, ranging from fifteen to nearly thirty per square mile. Hunting pressure has increased in Mackinac County in the past few years, but not as fast as the deer herd.

Ontonagon County

This is the county of the Porcupine Mountains State Park, and with the exception of that entire area plus the area immediately east of the park, the whole of the western part of the county offers improved hunting opportunity and excellent trophy hunting potential. The problem with the northern areas is the extreme maturity of the forests. The park itself is virgin timber; there's basically no whitetail habitat here at all, and hence very few deer. On the positive side, there are few hunters, and with a buck-to-doe ratio of roughly 1:4 or even 1:3 plus a highly skewed age distribution in favor of older animals, your chances of tagging a fully mature buck are very good.

From White Pine south, however, the habitat is much better. A flat to gently rolling countryside, this area is covered with hardwoods and some brush. There are a few scattered pockets of pine and hemlock throughout; ongoing logging operations are improving the habitat. The better areas are Berglund Township in the extreme southwest corner and the area south and east of Berglund.

The southeastern corner of the county has some nice cover. There's a band of private land running through the center of this area; the land both north and south of it is part

Deer in Cut Cedars. Cedars and other conifers are intentionally cut in winter so that the fallen tops can be utilized as food. Literally overnight—small cuts in large yards even faster—these tops will be completely stripped.

of the Ottawa National Forest. The entire area is unbroken forest except some of the private sector. South of Ewen, in the west-central area, are a dozen or so very active farms, mostly cattle and haying operations. Otherwise there's little agriculture anywhere in the county. The northern portion of southeast Ontonagon County, around the village of Paynesville, is a tractless wilderness. The northwest corner is flat and very heavily forested. Predominately soft hardwoods are found in this area. The northeast is solid forest, with a higher percentage of pine than the land to the west. Most of the hardwoods are poplar and birch; there's not much brush in this area.

The entire southern tier from M-28 south is the best-looking area. Its gently rolling landscape is covered with a good mix of habitat, mostly hardwoods but lots of edge areas. There are plenty of thickets, scattered brush and generous tracts of private land interspersed with the National Forest lands.

The northeast part of Ontonagon County is all solid; it's mostly private with some state and national forest lands around the perimeter. There's an excellent mix throughout the area of forest and open areas. There's a lot of edge. It's a shame that, overall, the habitat is too mature, winters are just too hard, and deer numbers remain low. However, they're increasing, now about fifteen per square mile. The extreme southern section below the villages of Rockland and Mass City provides the best bet.

I feel the best region in the entire county is the extreme west side of the southwestern corner. It encompasses Haight, McMillan and Rockland townships around Ewen as well as the southern portion of Matchwood Township. Deer numbers here are now running twenty to twenty-five per square mile.

Houghton County

With the exception of the area from Houghton–Hancock up to Laurium–Calumet and the northern county line, the entire county has pretty consistent habitat. The northern portion of the county is perhaps more rugged than the south, but that's about the only difference.

Predominantly forested, the county is blanketed with good stands of hardwoods, some of which are mast-bearing. Smatterings of cedar and hemlock intersperse with occasional cultivation, mostly in the form of haying operations, throughout the county. Overall, however, the combination is too mature for good whitetail habitat.

I believe the best areas are east of Portage and Hubbell Lakes over to Lake Superior, although deer numbers are low, about five per square mile, throughout this and the rest of the Lake Superior watershed area. I like the rather broken habitat around Bootjack and also the area down around Jacobsville. Farther south I like the area from Chassell, at the southern end of Portage Lake, down to the Baraga County line. Again, I particularly like those spots surrounding the broken habitat formed by the haying operations in this area.

In the southern region of the county, I especially like the east side, although the entire southern section is better than the area farther north. Deer numbers are up markedly and now run twenty to even twenty-five per square mile throughout the southern half of the county. The habitat of the northern sections is far too unbroken and too mature, and the winters too tough, to support sizable numbers of deer.

Baraga County

Most of the county is a heavily forested area, much of which are state and federal lands. The habitat in the northern areas is quite consistent, being mostly hardwoods—all too mature.

From M-28 south (the southern one-third of the county) there's a significant increase in pine and cedar. This is particularly true in the southeast corner. The county has some real rugged terrain in places. The area around Craig Lake State Park in the southeast is an example. There is one large peak after another, and good-size, extremely dense, cedar swamps in between; there is also a lot of water. Few roads penetrate this region and access is very limited. The west-central area of the county levels out a bit and is covered with an immense forest of poplar throughout, with the exception of a large area of planted pines in the Camp Baraga area.

There are several areas I like. The area surrounding Froberg in the northwest is an area of broken timber, lots of edge, some haying operations and a good solid mix of habitat. The peninsula north of L'Anse, especially the area between Aura and Point Abbaye, has promise. This is again an area of broken habitat, but mostly young poplars and alder thickets. The extreme northern area, however, is a huge cedar swamp, very dense but too mature. Local hunters will do best throughout the northern reaches. Deer numbers run about five per square mile throughout the northern half of the county. Trophy hunting potential is excellent.

From L'Anse east to Arvon, then south to Herman, are many rolling, timbered hills with a good mix of cover. Another good bet is the entire southern tier of the county. Try the cover surrounding the openings in the private lands throughout this area.

Collared Deer. First perfected by Louis Verme working out of
the Cusino Research Station in Shingleton, deer collaring has
erased the biologist's uncertainty on deer movement. It's vitally
important that we continue with our research efforts, however,
as there remains much more to learn.

Schoolcraft County

The extreme northwestern corner of Schoolcraft County is a scenic area of towering hardwoods, contoured terrain and sparkling lakes. However, it offers very limited opportunities except to the serious trophy hunter. Farther east you encounter a huge area of sparse, scraggly pines. This continues unbroken until just northeast of the town of Seney. There are no adequate wintering areas and little browse. Around Seney, the situation improves; there's more cover, more browse and a considerable amount of edge. If these elements are found in the right combination, a hard-working hunter should do all right in this area. Deer numbers run twenty to twenty-five per square mile—up considerably in the past five years.

Farther south is the Seney National Wildlife Refuge, which allows deer hunting. Up to this point in time, state regulations have applied to these hunts; no special permits have been required (check with Seney, the situation could change). If you camp in Seney, a permit is required. The habitat is a mixture of softer hardwoods and conifers. Those in the northern part of the refuge and west toward Shingleton are less mature, more open and hold more deer than those farther south. However, this entire region offers the hunter good opportunities.

Around the northeast corner of the Seney Refuge and north of Manistique to the south is some agriculture (mostly haying). But it creates much needed edge. There are good cedar swamps in these areas and hunters would be well advised to stay near them. The southeast corner of the county is also excellent; in particular, the area around, and both north and east of Gulliver.

The west side of the county shows some agriculture around the Cooks area, but the habitat is poor; deer number near fifteen per square mile. The nonlocal's best bet is in and around Seney Refuge, the southeast corner of the county, and along the M-94 corridor north of Manistique to Ashford Lake. The area just west of Seney is also good.

Try to locate those areas that have browse, cover, winter

habitat (at least nearby), and a broken forest canopy—you'll then find deer. They are not spread out uniformly in this area. Pay particular attention also to the river drainage areas throughout this region.

Alger County

Alger County is heavily contoured in the extreme north and then levels out quickly. The north is totally dominated by solid stands of hardwoods, all of which are far too mature. The canopy remains unbroken until you reach the southern half of the county. There are precious few pines and hardly any cedars in the north, hence no suitable winter habitat and few deer.

The southern portion of the county shows an improvement over the northern regions, and with recent increases in logging operations this promises to be even better in the future. However, right now it's still too mature. The Traunik area in the southwest corner shows promise with lots of woodlots interspersed with hay fields, primarily mature hardwoods (a lot of maples), some poplar and brush, with plenty of browse. But there's no winter habitat anywhere in the entire area. Visualize these hardwoods with two or three feet of snow on the ground. There's no food between the snowline and fifty feet up! Deer numbers run ten to fifteen per square mile.

Other regions, notably in Mathias Township in the south-central area, have some cedars to provide winter cover, but these are so mature they contain no food. In looking for deer in the north, you need to find food and winter cover. This area has little of either.

The situation improves somewhat in the extreme southeast corner of Alger County, in the lakes region. Also some of the habitat from there north to Munising is marginally adequate. The Hiawatha National Forest in Alger County, while perhaps improving in the future, is now disappointing with low deer numbers. Its hardwoods are too mature, with too many red pine in its southern areas.

In the area from Shingleton east to the county line along the face of highway M-28, and extending north for a couple miles, there's a major improvement in habitat and the size of the deer herd. This area is covered with young dense cedars, pines, heavy brush, and some poplars. Farther north, the area from Grand Marais south along the M-77 corridor to the county line is adequate; there's a real blending of tree types in this area and the cover is good, although too mature overall.

My hunting suggestion throughout the county would be to stick near those areas with cedars. You need not necessarily hunt the cedars themselves, but you should be within a few miles of adequate wintering areas. If you find broken edges, cedars, heavy brush, as well as young poplars, birch, beech, and so on, all in close proximity to one another, you'll find deer. Such areas, though constituting only a small percentage of the land area, do exist—seek them out. As is true of the entire eastern end of our U.P., pay particular attention to the river flood plains as well.

For nonlocal hunters, your best bet will be around the lakes region in the southeast, and east of Shingleton along M-28. The local hunter, locating the combinations mentioned above, may well find action anywhere in the southern reaches of the county.

Luce County

Luce County is yet another area that suffers terribly from a lack of winter habitat. There are scattered places where there's good browse comprised of young poplars, birch, willow, and even young hardwoods; yet there are no cedars or hemlock. Then there are areas where there are cedars, but due to their extreme maturity they're inadequate, and there's little browse. There are also areas with seemingly sufficient stands of densely planted young pines, which provide some winter habitat, but again there's little browse. Throughout much of the northern half of the county, the habitat is far too mature. In the western half, some areas have solid stands of mature mast-bearing hardwoods—again poor habitat. The overall results are very low numbers of deer throughout much of the county, running roughly ten per square mile in the north to as high as twenty in the southern third.

The best areas spread out around the village of Newberry. The extreme southeast corner of the county holds fairly good numbers of deer, as does the area east of Manistique Lake and from the county line north for a couple miles. The area running along highway M-123, north of Newberry for ten miles or so, is quite good also. There's a huge yarding area west of Newberry, along the Syphon River and surrounding the Dollarville flooding, which can be successfully hunted around its perimeter.

Hunting will be tough throughout the county, and those doing best will be those hunters exerting the most effort. Try locating those areas with plenty of browse and winter cover. Stay away from the Lake Superior area. Trophy hunting potential is excellent.

Keweenaw County

A very rugged, beautiful area, Keweenaw is perhaps the most rugged in all of Michigan. Large hills dominate the terrain. The habitat is essentially unbroken throughout. The forests are extremely mature, mostly hardwoods except along the southern shoreline where hemlock and jack-pine are common in areas.

Keweenaw County is a beautiful place to see, fish, take a family vacation or a sight-seeing tour, but it's no place to hunt deer. There are very few deer anywhere (plus or minus five per square mile throughout), and I think that the vast majority of the local hunters head south speaks for itself.

Epilogue

Michigan's sportsmen are blessed; we have a beautifully scenic state, plenty of game, and a DNR that, overall, has done a remarkable job of safeguarding our wildlife resources. I'm confident that controlled sports hunting is, and will continue to be, the most logical vehicle through which to maintain a proper balance between our game animals and their habitat. Nonetheless, I'm concerned about our hunting future. And, although I'm concerned about the future of our game animals and their habitat needs, my deepest concerns are about us.

Hunters are, by the very nature of our sport, a highly visible group; the clothing we wear, the weapons we carry, and the specialized equipment we use all serve to make us clearly identifiable. We need to be constantly mindful of the image we project. Survey after survey has shown that the vast majority of Americans are neutral on the issue of hunting. But let someone who's neutral have just one negative experience with a hunter and that neutrality will disappear. "Hunting" and "hunter" assume a negative connotation that will easily be turned against us at the ballot box.

I'm offended by the sight of a deer's carcass slung over the hood of a car. I'm offended by the slogan, and the T-shirts, that read, "Happiness is a big gut pile." I'm offended by the hunter or shooter with a gun in one hand and a beer in the other. It's the responsibility of hunters who take this sport seriously to let those who threaten it know just how we feel; we need to do a much better job of promoting a positive public image.

One of my real concerns about deer hunting is that an entire generation of hunters may never learn how to hunt deer by using a working knowledge of the animal's behavior and habitat. Of particular concern to me is the issue of baiting. Whether baiting actually improves the success rate is open to question, but it's estimated that some 35 percent of our hunters today employ bait. That I have not suggested or discussed baiting as a tactic, despite its widespread use, gives away my feelings. In my eyes, baiting is a lazy way to hunt deer. There is little or no need to ever learn anything about deer or deer hunting. This is not the place to debate this issue. Suffice it to say that baiting is an emotional issue for hunters and, especially, for nonhunters. Again I ask: is this the image we should be projecting?

A friend of mine lives up in Indian River—not exactly the metropolitan hub of Michigan. Way back in the early 1970s, Don was lamenting to me that when he first moved there the townspeople respected the local hunters, but now (1974) they viewed them with a jaundiced eye. He was afraid of what the future might hold for hunters and hunting. Now, in March 1990, I don't believe things have improved. I share Don's concern; we all should. If we want a bright hunting future, we must be more concerned about ethics and do everything we can to improve the nonhunter's image of our sport.